The Return of the Left in Post-communist States

STUDIES OF COMMUNISM IN TRANSITION

General Editor: Ronald J. Hill

*Professor of Comparative Government
and Fellow of Trinity College
Dublin, Ireland*

Studies of Communism in Transition is an important series which applies academic analysis and clarity of thought to the recent traumatic events in Eastern and Central Europe. As many of the preconceptions of the past half century are cast aside, newly independent and autonomous sovereign states are being forced to address long-term, organic problems which had been suppressed by, or appeased within, the Communist system of rule.

The series is edited under the sponsorship of Lorton House, an independent charitable association which exists to promote the academic study of communism and related concepts.

The Return of the Left in Post-communist States

Current Trends and Future Prospects

Edited by

Charles Bukowski
Associate Professor of International Studies, Bradley University, USA

and

Barnabas Racz
Professor of Political Science, Eastern Michigan University, USA

STUDIES OF COMMUNISM IN TRANSITION

Edward Elgar
Cheltenham, UK • Northampton, MA, USA

Published by
Edward Elgar Publishing Limited
Glensanda House
Montpellier Parade
Cheltenham
Glos GL50 1UA
UK

Edward Elgar Publishing, Inc.
136 West Street
Suite 202
Northampton
Massachusetts 01060
USA

A catalogue record for this book
is available from the British Library

Library of Congress Cataloguing in Publication Data

The return of the left in post-communist states : current trends and
    future prospects / edited by Charles Bukowski, Barnabas Racz.
        (Studies of communism in transition)
        1. Communist parties. 2. Post-communism. 3. Right and left
    (Political science) I. Bukowski, Charles J. II. Racz, Barnabas.
    III. Series.
    HX44.5.R475 1999
    320.53'22—dc21   99–30950
                                                                    CIP

ISBN 1 85898 815 2

Printed and bound in Great Britain by Bookcraft (Bath) Ltd.

In memory of Max Kele

and for Jeanie

C.J.B.

To all those who deserve a better world to live in

B.R.

Contents

Tables

Contributors

Charles Bukowski is an associate professor of international studies at Bradley University, Peoria, IL, USA

Mark A. Cichock is an associate professor of political science at the University of Texas–Arlington, Arlington, TX, USA

Terry D. Clark is an associate professor of political science at Creighton University, Omaha, NE, USA

Danica Fink-Hafner is an associate professor of political science at the University of Ljubljana, Ljubljana, Slovenia

Nicolae Harsanyi is administrative director of the Centre for Slavic, Eurasian, and East European Studies, University of North Carolina, Chapel Hill, NC, USA

Barnabas Racz is a professor of political science at Eastern Michigan University, Ypsilanti, MI, USA

Robin M. Tucker is an account associate with Sterling Communications, Inc., San Jose, CA, USA

Janusz Wrobel is a professor of linguistics and Polish studies at St. Mary's College, Orchard Lake, MI, USA

Preface: Defining the Left

This book is about more than ex-communist parties. We view the term 'left' more broadly than many who study post-communist polities. The common conception of the left seems to be parties emerging directly from the dominant Marxist–Leninist parties of Soviet-style communist systems (often referred to as successor or ex-communist parties) and now espousing a more moderate or socialist ideology along with a commitment to the democratic political process. We understand the left to be any party which emerged originally out of Marxist ideological roots and which continues to have a corresponding interest in issues of social justice. We include in this definition the successor or ex-communist parties, the more radical, Marxist parties laying claim to the communist heritage of the old one-party state (and with a more dubious commitment to democracy) and traditional parties of the left that have drifted away from their Marxist roots. Included in the third category are those reconstituted parties (primarily social democratic in orientation) which were disbanded or were captives of the dominat Marxist–Leninist parties during the communist era.

Our decision to be more inclusive in our conception of the left was predicated on our desire to explore as fully as possible the political dynamics that have emerged in post-communist polities. The great diversity of experiences they have had since beginning their transitions from authoritarian rule recommends a broad perspective, and, in recognition of this diversity, we wished to give the authors of the country studies maximum flexibility to pursue their analyses. We believe that a full understanding of the political experiences of post-communist polities requires examining more than just the communist successor parties and that the fates of the successor parties are, in part, determined by the dynamics of the entire political left. We hope this volume represents a useful start to gaining such an understanding.

Charles Bukowski   Barnabas Racz

1. The Return of the Left: Causes and Consequences

Charles Bukowski

The end of the Cold War has presented analysts with many surprising puzzles, not the least of which has been the extreme and ongoing variation in the fortunes of the political left in many post-communist states. Broadly defined here, the political left is understood as those parties which have Marxist ideological roots and a corresponding interest in issues of social justice. Obviously included in this definition are the communist successor parties, both direct and indirect, as well as traditional parties of the left that have drifted away from their Marxist roots. In the case of the latter, included are those reconstituted parties which were disbanded or were captives of the dominant Marxist–Leninist parties during the period of the Cold War.

Thus far the parties of the left, especially the direct communist successor parties, have experienced a surprising variety of fates. Just the experiences of Eastern Europe present a useful microcosm of the entire former communist world. Perhaps most surprising have been the cases where communist successor parties were soundly defeated in initial elections only to return to power after a few years of economic decline or mismanagement by the opposition. Poland and Hungary stand as the most prominent examples of this course of events. At the other end of the spectrum lie cases where the communist leadership never truly left power. Assenting only to a few cosmetic changes and a purging of the most visible Cold War elite, events in countries like Bulgaria and Romania were not unexpected by many analysts (putting aside the very unexpected initial chain of events in Eastern Europe and the Soviet Union that led to the collapse of the Soviet bloc and the disintegration of the USSR). Somewhere in between lie cases such as the marginalization of the communists in the Czech Republic. All of these cases are further complicated by the reconstitution of more moderate parties (social democratic) of the left and the fragmentation of many of the communist successor parties led by true believers who refused to give up their Marxist–Leninist orientation.[1]

The surprising success of the communist successor parties' portion of the

1

left in many post-communist systems has generated several explanations. Perhaps the most popular, at least from the point of view of the news media, views the success of the left as part of an electoral backlash to the consequences of economic reform. Popular discontent with Poland's 'shock therapy' economic policies was well documented in the press, and the overwhelming victory of the Democratic Left Alliance in the 1993 general elections was widely viewed as the result of that discontent.[2]

The fragmentation of the democratic opposition in the aftermath of its initial triumph is also a popular explanation. The Polish example is typical of this point of view. The victory of the former communists can be understood as a consequence of the inability of the various Solidarity-associated or Solidarity-successor parties to work together. By fragmenting the anti-left vote, the democratic leadership all but guaranteed a victory by the left.[3] This phenomenon is common in the study of democratic consolidations. In order to be successful in bringing about a transition, advocates of democracy must cooperate in their opposition to an authoritarian regime. Yet, once the transition has taken place, the various pro-democracy elements find themselves in competition with one another.[4] The complexities of governing during a democratic transition are enhanced by this fragmentation and public perceptions of the government are damaged. The inability of the parties of the democratic right and center to cooperate is further hindered by their political inexperience. A corollary to this situation lies in the possible advantage enjoyed by the post-communist forces by virtue of their long experience as an organized political group. They had an organization in place, and, although membership was substantially reduced, the party machinery was still superior to that of any opposing force. Obviously, the political landscape was radically changed, but the organizational skills and the personal connections remained as did the bureaucratic legacy. While the communist party leadership had been forced to relinquish power, government bureaucracies throughout virtually all post-communist states remained largely influenced by former party apparatus appointees.

A more nuanced explanation for the left's success is offered by Jane Curry.[5] She refers to the separate path taken by the former communist parties as a result of their 'pariah' status among the electorate. Forced to fend for themselves in the new democratic environment while the opposition parties received financial support and advice from the West, these parties adapted well to their new circumstances. The party apparatus, by virtue of their governing experience, already knew what was necessary to get things done in a dysfunctional system. In particular, according to Curry, 'They were the local power brokers with the resources to buy support and make things happen on the local level'.[6] What remained for the former communists was to learn how to gain popularity with the electorate. By distancing themselves from their communist roots and by remaining unified at a time when politics among the opposition parties grew more and more fractious, the former communists rebuilt their image. They came to be viewed 'increasingly as consummate professional politicians and local representatives'.[7] For Curry, a great irony lies in the fact that the pariah status of the former communists probably played a key role in keeping these parties united. Since no one would deal with them politically or legislatively, they looked to themselves. As political organizers they invested in 'faxes, telephones, and staff' and as legislators they worked as a cohesive group appearing 'above partisan battles' and 'devoted themselves to representing their districts'.[8]

Finally, one cannot overlook the possibility that the fate of the left is the result of a broader phenomenon in which the voters in a post-communist society use an election simply to reject those in power regardless of the leadership's party affiliation or ideology. The option of turning out a standing government represents a new opportunity for the electorate in a post-communist state. Assuming a long-standing mistrust of governmental authority, it would not be difficult to imagine an electorate that routinely turns against the incumbent leadership. Certainly the defeat of the Democratic Left Alliance in Poland's 1997 parliamentary elections and a similar defeat suffered by the Hungarian Socialist Party in May 1998 can be understood from this point of view.[9]

Given the great diversity of experiences of the successor parties among the former communist states, it is unlikely that a single explanation can be uniformly applied to this puzzle. Instead it will be necessary to look at both possible uniform causes applicable to the entire range of cases and factors specific to each country. It is the purpose of this volume to seek a better understanding of the fortunes of the successor parties and the left in general in the post-Cold War era. It will use a case study approach to examine the immediate fates and characteristics of the left and the broader challenges that the left is likely to face in the future. The case study method permits at least partial accommodation of the variety of fortunes experienced by the left since 1989. Such an inductive approach should yield a useful categorization scheme and assist in the building of more generalizable explanations.

This volume, however, seeks to go beyond the backward-looking puzzle of what the left has experienced thus far. It is also concerned with the current appearance of the left and with the challenges the left is likely to face in the future. Each case study addresses the issue of the left's characteristics as a political party(ies) competing in a democratic environment. The chapter authors also discuss what are likely to be the major challenges facing the left, including an evaluation of the left's ability or inability to meet those challenges. Regarding the former, a primary concern will be the internal characteristics of the major parties of the left. Among the characteristics warranting attention are the level of democratization and the demographic features of the membership as well as the voting constituency. In the case of the latter, future challenges present a diversity at least equal to that of the left's current political fortunes. The relevance of these challenges will vary for each country as will become obvious to the reader.

Eventually all of the systems examined in this volume are confronted with the comprehensive test of democratic consolidation. Given this common thread, the study of democratic consolidations suggests some key categories of challenges that the left (or any other political movement) must be able to confront successfully if it is to remain a significant force in the post-transition political environment:

1. *Historical legacy* The literature on democratic consolidations gives much attention to the impact of the historical legacy that every political leadership in the former communist world must deal with. Clearly the historical legacies confronting post-communist regimes will have political, economic, social and even cultural implications, but the most direct impact can be seen in the political realm. Two of the most widely discussed variables in this category are the impact of the previous authoritarian regime and the mode of transition experienced by the political system.

One perspective on the impact of regime characteristics on consolidation concerns the level of success of the authoritarian regime. Huntington finds it possible to hypothesize in both directions. On the one hand, it seems plausible that an unsuccessful authoritarian regime might be a positive incentive for consolidating a new democracy. On the other hand, a society that was unsuccessful in building an authoritarian regime may be no more likely to build a functioning democracy.[10] O'Donnell prefers the former point of view, although for slightly different reasons. A successful (particularly economically successful) authoritarian regime will leave behind a cache of positive memories (or at least a lack of negative ones) resulting in less reluctance on the part of society to return to the past. As a result, one can expect consolidations to proceed more smoothly in the wake of an unsuccessful authoritarian regime.[11] Valenzuela suggests that those leading a transition often invite comparisons with the unsuccessful authoritarian regime in order to generate public support for the transition and consolidation. He refers to this tactic as 'inverse legitimation'.[12] It will be important here to understand how the left is prepared to deal with its past record and whether a relatively successful past foretells a brighter future for the left, especially the successor parties.

The historical legacy of communism also requires an understanding of the structure of the previous regime. Huntington defines two types of regimes that are relevant to the examination of socialist systems: one-party systems and personal dictatorships.[13] With the exception of Romania all of the country studies that make up this volume can be categorized as one-party systems. The distinction between the two categories can have important consequences for democratic consolidation and for the future success of political parties of the left. Huntington finds that personal dictatorships are more likely to end in violent transitions which, in turn, increase the difficulty of the consolidation.[14] And yet a very personal rule, such as Nicolae Ceausescu's, may make it easier for the communist successor party to distance itself from his legacy and invoke inverse legitimation. Short-term success, at least, might be more likely under such circumstances.

Another perspective on the importance of regime type is offered by Ishiyama. Based on an analysis of 18 successor parties in Eastern Europe and the former Soviet Union, he finds that the success of ex-communist parties can be understood partially by the political environment under communism from which the new parties emerged. Ishiyama identifies three types of communist political environments: patrimonial (for example, Russia and Bulgaria), national consensus (for example, Hungary and Poland) and bureaucratic authoritarian (for example, Czechoslovakia). The most successful successor parties have emerged out of national consensus systems, and Ishiyama believes these parties have the brightest futures as well because, as a result of their transition experiences, they have evolved into 'genuine political parties'.[15]

The success of an authoritarian regime has also been considered a factor in understanding why a transition assumes a particular form or mode. Successful regimes are perceived as better able to control events, thus the character of such a transition will be more top-down in structure. In contrast, transitions arising from poorly performing regimes are likely to have events driven from the bottom-up.[16] Given this, it is not surprising that much of the work on democratic consolidations focusses on the relationship between the mode of a transition and the path of the subsequent consolidation.

A common contention among those examining the link between mode of transition and democratic consolidation is that the more peaceful a transition, the better the climate for consolidation of democracy. Karl proposes this hypothesis in her work on democratic transitions in Latin America.[17] Huntington and Valenzuela concur. For Huntington, a 'transplacement', in which a transition is peacefully negotiated by roughly equally matched regime and opposition forces, is most likely to lead to a multiparty democracy. Transitions which involve force, or the threat of force, whether from elite or opposition, have dimmer prospects for success.[18] Valenzuela chooses to focus on the origins of a transition from the perspective of the elite. This view requires that one understand the elite's attitude toward democratization and how that attitude emerged. An elite that is favorably disposed toward building democracy is likely to result in a peaceful transition and a successful consolidation. Successful consolidations are likely because those in the elite who were resistant to democratization have already been marginalized by reformers. Once reformers win the initial struggle for political power, reversal of the transition becomes difficult and consolidation easier.[19]

In her study of transitions in Eastern Europe, Welsh draws on both Huntington and Valenzuela. She argues that successful communist transitions are most likely to emerge out of prolonged periods of bargaining. Such transitions produce political leaders who are receptive to the requirements of a competitive democratic electoral system, especially conflict resolution.[20] Agh makes a similar argument in his analysis of the Hungarian Socialist Party, noting the existence of a reform-minded regime which tolerated reform sentiments among both the intelligentsia and the masses. The result was a negotiated, peaceful transition in which the Socialist Party retained substantial support. Although the socialists lost control of parliament in the country's first democratic election in 1990, they were well placed to make a successful return in 1994.[21]

Munck and Leff also argue for the importance of studying the mode of transition in order to understand the course of the subsequent consolidation. While agreeing with those that make this link, they criticize earlier studies for their lack of clarity in not specifying exactly how the mode of transition may affect the consolidation. Munck and Leff hypothesize three components of consolidation that are influenced by the transition: patterns of elite competition, post-transition institutional rules and acceptance or rejection of those rules by the key political actors. Also significant is the broadly comparative nature of the study. Munck and Leff apply their hypotheses to brief case studies of transitions in Latin America (Argentina, Brazil and Chile) and Eastern Europe (Bulgaria, Czechoslovakia, Hungary and Poland).[22]

Once again, understanding the future prospects of the left requires that we temporarily look backward. But since the historical legacies of all post-communist systems are by definition the legacies of the left (or a major part of the left), it is vital to understand those legacies. Clearly the past matters.

In addition to the general legacy attributable to the left, it may be useful to examine the sequencing of events following the transition. Given the diverse fates experienced by the left in the immediate post-transition period, one must ask whether early defeat or victory by these parties will subsequently affect the future ability of the left to compete. Is it beneficial, for example, for the left to be defeated electorally early in the consolidation phase, thus allowing it the opportunity to remake itself away from the scrutiny that comes with holding leadership?

2. *Economic challenges* The need for economic reform has been a crucial factor for all post-communist regimes. The necessity of undertaking radical

economic reform along with a democratic political transition has been the norm for the post-communist world and distinguishes it from other cases of democratic transition and consolidation.

Przeworski's treatment of this issue is among the most ambitious of the initial theoretical studies of democratic transition and consolidation. His conception of the consolidation process leads him to place enormous importance on the ability of the new democratic government to deal with economic crisis. Przeworski proposes a dynamic model which centers on the political choices available to the key actors. His analysis suggests that the most likely outcome of attempts at radical reform of an economy yield an uncertain path where radical reforms 'are eventually slowed or partly reversed'.[23] This cycle can repeat itself with the result being that economic reform never entirely succeeds or fails. Despite this pessimistic assessment, Przeworski does not believe that the situation is hopeless. While acknowledging that economic reform is politically risky, he argues that reform can be successfully pursued if the pro-reform forces (whether government or opposition) can achieve political hegemony. For this to occur, the pro-reform groups can either seek to broaden their own base of support or act to narrow the support of their opposition.[24] Unfortunately, the former strategy is difficult to accomplish and the latter jeopardizes the democratic process. It should not be surprising that the problem of economic reform still bedevils all post-communist states, and a political party which is incapable of dealing with this challenge faces a very uncertain future.

Economic reform represents a particularly sensitive issue for the left as it seeks to maintain its reputation of protecting the interests of the working class without giving the impression of backtracking on the fundamentals of the economic transformation. In some cases, however, the mainstream left seems to have abandoned any pretext of protection of the working class. In Curry's words, 'something akin to "trickle down economics" of the Reagan era was their [the successor parties'] vehicle for saving the victims of the transformation'.[25] It is unclear whether the left can continue with this approach and still lay claim to the loyalty of the working class. Nor is it clear whether the left will be able to differentiate itself effectively from the policies of the parties of the center if it champions radical economic transformation.

A more distant problem rests in the transformation of the entire global economic system. One must ask what will the working class look like in a fully transformed, high-tech economy. Although this is an issue which will confront the advanced capitalist states first, the economies of most post-communist systems eventually will find themselves at this stage too. Will the social policies of the left, moderate or radical, have any attraction to a transformed working class in a post-industrial society? On the other hand, it is possible to conceive of the left as a social and political counterbalance to the dominance of capitalism, thus creating a long-term rationale for the left's existence.

3. *Management of social and political conflict*   A successful democratic transition will result in competition for influence among a variety of political and social actors.[26]   In order for democratic consolidation to proceed, the conflicts generated by this competition need to be controlled.   If a political party is to be successful, it must show itself to the electorate as capable of managing social and political conflict and, once in power, must implement successful policies to control conflict.   In more general terms, Schmitter argues that the challenge is for political leadership to devise new 'social demand and conflict processing settlements'.   These arrangements must, on the one hand, include all of the significant political and social actors, and still manage to be 'insulated within the narrowest possible boundaries in terms of the specificity of the issues and the state political and social actors who are involved'.[27]

Meeting the challenge of social and political conflict in post-communist states raises three issues for the left.   First, it will be necessary to examine the adaptability of these parties in adjusting to the post-transition political environment.   To some extent, the parties of the left can be evaluated according to their performance since 1989.   While this may be the best indicator for which there is data, it is by no means a guarantee of future success.   The left must be analysed in terms of its ability to compete in the future and to confront the problems of consolidation that lie farther down the road.   One useful method would be to examine generational change in a party. Party leadership that came of age in the post-communist era might be better prepared to deal with such challenges.   In terms of Schmitter's contention, their minimal ties with the communist past would make it easier for them to gain the support of the broad spectrum of actors necessary to manage social and political conflict.

Level of party democratization represents another potential indicator of adaptability.   To some extent, this represents a two-edged sword.   A party with a high level of democratization should be more capable of understanding the changing needs of the electorate.   In new democracies, where the electorate is likely to be volatile as its voters seek to develop an awareness of their political interests, the ability to understand such trends quickly and accurately can be an important competitive advantage.   On the other hand, a party that is fractious risks being incapable of responding to the changing nature of the political environment.   Firm leadership, with some top-down decision-making and implementation, can be beneficial.

A complicating factor here will be public perception.   The communist successor parties must be especially cognizant of how their commitment to a democratic political system is perceived by the electorate.   They will continue to be vulnerable to their communist past for most of the current generation. This was clearly a concern of the Hungarian Socialist Party after the 1994 election when its leadership, despite controlling 54 per cent of the seats in the new parliament, invited the Alliance of Free Democrats to join the government. Meanwhile, all parties of the left will need to cultivate an image of competence with the voters. They must demonstrate, for example, an ability and a willingness to work within the parliamentary system. Such an image would probably include convincing the electorate that they are willing to work with other parties of the center and that such parties would be willing to work with them.

An intervening variable affecting party adaptability will be the level to which the electorate has come to understand the democratic process. There appears to be considerable variance among the post-communist states with respect to the sophistication of the voters. A major question centers on the extent to which voters perceive differences among the political parties and are able to arrive at informed decisions regarding support of a party that conforms to their interests. A country with a relatively sophisticated public will exhibit signs of class politics. Social classes will come to regularly support political parties based on a sharing of values. This relationship is the result of economic transformation that has given rise to the re-emergence of social classes.[28] In countries where class politics exist, the left must be concerned with developing as broad a constituency as possible while still holding on to its loyal core. It will be important to determine the nature of the left's appeal to various social classes. In cases where the data can be sufficiently disaggregated, it would be useful to determine whether certain social classes emerge first in a post-communist society and whether the order of emergence benefits the left or its political opposition.

A second issue facing the left in meeting the challenge of managing social and political conflict is its ability to attract support in both the present and the future. One concern must be sustaining, if not enhancing, party membership. An active party membership is vital for conducting a successful campaign and for cultivating candidates for office. The characteristics of party membership can be included here. For a party to be successful in the future, it will need to attract younger members to replace retiring members and candidates. Similar concerns can be raised about the types of voters likely to support a party. Clearly it will be necessary to determine what interest groups the left is supported by and how much electoral influence those groups are likely to accumulate in the future. Related questions include whether the left is attracting the constituencies one might expect to support the left and what the left must do to attract such constituencies. A key example here is the relationship between the left and labor unions, as well as whether labor unions represent an important, or potentially important, political force in a country.

Funding is also a function of constituency support, so it will be useful to examine existing and potential sources of financial support for the parties of the left. A better understanding of the left's funding potential will help to better estimate its competitiveness *vis-à-vis* other political parties.

Finally, the individual or idiosyncratic factor deserves attention. To what extent can the left's present and future success or failure be explained by individual personalities? Does it matter who is or will be in charge of a party? Are individual leaders capable of overcoming hindrances to the future success of the left? Although broader economic, social and political forces merit the bulk of our attention, it would be unwise to overlook the occasional importance of individuals. One wonders what the political face of Eastern Europe would look like today if Leonid Brezhnev or Yuri Andropov were still alive.

4. *External factors* External factors traditionally have attracted little attention among those studying transitions from authoritarian rule and only slightly more attention in the study of democratic consolidations. Recent literature has become receptive to the international context of consolidations. With the collapse of communism in Eastern Europe, external factors have received a higher priority in scholars' efforts to understand the dynamics of regime change and development. Clearly without the actions of Mikhail Gorbachev, the momentous events of 1989 would not have happened.

Pridham argues that considerable attention must be paid to the role of external factors in the democratization process, and that this is especially true with consolidations occurring in Eastern Europe.[29] The most frequently mentioned international factor relates to what Huntington refers to as 'snowballing'. The rapid chronological sequencing of the East European transitions meant that events occurring in one country were likely to affect affairs in other countries in the region. With respect to consolidation, Huntington writes that a country's success in achieving democratic consolidation will depend partially upon whether a favorable international climate exists to facilitate the growth of democracy. The interests of the most significant international actors in the region will be particularly important in understanding the course of events.[30] For Pridham, external actors become a more significant factor in East European consolidations because of the great extent to which the international system changed as a result of the fall of communism in the region. Western Europe and the United States found their interests and priorities in the region radically changed and were obliged to seek re-engagement.[31] Schmitter offers a different perspective on the snowballing effect. While acknowledging that late arrivals in a wave of democratization are more apt to be subject to external forces, he speculates that this may be an advantageous situation. Successive democratizations have led to the emergence of an international 'infrastructure' which encourages and protects democracy. The late-coming countries of Eastern Europe are well placed to take advantage of this infrastructure by receiving advice and assistance from a variety of governmental and nongovernmental actors, especially the network of organizations and institutions that pervades Western Europe.[32]

This volume will be concerned with how the left will be affected by various external factors that impact on democratic consolidation and how successful it might be in meeting the challenges posed by external factors. The snowballing phenomenon suggests the need to understand how the experiences and activities of the left in one country might affect the fortunes of the left in a neighboring country. Is it possible to locate instances where the left in one state learned from the fortunes or misfortunes of the left in a second state? The ability of the left to face successfully the regional (European) environment must be scrutinized. How has the left come to terms with the potential for membership in the North Atlantic Treaty Organization (NATO) or the European Union (EU)? Does the willingness of NATO or the EU to accept a country into membership help to validate the transformation of the moderate left parties? Can the successor parties use pressure from external actors to continue with economic reforms as a means of reducing some of the public ill will previously directed at the communist past? What assistance from external actors can the left count on; will the left's political competition be the principal beneficiary of Schmitter's international infrastructure? To what extent is the left able and willing to work with this infrastructure?

The purpose of this discussion of challenges facing the left is meant to set the conceptual stage for the country studies that will follow. It is not intended to be a comprehensive review of all challenges facing the post-communist left, but rather it is meant to raise issues for discussion. It is recognized that not all of the challenges described here will apply to every post-communist country. Indeed, it is likely that knowledge can be gained simply by discovering which challenges apply to which countries. The country studies will function as a guide for theory-building and the formation of tentative conclusions. But the journey for the post-communist left has just begun and probably will include several more stops. No doubt more surprises will be in store for 'successor' scholars studying successor parties.

NOTES

1. For example, the 1989 split in the Hungarian Socialist Workers' Party in which a majority of the membeship remade itself in to the reform-minded Hungarian Socialist Party while the orthodox communists continued on under the old party banner.
2. For example, see the editorial in the *New York Times*, 23 September 1993, A26.

3. Alison Mahr and John Nagle, 'Resurrection of the Successor Parties and Democratization in East-Central Europe', *Communist and Post-Communist Studies* **28**, 4 (1995): 406.
4. Adam Przeworski, *Democracy and the Market* (New York: Cambridge University Press, 1991), pp. 88–94.
5. Jane Curry, 'The Return of the Left', *NewsNet: The Newsletter of the AAASS* **37** (May 1997): 1–3.
6. Ibid., p. 1.
7. Ibid., p. 3.
8. Ibid., p. 3.
9. I am grateful to Richard P. Farkas for this observation.
10. Samuel P. Huntington, *The Third Wave: Democratization in the Late Twentieth Century* (Norman: University of Oklahoma Press, 1991), p. 277.
11. Guillermo O'Donnell, 'Transitions, Continuities, and Paradoxes', in Scott Mainwaring, Guillermo O'Donnell, and J. Samuel Valenzuela, (eds), *Issues in Democratic Consolidation: The New South American Democracies in Comparative Perspecteve* (South Bend: University of Notre Dame Press, 1992), p. 25. O'Donnell notes that this advantage is partially offset by the damaged economy the old regime has left behind.
12. J. Samuel Valenzuela,'Democratic Consolidation in Post-transitional Settings: Notion, Process, and Facilitating Conditions', in Scott Mainwaring, Guillermo O'Donnell, and Samuel Valenzuela, (eds), *Issues in Democratic Consolidation: The New South American Democracies in Comparative Perspective* (South Bend: University of Notre Dame Press, 1992), pp. 78–9.
13. Huntington, pp. 113–15.
14. Ibid., pp. 113–15, 276.
15. John T. Ishiyama, 'The Sickel or the Rose? Previous Regime Types and the Evolution of the Ex-communist Parties in Post-communist Politics', *Comparative Political Studies* **30**, 3 (June 1997): 299–300.
16. Guillermo O'Donnell and Philippe C. Schmitter, *Transitions from Authoritarian Rule: Tentative Conclusions about Uncertain Democracies* (Baltimore: Johns Hopkins University Press, 1986), pp. 16–17.
17. Terry Lynn Karl, 'The Dilemma of Democratic Transitions in Latin America', *Comparative Politics* **23**, 1 (October 1990).
18. Huntington, p. 276.
19. Valenzuela, pp. 75–6.
20. Helga A. Welsh, 'Political Transition in Central and Eastern Europe', *Comparative Politics* **26**, 4 (1994).
21. Attila Agh, 'Partial Consolidation in the East-Central European Parties: The Case of the Hungarian Socialist Party', *Party Politics* **1**, 3 (1995). Also see Barnabas Racz, 'The Socialist Left Opposition in Post-communist Hungary', *Europe-Asia Studies* **45**, 4 (1993).
22. Gerado L. Munck and Carol Skalnik Leff, 'Modes of Transition and Democratization: South America and Eastern Europe in Comparative Perspective', *Comparative Politics* **30**, 3 (April 1997): 343–62.
23. Przeworski, p. 179.
24. Ibid., pp. 180–82.
25. Curry, p. 3.
26. Schmitter refers to these actors as 'intermediary institutions'. Philippe C. Schmitter, 'Transitology: The Science or the Art of Democratization?', in Joseph S. Tulchin (ed), *The Consolidation of Democracy in Latin America* (Boulder: Lynne Rienner, 1995), p. 27.
27. Ibid., pp. 27–9.
28. H. Kitschelt, 'The Formation of Party Systems in East Central Europe', *Politics and Society* **20** (1992).
29. Geoffrey Pridham, 'The International Dimension of Democratization Theory: Practice and Inter-regional Comparisons', in Geoffrey Pridham, Eric Herring, and George Sanford,

(eds), *Building Democracy? The International Dimension of Democratization in Eastern Europe* (New York: St. Martin's, 1994).
30. Huntington, pp. 100–106; 273–4.
31. Pridham, p. 29.
32. Schmitter, pp. 35–6.

2. The Russian Left in Transition

Mark A. Cichock

We are the communists. Not pink, not brown. But real, red communists.
(Yuri Terentyev, member of the Communist Workers of Russia, 10 December,
1995)

Of all the political forces to emerge from the chaos of the demise of the Soviet
political system the left has proved itself to be the strongest and most
consistent contender for political power. Only in the Baltic states, Armenia
and Georgia, where strong nationalist movements captured public affinities,
has the left been unable to dominate the political agenda (and even in these
countries several left-oriented parties transformed their identities and
continued to govern). In virtually every other successor state – and especially
the Russian Federation – the left in varied form became either the inheritors
of power (primarily in Central Asia and Azerbaijan, and also Belarus), or an
opposition force capable of stymying reformers (Russia, Ukraine, Moldova).
Viewed in broad, macro terms the left had been on the brink of political
oblivion in 1991 and yet staged a comeback at a time when the forces of
change seemed arrayed against it.

In the Russian Federation the left has survived the immediate travails of
system transformation and in some respects prospered. Even so, the left –
particularly the communist left – has not been able to control or direct the
process of change. It is this inability of the left to seize the moment in Russian
politics despite its resources and clear organizational advantages that moves
us to take a closer look at the phenomenon of the left in post-Soviet Russian
political society. Why has the left not been able to effectively rise to the
occasion of leadership? Why have left-oriented parties demonstrated a
strikingly high degree of fragmentation and intractable attitudes toward
reconciliation and compromise?

Forced into coalition arrangements among themselves the elements of the
left have squabbled over priorities, laid conflicting claims to elusive leadership
mantles and not infrequently treated each other as enemies rather than allies.
Seemingly every party or movement of the left has attempted to establish its

credentials as the inheritors of Soviet communist legitimacy and as a result tried to discredit other claimants to the mantle of Lenin. How, then, could a unified left be expected to take center stage in the overall policy process if it cannot get its own house in order?

This chapter tries to explain both what the Russian left is and what it means in Russian politics today. To do this the legacy of communism is examined from the last days of *perestroika* (1990–91) when the Communist Party of the Soviet Union (CPSU) was in crisis to the evolution of communism and socialism into but one side of a multi-facted, pluralistic policy-making process. In particular, this chapter focusses on the re-emergence of communism as a viable, albeit dramatically altered, ideological force in the post-Soviet era. The fact that this parallels the evolving character and structure of the Communist Party of the Russian Federation (KPRF) requires that we understand the primary developments which have shaped this largest of Russia's political parties. But whatever the story of the KPRF it cannot be complete without profiling its varied allies and adversaries; it is these organizations, parties and movements which give scope to the category 'left'. Ironically, these collective forces have become an important aspect of the general phenomenon of Russian political pluralism and within that a specific subset which flies in the face of the principle of democratic centralism developed by V.I. Lenin. Here it is proposed that the Russian left, despite its electoral strength, is in fact a victim of factors beyond its control and not likely to regain either the political strength or the internal cohesion the CPSU possessed during the Soviet period. We are thus bound to examine not what the left used to be but rather what the left has become.

The Russian Federation represents the best case study of the fate of the new left in the former Soviet space. The sheer size of the Russian Federation recommends it to our course of study; within its political spectrum we find every aspect of political debate current anywhere else in the Eurasian republics. Whether right, center or left, the forces of the Russian political scene represent movements in only the loosest sense of the term. The importance of the left as compared to the other two designations lies in its proximity to power. In contrast to the political right which stands no realistic chance of gaining either parliamentary or presidential power in the near future, or the center where the so-called 'democrats' have not been certain what they wanted to do with the authority they held, the left has come close. A loose coalition of leftist parties holds a plurality of power in the Russian State Duma, the lower chamber of the legislature; it has achieved increasingly greater support in the Federation Council, national the upper chamber; and finally it has managed to secure wins in presidential, gubernatorial and legislative elections in a number of Russia's republics and regions. This situation has permitted the left to challenge the reformist agenda of the Yeltsin administration at the national level and of change-oriented elites at the regional level. The left has subsequently taken the opportunity to prepare its own positions and familiarize the public with them should it, through any of its myriad organizations, manage to overcome the many obstacles to power.

On the heels of the important KPRF victory in the December 1995 elections to the State Duma, Russian and Western media proclaimed the resurgence of communism and the end to the reform era. Having won 22 per cent of the national vote the KPRF was by far the largest faction in the new Duma. Along with the candidates who had won seats by running in single-member districts, the KPRF was in control of 157 seats overall, or 34 per cent of the Duma's total of 450 deputies. With support from the Agrarian bloc and other left-wing forces at their disposal, the KPRF was in an advantageous position for the first time since the suspension and siege of the parliament in the events of September–October 1993.

Moreover, once the new State Duma came into session in January 1996, the parcelling out of committee assignments and chair positions put the communists in charge of nine of the lower house's 28 committees. Their allies in the Agrarian Party were allocated two chairmanships. In addition, with the support of the reform-oriented Yabloko bloc, the communists were able to name one of their own – Gennadii Seleznev, a member of the party's Politburo – as speaker of the Duma thereby giving the KPRF even greater control over the Duma's agenda (in the previous Duma the KPRF had held the deputy speaker position). All of this seemed to reflect a sense of momentum, of strategic placement for the left and the communists in particular and a reversal of fortune for the forces of reform centered around President Boris Yeltsin. Certainly the left had recovered from the body blows dealt it by Yeltsin and the public in the initial days of the post-Soviet period. This chapter contends, however, a different prospect, namely that the unity of Russian leftist forces generally and communist forces in particular are not as cohesive as generally thought. It is instead hypothesized that given the diversity of goals and policies expressed by the various communist parties or factions the prospects for continuing electoral or policy solidarity are minimal. The left itself may fare well, but cohesion is another thing and presents the left with as big of a challenge as winning the elections themselves.

To test the validity of this prospect this chapter examines the considerable variation which exists within the framework of the Russian left. Thus, the pattern of support that the various communist factions offer each other is a direct result of how well they adhere to each other's stated goals. Further, the degree of factionalism that exists within the largest of these parties, the KPRF, determines how they will fare in putting forth a parliamentary agenda and realizing it through legislative action. But there is more to the issue than just the fate of communism: there are also the more moderate elements of social democracy and the less-certain non-communist parties, blocs and movements which ally themselves with the KPRF but may not agree with that party's goals. Gaining a significant electoral following is only part of what the left needs in order to survive: it also needs a sense of who it is and a willingness to compromise within itself. This is not the easiest of tasks given the divisiveness of the various elements of the left. Thus, unification within this part of the political spectrum is the barometer by which we may best judge the left's success.

1 WHAT IS THE LEFT?

It is something of a stereotype to think of the left purely in terms of political parties. And yet since the beginning of the twentieth century and Lenin's organization of the Bolshevik faction within the Russian Social Democratic Labour Party the political party has been the principal identifier of the left. A truer reflection is that the left is an integral element of the larger Russian political culture. It is within this environment that political parties, movements and underground organizations have traditionally existed and sometimes flourished. The left is a prism through which much of Russian society has typically seen the world, and it has left a clear physical imprint upon both the land and its peoples.

The political ecology of the left exists to a degree unthought of in the United States or even in most West European countries. Leftist ideals, whether socialist or communist, are deeply rooted in such institutions as the collectivism of the Russian village, or *mir*. Communitarian and egalitarian values that characterized village and small town in the Tsarist Russia passed slowly into the cities of the empire in its latter days. The process was furthered in the Soviet period with Stalin's industrialization drive feeding millions of peasants into the Soviet Union's factories, forever after to be city dwellers, but still possessive of their collective ideals. As such, a melding of rural and urban values in Russia took place fairly late compared to those experiences of West European nation-states. Both Yeltsin and KPRF leader Gennady Zyuganov were raised in rural confines and bring to their governance much that they learned from these experiences.[1]

For Russia the twentieth century has been a time of vast upheavals in terms of social and political revolutions, civil and world wars, famine, industrialization, economic expansion, mass education and a host of other systemic changes. Change for Russia has largely been a dichotomous process based on ideological interpretations of economic development within society; change was the result of challenges and responses that pitted large segments of the population against one another. Out of the crucible of such revolutionary conditions has come a sense of self-righteousness that is not given over to compromises or inclusory politics. Coupled to an ideological dogma that pronounced itself to be scientific in nature (Marxism–Leninism) and therefore rejected alternative organizational schemes the political system of the communist period was decidedly intolerant of competition. The implications of communism's legacy for the post-Soviet successor state have been a political culture of conflict wearing the ill-fitting clothing of democratic participation.

The associations of the Russian citizenry with the goals of the revolutionary movement – whether underground or in statist form – are long and deep and not readily eradicated. On the cusp of the millennia Russian citizens are much less frequently men and women of Soviet making. Russian youth especially have their political experiences shaped not by the weight of Soviet achievements and failures but instead by the politics of the transition period. Whereas Lenin saw the then-new communist state as bearing the birth marks of developing Russian capitalism[2] the reverse is true today with capitalism, social pluralism, and democratic governance being molded by the birth-mother of communism.

Even those citizens who have rejected outright the legacy of communism find themselves still affected by all that the Soviet system provided or prevented. In particular, an impressive number of citizens belonged to the CPSU which at its height in 1989 consisted of 19.4 million people out of 292 million Soviet nationals, or 6.6 per cent of the total.[3] For whatever reasons members belonged – usually careerism or ideology – the system shaped them. As well, virtually every Soviet citizen benefitted from common health care, education, job security and a host of other programs all decided upon for them by the CPSU. For the many who left the party or refused to support it at the time of the coup in August 1991, dissatisfaction had been fostered by abuses and gross manipulations of power and human rights. The downfall of an entire national–political–ideological concept obviously presents a major shock to any public and the fall of the Soviet Union was not taken lightly or without some regret by a sizable portion of the public. The loss of support for the statist concept did not mean that the public no longer accepted left-oriented ideals, but rather that a particular element of this support – granting the CPSU monopoly decision-making powers – had diminished considerably.

If the left is about a way of life that is very much a part of Russian politics there is an obvious need to pay attention to its organizational component. Political parties have become for Russia in the 1990s a concrete form for expressing and realizing political viewpoints and ideologies. The Russian left is a composite and largely non-cohesive grouping of communist, socialist and social-democratic parties. Since 1993 approximately 13 parties, movements and associations have come to define the parameters of the Russian left. For the most part these groups call for a reorientation of society giving a strong degree of preference to state direction in economic planning, centralized decision-making over political and social issues and a reorientation of society's resources in favor of the economically and socially disadvantaged. Nevertheless, the left can be divided into two major branches, each of which encompasses its own distinct thematic focus beyond which each has difficulty seeing. The first of these we turn to is that of social democracy.

2   THE SOCIAL-DEMOCRATIC LEFT

As in the last several decades of the tsarist empire so too today the major branches of the Russian left are separated despite their common ancestry. While the social democracy pedigree is as well founded as that of communism and literally comes from the same roots, social democracy has not had the organizational success or societal attachment attained by communism. Attributing these shortcomings entirely to the superior organizational skills of Lenin and his followers gives us only part of the picture. Communism did develop for itself a more definitive set of goals and proved more adept at mobilizing than its ideological cousin, but more importantly social-democratic ideals never resonated deeply within the Russian political culture. The goals of social democracy seemed more suited to the advanced economic infrastructures of Western Europe where political participation was more a matter of established practice than to the continuing political struggles of Russia. As the social and political pressures built up behind the CPSU in the *perestroika* period it was not social democracy which was accepted in lieu of communism. What prevailed instead was a rejection of the principles upon which the CPSU's monopoly of political power was maintained and with this rejection came a search for another option.

In the immediate post-Soviet period it may have seemed that a clear niche had opened up within the Russian political spectrum for social-democratic parties. Stating, among other things, that 'Marxism's claim to be scientific is nothing more than a pseudoscientific neoreligion ... subordinate to the interests and caprices of a monopolistic, absolutist power'[4] former CPSU members who were by this point calling themselves social democrats rejected out of hand the authoritarian tendencies of the communists and pledged themselves instead to a pluralist society. By casting off the vestiges of centralized power and any association with the Stalinist legacy, Russian social democrats positioned themselves for the political fallout they were certain would benefit them in electoral politics.

The basic ideas of the social democrats were, however, almost always in competition with other more established ideas. At first it was the middle of the road socialism proposed by Mikhail Gorbachev which prevented a true socialist alternative from developing. And under other circumstances the temporary banning of the CPSU (1991 to 1993) might have afforded the social-democratic groups the time and space necessary to forge organizations capable of electoral competition. But the long years of the CPSU's monopoly on political ideas meant that social-democratic ideals were largely unknown to the public or undifferentiated from that of the communists to their left. Other imported Western concepts of democracy and free market reform presented clearer, more differentiated alternatives to state socialism at a time when the Soviet public was largely disenchanted with the ways that things had been done. As a result social democracy was effectively squeezed into a political corner at the very time when it should have been developing ties with a dissatisfied public.

The social-democratic movement in Russia sprang from the premise that party membership would not and could not be a monopolized commodity. The successful effort to get the CPSU to abandon its hold on political power in 1990 did not guarantee that any other party would be the natural inheritor of what the CPSU had left behind. Social-democratic parties instead committed themselves to freedom of conscience in choosing party organizations and a rejection of strict party discipline. This included most obviously Lenin's democratic centralism precept which was unceremoniously dropped by virtually all other components of the Russian party system but still religiously maintained by the KPRF and the other splinter groups of the far left.

Better known for the personalism of their political leaders than for their organizational skills, the social-democratic parties have thus far experienced identity crises as the public did not respond to their electoral messages in either the 1993 or 1995 federal elections or the numerous regional elections held since 1996. The banner of social democracy has been taken up by prominent ex-CPSU members such as Gavriil Popov, the former mayor of Moscow who founded the Russian Movement for Democratic Reforms, and Alexandr Yakovlev and former CIS military commander Evgenii Shapashnikov, the co-chairs of the Russian Social Democracy Party. Yakovlev was not just the primary architect of the program of *perestroika* but also one of the few who would seek answers as to why the Soviet system fell apart. Notable also for its leaders rather than any electoral successes is the Social Democrats Election Bloc composed of the Russian Social Democratic Union (RSDU), co-chaired by Vassily Lipitskiy, an organization which in 1994 was aptly described as 'without influence'. At the founding of the RSDU in that year Lipitskiy described both his party's platform and unwittingly its problem when he rejected the calls of the extreme left for rebuilding the Soviet Union but also refused to embrace 'drastic revolutionary reformism' such as the democratic groups demanded.[5] Even more obscure social-democratic groups than these have tried to mold themselves as viable options in the search for solutions to Russia's problems. But all seem to fail by their emphasizing Western European traditions of social democracy and pluralism which the public finds at odds with Russian traditions of political development. Moreover, the social-democratic parties especially, as well as the more radical elements of the communist left (see below) lend weight to the supposition that the leadership variable is not an adequate substitute for a concise, well-formulated and popular ideology to which a mass voting public can adhere.

3   THE COMMUNIST LEFT IN TRANSITION

If the social-democratic component is a political concept which embraces compromise, the communist left largely rejects it and instead promotes a regressive political vision. The communist left endorses a return to the dominant role that the state held during the Soviet era. Within this context the more radical left parties or groups prefer the strict, iron-handed Stalinist control over economic and social functions and profess the desire to return to a one-party political system. Playing a more middle-of-the-road strategy other components of the communist left, notably the KPRF, support a quasi-pluralist approach such as that which was fostered by Gorbachev toward the end of the Soviet period. As already noted, Gorbachev's reforms and most particularly the CPSU's loss of its monopoly on political power caused a splintering which formalized the birth of a pluralistic process. The *perestroika* era revealed the disparate opinions within the CPSU that had long been papered over by democratic centralism. The so-called liberal or democratic reform movement within the party eventually divorced itself entirely from leftist ideologies and what remained of the CPSU were principally the hard-line conservatives opposed to the reformist program of Gorbachev.[6] The failed August 1991 coup resulted in the CPSU being banned outright and when the state structure imploded in late 1991 a number of communist factions seized the moment to lay claim to the CPSU's legitimacy, ideology and resources. The single most significant part of all this was the millions of party members. Since the KPRF and other 'radical' left organizations eventually would account for only about 3 per cent of the CPSU's former membership, the real question seems to be where these millions of party stalwarts, careerists, hangers-on and the politically marginal had gone. It would appear that the great majority of former members have become part of the amorphous mass electorate which has taken shape in the Russian Federation. Inevitably most ex-CPSU members are still deeply affected by the values of Marxism–Leninism, state socialism and the struggles implied by class conflict. Some of these millions are undoubtedly waiting for the KPRF to convince them of its value, while possibly the great majority are waiting for the political system to finish shaking itself out prior to their adopting new identities. But in the 1993 State Duma elections neither the general voting public nor former party members found any special reason for joining or staying with any of these parties.[7] By 1995, however, the economy was the priority issue determining party affiliation although not necessarily whether individuals participated in the first place.[8]

As political parties often reflect the priorities and personalities of their leaders, so too the KPRF seems to be the party of Zyuganov. With the sponsorship of Ivan Polozkov the former First Secretary of the Communist Party of the Russian Federation in the Soviet period, Zyuganov rose through the ranks eventually gaining the position of deputy chairman of the Central Committee of the CPSU's Ideology Department. Polozkov, who had been an opponent of Gorbachev's reform program, supported Zyuganov knowing full well that his protégé was ideologically parallel to himself. Zyuganov's post-Soviet stances on reconstructing the Soviet system, his close association with the ideology of national patriotism, his calls to abolish the powerful nature of the Russian presidency in favor of a resurrected Supreme Soviet[9] and voiding the constitution promulgated under Boris Yeltsin in 1993 demonstrate Zyuganov's deep sense of conservatism. And yet the party chairman has not been a leader of great stridency such as is encountered in the intransigent elements of the communist left. Instead Zyuganov's hallmarks have been those of a compromiser intent on gaining power within the system first and then changing it by means of the system's own institutions.

Zyuganov has been given much of the credit for resurrecting what had been a moribund party organization and making it electorally viable.[10] This has been due not so much to his organizational skills as to his popularity within the party organization. As may be discerned from his writings Zyuganov is not a theorist, nor does he frequently discuss the concepts of Marx or Lenin in his own writings; generally this is left to other members of the leadership such as the KPRF ideologist Alexandr Shabanov while Zyuganov himself focusses on explaining the party's political stance. Elected to the leadership of the newly-founded KPRF in 1990 Zyuganov became General Secretary when the party was reconstituted in February 1993; his tenure has not been uncontested, however, as many within the KPRF have disagreed with his policies and on occasion sought his removal from power (as was the case prior to the Fourth Congress in April 1997 and again in October of that year). His ideological pronouncements show him to have diverged considerably from mainstream Leninism, especially since Zyuganov has so closely intertwined his pronouncements on political economy and class conflict with calls for popular patriotism. Rhetorical flourishes as demonstrated in his contention that 'in broad historical and cultural terms, Great Russia is the Soviet Union .... Today it is criminally dismembered',[11] or that the 'capitalist restoration' under Yeltsin was equal to the devastation caused to Russia by Batu Khan, Napoleon and Hitler combined[12] show that he has strong affinities for the so-called 'radical patriotic movement' within the KPRF, although this group sometimes also questions Zyuganov's commitment.

At the close of the twentieth century a truncated Russian population of approximately 147.5 million citizens is largely apolitical if measured in terms of party affiliation. Collectively the communist left has the largest number of adherents of any group within the Russian political spectrum. The KPRF itself claims 540,000 members, a not-inconsequential figure even given the dramatic fall-off this implies from the previously mentioned figure of over 19 million. Rather glaring discrepancies in party membership are apparent, however, in that members are primarily drawn from white-collar professions with relatively few coming from the working class or the peasantry. Valentin Kuptsov, for instance, admitted that 'we have been unable to create an organized workers' movement, although this should have been one of the main aims'.[13] Perhaps recognizing a sense of unease within the party ranks over such a traditionally important issue, Zyuganov built on this theme himself at a party plenum and characterized party recruitment efforts among workers as having 'paid utterly inadequate attention' to labor collectives. As a result the party faces the dilemma of becoming a party of seemingly disenfranchised members of the *apparat* who mourn their loss of influence rather than a party of working-class interests.

More problematic for the KPRF is the generation gap in membership. The KPRF leadership has consistently recognized the lack of younger people in the party's ranks especially given the fact that those young members who are brought in are barely replacing those who are leaving or dying. At the time of the Third Congress in 1995 the average age of all members was nearly 50 years,[14] and only 10 per cent of the 363 delegates to that meeting were under the age of 40.[15] This has led the party leadership to the conclusion that if the KPRF hopes to keep its social base from shrinking it will need to convince the general public that it is not just a hold-over from the Soviet era. Toward this end the KPRF took the unprecedented step at the Third Congress of lowering the minimum membership age from 18 to 16 and the number of years a sponsor must know a candidate from three years to one. The problem is a critical one for the party, however, for if the core values of a free market system and limited government involvement in the economy are accepted by this group, and this group votes, then the KPRF's electoral and societal influence will certainly diminish.

The KPRF's structural organization is quite similar to that of the CPSU. The party is headed by a chairperson (formerly Secretary General) of the Central Executive Committee (more commonly just Central Committee) from which he/she derives authority. It is at the party congress that the Central Committee is elected, rules are decided or amended and policy is determined. At the Fourth Congress held in April 1997 the majority of the Central Committee was re-elected and a number of new members were elevated in rank bringing this body's size to 149 members.

As in the Soviet period the KPRF's other leadership positions are also settled during the congress and the number of positions may either expand or contract. At the Fourth Congress the position of first deputy chairperson was formally created (it had already existed de facto) and filled by Zyuganov's second in command, Valentin Kuptsov, at once a more orthodox communist than his immediate superior. The number of deputy chairpersons was reduced from four to one at this time (I.I. Melnikov) and the Presidium, or Politburo, was affirmed. As it did in the Soviet period the Politburo today represents the elite power structure within the KPRF, and Zyuganov must work through it rather than above it. With Zyuganov, Kuptsov and Duma speaker Gennadi Seleznev among its 17 members it is the primary decision-making body in the party hierarchy. Other bodies such as the Secretariat (which has only two members who simultaneously sit on the Politburo) and the Central Control and Auditing Commission are subordinate to the Central Committee. Collectively these bodies have become responsible for party policy including that which governs voting strategies for KPRF deputies in the State Duma.

Paying for all that the party does is an expensive proposition. The party is less wealthy than in the past especially without the state support of the past which permitted the party to develop a massive bureaucracy for the purpose of applying its standards and rules within the Soviet state. The KPRF's actual net worth and operating costs are not specifically known. This is one element of the old CPSU operating procedure which has remained a secret due in part to the unwillingness of party officials to tip their hand to their opponents in the administration and in competing parties. It is also a response to the need to protect the identities of those who support it but are not yet inclined to announce their affinities publicly, such as Duma member and chairman of Mosbiznesbank, Vladimir Semago.[16] The party claims that its dues account for 1 per cent of total party income while the rest comes from secret contributions.[17] Other resources have assisted the party such as the allowances made for all Duma deputies to hire five aides of whom four may be 'given' to their party; this effectively permits the hiring of party staff members at government expense. But the issue of finance loomed heavily over the party in the 1996 presidential elections when in the second round Zyuganov waged a lackluster effort prompted by its admission that it had simply run out of money.

The KPRF's structure beyond the national level is sketchy although the party claims to have 24,000 local organizations. The party has had to come to grips with the desire of autonomy-minded regional organizations which have only slowly opted for inclusion in the KPRF itself. For instance, it was not until 1997 that the communist parties of Tatarstan and Yakutia formally sought association with the main body of the KPRF. And while this points to the general difficulties that the KPRF has had in establishing its authority within the entire communist movement the party has unquestionably had more success than any of its competitors in building or attracting regional organizations to its ranks. Information concering the Novosibirsk organization, for instance, might be typical of other regional organizations. In 1994 the *oblast* party claimed a local membership of 4,500; the *oblast* committee was composed of 56 people from the *raions* which indicates that regional parties adhere to regional representation principles. Plenary sessions of the *oblast* committee were held on a bi-monthly basis, and the local leadership worked on a voluntary rather than a paid basis. This latter point was most likely the result of the ambiguous nature of the defunct CPSU's property which had been confiscated after the events of August 1991, and to which the KPRF had not at that point been able to lay claim.

Compared to other communist parties in Russia and the Eurasian states the KPRF has moderated the general orientation of ideology, particularly in its desire to participate in the instruments of federal power established under the 1993 constitution. Unlike the Bolsheviks prior to the outbreak of the First World War the KPRF leadership has seen the merit in participating in organs of state power such as the State Duma. With few other avenues of influence open this seemed like a logical choice for the KPRF leadership; and with the exception of all but the smallest of the fringe parties, it is a strategy that has been attempted by even the most hard-line communist elements. Moreover, the KPRF has proved itself to be an organized, relatively well-disciplined parliamentary faction quite capable of preventing the Yeltsin administration from carrying out key parts of its reformist agenda. For instance the Yeltsin administration's efforts to gain passage of a land code permitting the buying and selling of agricultural land has been blocked by the KPRF on numerous occasions. The party leadership has also recognized that it can hold much of the state budget hostage to its interests to the frustration of the Yeltsin administration.

At the Third Congress the KPRF leadership declared that the party had at last achieved a measure of stability after the tumult of the previous two years. They used this opportunity to begin the process of organizational reinforcement and rejuvenation of the party by bringing in younger members.

Speaking before that congress Zyuganov rejected the concept of revolutionary leaps and forceful solutions to problems and instead embraced what was to become the KPRF's most controversial policy, that of 'popular state patriotism'.[18] While this was a concept that has long been of great importance to Zyuganov, the Third Congress marked a turning point in the party's strategy. Two years later at the Fourth Congress the policy was forcefully reiterated as the leadership had come to believe that patriotic issues held the key to gaining political power. Thus, speaking before the congress Zyuganov could emphatically declare that the urgent task before the party organizations was their recognition that the issue of national patriotism was literally co-terminous with that of socialist development.

Probably the most interesting divergence that the KPRF exhibits from the standards of the CPSU is the lack of attention paid to the life-and-death struggle against world capitalism. For the KPRF it is still an important issue but in the party's short history and under the direction of Zyuganov there have been notable omissions in the development of economic and class struggle theory. One brief statement by Zyuganov demonstrates this point. Writing mid-way through his 1996 losing presidential campaign the KPRF chairman reflected on what form Russia's economic policy should take:

> It must be modern and national, that is, it must incorporate and reflect all the newest tendencies of world development, take into account our country's traditions, and respond to our national interests. Such a policy would then enjoy the broadest support of the Russian people, and Russia would then be able to recover quickly from its crisis and regain its former position in the world.[19]

Recovery and re-emergence seem to be the immediate concerns for Zyuganov while development of a socialist society takes a decidedly secondary place. Preservation of what remains of the Soviet Union's power, restoration of the army to its former greatness and creation of a volunteer association of states in the former Soviet space are frequently portrayed as being equally important, if not outright superior elements for the party's agenda in comparison to the struggle against capitalist enemies who are seen as robbing the state. All of this again raises the question of how unified the party hierarchy and rank-and-file membership are on these issues but there have been no specific outcries from within the party to change the emphasis in policy.

In discussing the inner workings of the KPRF there remains the continually perplexing issue of party discipline. The KPRF still subscribes to the notion of party discipline in both internal and external dealings; the entire concept is one of the most time-honored in the history of twentieth-century socialism. It is, however, also one of the most difficult to enforce if the leadership is not willing to accept splits, or the membership sees real distinctions characterizing the approach to policy and social development. For the KPRF the revival of the organization in 1993 meant new informal rules of organization and procedure. Since the party could or would not identify Russia's stage of development as being at the take-off point of revolutionary change, ideological conformity could not be justified. This effectively meant that factionalism had a de facto right to exist. As a result, over the first five years of the KPRF's existence three groups or factions had developed including the already mentioned 'patriotic' group, the 'ideological' group and the 'nomenclature' group. Zyuganov and Kuptsov themselves held different positions which occasionally put them at odds with each other;[20] their relationship, however, seems to be accurately portrayed as complementary rather than confrontational.

The existence of different camps or factions within the party not only presupposes policy differences but also has presented the party with one of its greatest challenges. In April 1998 in the crucial third Duma vote for the approval of Prime Minister Sergei Kirienko, the KPRF leadership allowed a secret ballot, effectively turning Duma deputies loose to vote as they desired. Having seen its much vaunted party discipline erode in the face of Seleznev's desire to keep the Duma from being dissolved, the KPRF lost one of its most visible struggles with the president. Although the party later considered the possibility of purging the mavericks who had voted to confirm Sergei Kirienko's candidacy for prime minister, pragmatic considerations such as how the public might view the dispute prevented a rupture. In this sense, then, the KPRF found that the political environment controlled it rather than the other way around.

The KPRF's views on governance have focussed on gaining greater power for the legislative branch of government at the direct expense of the powerful executive created by Yeltsin. Zyuganov and others in the party have attempted to cloak their willingness to use and sustain the current political and administrative organs in the guise of being a 'responsible and intransigent opposition'. But having developed this catch-phrase at the Fourth Congress Zyuganov himself could come up with no strategy to complement it, whether in legal or extra-legal terms.[21] Here again the differences with mainstream Leninist thought stand in sharp contrast; as Lenin succinctly stated it:

> We cannot imagine democracy, even proletarian democracy, without representative institutions, but we can and *must* [italics in the original] imagine democracy without parliamentarism, if criticism of bourgeois society is not mere words for us, if the desire to overthrow the rule of the bourgeoisie is our honest and sincere desire, and not a mere 'election' cry for catching workers' votes.[22]

For its part the KPRF has also argued that the presidency should be elected by the parliament rather than directly by the people, or be eliminated altogether. This view did not deter Zyuganov from running for the presidency in 1996 nor, one might speculate, from considering keeping such a powerful institution intact to further his party's agenda if he had come to power.

One of the most telling changes to come over the Russian left since the end of the Soviet Union has been the wedding of Russian nationalist traditions to the policy priorities of state socialism. Russian communists, especially those in the KPRF, have grafted calls for nationalist economic development onto the general doctrine of Marxist–Leninist thought. In the process the tenet of international solidarity of working classes has been downgraded both in terms of realistic prospects and as a desirable goal in itself. Not formally rejected by party ideologues, internationalism no longer occupies the privileged position it once did within the CPSU's operational code. The coming to the fore of nationalism did not occur immediately and in fact the constraints on Russian nationalism had already begun to be loosened as early as the 1970s.

It does not appear that at any time in the near future true unity will be achieved within the communist left, much less within the left taken in its entirety. Another half dozen minor parties have consistently challenged the KPRF for ideological supremacy and the all-important mantle of Marxist–Leninist standard bearer. The most immediate competitor to the KPRF is the Russian Communist Workers' Party which claims 50,000 members; a handful of lesser parties and movements – among them the more radical elements of the left – make up the remaining 10,000 members.[23] Of all other left-oriented parties, whether communist or non-communist, only the Agrarian Party led by Mikhail Lapshin has had much electoral success. The Agrarian bloc, which is composed of several small agriculture-oriented parties, favored the development of farmers' associations and the agro-industrial complex. The Agrarians have been vehemently resistant to the idea of privatized agriculture and have supported reinstitution of state agricultural subsidies. With many of its members coming from the ranks of collective farm management (the agricultural *nomenklatura* of the Soviet era) the party has been predisposed to electoral cooperation with the KPRF and in the Duma; their close association therefore places them within this part of our discussion. The Agrarians have also been hostile toward the Yeltsin–Chernomyrdin market-oriented reforms as they relate to land reform especially. But the Agrarians, who won 53 deputies in the first Duma elections in 1993, failed to retain the allegiance of their voters in 1995. The party failed to pass the 5 per cent electoral barrier and seated only 20 deputies from single-member districts. If it had not been for the KPRF 'loaning' 15 of its members to the Agrarians to bring its numbers up to 35, the Agrarian Party would have lost its status as a registered faction in the assembly. The KPRF has managed to make the Agrarians beholden to it, one might suspect, primarily to maintain the artificial cover of pluralism.

For various reasons other parties of the communist left have not proved themselves to be electorally significant. What to the voters must appear to be arcane differences in policy are sufficient for factional party leaders to distance themselves from one of the few realistic means they have for gaining power. One such group is the Socialist Party of the Working People headed by long-time Marxist dissident and respected historical author Roy Medvedev. The party, or more likely Medvedev on his own, sees the KPRF as an acceptable ally but does not receive most of the more radical parties of the left as warmly. Among the kinds of policies proposed by Medvedev are governmental guarantees of food and essential items to the population, especially children, the stimulation of productive rather than speculative activity in the economy and income redistribution that would not affect citizens' labor savings.[24] The significance of such a party is certainly not to be found in a burgeoning membership which has largely escaped it anyway, but rather in the power and influence of the ideas put forward by an individual of Medvedev's caliber.

4 THE 'RADICAL LEFT'

Further to the left of the KPRF several other communist parties have taken up the cause of resurrecting socialism. These groups were formed when the CPSU opened itself to divergent viewpoints (a 'Unity' faction of hard-liners emerged within the CPSU in 1988), or later in opposition to the KPRF's perceived lack of attention to the goals of the revolution. Their long-term importance is not to be found in the presence of any particular party or leader but rather in the divisiveness of political goals and the strategies adopted for realizing these goals. Most of the communist left is implacably opposed to the 1993 constitutional system and view Yeltsin as a traitor directly responsible for the fall of the Soviet system. Most of the radical left actively seek the restoration of the Soviet Union and publicly pronounce this to be their goal. Among these may be counted the Russian Communist Workers' Party, which is led by Viktor Tyulkin; Working Russia under the direction of Viktor Anpilov; and the Russian Party of Communists, headed by Anatoly Kryuchkov. The antipathy of these groups to the Yeltsin regime led many of their members to take part in the parliamentary uprising of September–October 1993, for which some, such as Anpilov, were jailed. At the same time some of these groups also harbor animosity toward Zyuganov and the KPRF which they consider as social democratic rather than Marxist–Leninist and too conciliatory toward the Yeltsin administration.[25]

The participation of several of these parties in the 1995 Duma elections did much to charge the political atmosphere since they were opposing not only the administration but the power structure of the KPRF as well. Several small parties formed an electoral bloc called Communists, Working Russia – For the Soviet Union. While they eventually proved unable to break the 5 per cent threshold this group did poll 4.53 per cent of the vote, which sent a clear message of dissatisfaction to the KPRF. The sole deputy awarded to this coalition came from a single-member district victory, but the importance of the election for the coalition was that it pressed the KPRF to the wall and required that party to abandon any pretence that it was truly representative of the entire left political spectrum. Particularly notable were the votes that Communists,Working Russia collected in the Republic of Tatarstan and Kirov *Oblast* where the coalition polled 47 per cent of the KPRF's total in each locale, Udmurtiya where it pulled in 56 per cent and Tyumen *Oblast* where it scored nearly 79 per cent! The fact that the KPRF failed to represent the most dissatisfied portion of the communist electorate gives the impression that the KPRF is at once much more of an establishment party than the radical 'intransigent opposition' of Zyuganov's claims.

    Less extreme but still farther to the left than the KPRF is the Union of Communist Parties – CPSU headed by Aleksey Prigarin. Calling itself a revived version of the CPSU, the UCP attempted to forge alliances with the various splinter groups on the far left such as Anpilov's and Kryuchkov's groups and the All-Union Communist Party (Bolsheviks), the Union of Communists and the Leninist Platform within the KPRF. In 1995 the UCP leadership described its relations with the KPRF as 'amicably hostile' due to what the UCP saw as the KPRF's social-democratic and less-than-Marxist tendencies.[26] At that same point Prigarin described Anpilov's group as too intent on old-style centralism in contrast to the UCP's calling for decentralized economic management alongside state planning and a regulated market. Rather accurately the UCP leadership determined that the people's lack of faith in the left was largely a condition of the unending factionalism among the communist parties.[27]

    In April 1995, in a bid to narrow the political spectrum and to preclude the radicalism represented by the communist left, Yeltsin convinced his prime minister, Viktor Chernomyrdin, and the then-speaker of the Duma, Ivan Rybkin, to form electoral blocs of the right and left respectively. This was perceived by Yeltsin as the moment that Chernomyrdin would require to consolidate his government's hold on power and to marginalize those parties of both the left and the right which were beyond the control of Yeltsin. If these parties could, in fact, be marginalized it would be much easier to fashion a conciliatory majority in the State Duma with which Yeltsin could work. Rybkin's task was the more difficult of the two since it essentially meant creating an opposition force that simultaneously had the blessing of the very person to whom it was to be opposed. Moreover, it would exclude the most significant group in the opposition – the KPRF.[28]

In June 1995 Rybkin tentatively put together a coalition of 25 small parties and groups, most of which were left-center but not diametrically opposed to the system as the communist left claimed to be. The most important potential supporters for Rybkin's bloc were the Agrarians, but despite his being on good terms with his former party members the Agrarians and most of the rest of the non-communist left held back. Since it had failed to identify itself in the minds of the voters Rybkin's bloc received a dismal 1.11 per cent of the total national vote and just three deputies elected from single-member districts. As a result the left's fortunes were to stand even more in opposition and the prospects for a system-supporting role evaporated. In a sense this contributed to the radicalization of the left since what had been planned as a moderate center for the political system had now fallen out. Yeltsin's half-hearted experiment in political engineering had failed as much due to his and Rybkin's personal lack of efforts as the KPRF's clarity of purpose and organization.

Forming coalitions has consistenly been one of the more time-consuming activities of most Russian parties. After the 1996 presidential elections a number of social-democratic parties called for the creation of a new left-center coalition with an emphasis on moderate approaches to politics. This event was, however, overshadowed by the formal founding in August 1996 of a Popular Patriotic Union of Russia (NPSR) headed by Zyuganov and including former vice-president Aleksandr Rutskoi, as well as members of the Agrarians and the Power to the People movement of former Soviet premier Nikolai Ryzhkov. Founded as a means to promote patriotism and social justice, the NPSR also allowed the left opposition to develop a national base of support while keeping up its pressure on the Yeltsin administration. Prior to the 1999 elections the NPSR's significance lay in how successful it would be in both organizing a sustainable faction within the Duma and rallying public support. Many of the radical left parties have remained aloof from this creation including Prigarin's UCP–CPSU, Anpilov's Working Russia and others who perceive a contradiction in terms for communists to coexist with nationalists. While they have also accepted national patriotism in their public pronouncements this issue is unconditionally subordinated to that of the goal of a new socialist internationalism. For the radical left this is a point of definition between them and the KPRF.

It is obvious to virtually all of the radical left that the KPRF stands the best chance of attaining power and galvanizing a significant portion of the electorate over a number of years. But the radical parties question the KPRF's goals. While on the one hand there is an appreciation by the radical left for the Stalinist–Khrushchevite–Brezhnevite strain within the KPRF, many are convinced that Zyuganov is more of an heir to the Gorbachev phenomenon due to his lax attitudes toward intra-party pluralism. Other elements of the left have attacked the KPRF for its lack of commitment to the revolutionary cause, but the KPRF has taken what may arguably be the more difficult course, that is, playing the political game with all of its consequences instead of standing aloof from the fray and loudly proclaiming revolutionary slogans. That essentially is the job of the radical left.

There also remains considerable envy of the KPRF's successes by the radical left fringe. The KPRF is a convenient target for discontented voices within the left and it is often taken to be the source of all the left's troubles, both electorally and organizationally. The KPRF has been said to have 'abandoned communist principles, and turned nationalistic' by some,[29] while others have castigated it for its 'opportunistic neo-Gorbachev' line in playing opposition politics. KPRF officials like Grigory Rebrov have responded in kind, labeling the UCP–CPSU an 'apogee mutation of the left wing',[30] and generally deriding these groups' chances for electoral success. The lack of respect accorded the KPRF points to something that goes much deeper than just campaign rhetoric and as a result Zyuganov and other party leaders have not been able to gain their desired unification. Given that the unity within the CPSU had always been an artifice of the party leaders to dispel criticism it seems unlikely that these conditions could be recreated in a pluralist political system. And while the membership and vote differentials between the KPRF and the various elements of the left do not seem to indicate that the KPRF has much to worry about, the voices from the political fringe always have a way of making themselves heard, especially in hard economic times.

5   CONCLUSIONS: THE FUTURE OF THE LEFT

Seen solely in terms of party performance in elections the future of the Russian left on the whole seems assured for at least the short term and most likely the next several years. The KPRF in particular will continue to draw a significant share of electoral rewards as voters call upon it to speak to their concerns in a continuing time of uncertainty. The dissatisfaction with social and economic conditions experienced by the Russian public are so far best answered by the left and not the right, whose solutions the public may see as too draconian for its own interests. Other opposition movements may yet emerge but it is difficult to see what basis for support they could control given the left's strong organization and command of issues.

And yet there are clear problems to the left's continuing successes. The shrinking base of leftist support based on age can only be offset by the various organizations – particularly the KPRF – returning to their original core purpose, that is radical economic change. Whether or not voters and citizens in general will ever again buy into a revolutionary form of rhetoric, which the KPRF itself no longer really offers, is a question that cannot be answered in the present. It does seem likely that the KPRF may continue its move to the right already demonstrated by its embracing of nationalist and xenophobic virtues. In so doing it may prevent the social-democratic parties from ever finding a grounding for their ideals within the public as a whole. And unless these parties manage to gain some kind of foothold in government – deputies in the Duma, governorships – they will fade from the political scene leaving the moderate center-left to go undeveloped in Russian political society, or to be taken over entirely by the KPRF. Neither scenario would be in the interests of Russia's experiment with democratic procedure.

The radical left poses more of a challenge to the KPRF than it does to Yeltsin or other reformers. It is so directly opposed to the liberal reformers and their entire process of change that they present no realistic possibility for seizing power without a crisis of near-epic proportions. However, for the KPRF they may pose enough of a nuisance that they prevent the KPRF from moving toward the right in the pursuit of more public support. Stuck in the middle the KPRF needs to retain its credentials as a party of socialist/communist ideals, but also interest the public in their platform and other, more specific goals.

Whichever way it is viewed, the left operates from a disadvantage so long as the current framework of politics remains in place. The Yeltsin 'system' including the constitution and all its governing instruments represents a system to which most of the left is unreconciled. The KPRF has tried to operate from within this system but since the presidency has stayed beyond its control the overall influence of the left will be muted to the point of being a perpetual opposition. Under such circumstances the left will remain in a state of disunity as the various elements become increasingly dissatisfied with party 'policies, leaders and political results.'

NOTES

1. Boris Yeltsin, *Against the Grain* (New York: Summit Books, 1991); Gennady Zyuganov, *My Russia* (Armonk, NY: M.E. Sharpe, 1997).
2. V.I. Lenin, 'The State and Revolution', *Collected Works*, v.25 (Moscow: Progress, 1980), p. 470.
3. *Current Politics of the Soviet Union* 1 (1990), p. 81.
4. Aleksandr Yakolev, *The Fate of Marxism in Russia* (New Haven, CT: Yale University Press, 1993), p. 102.
5. ITAR-TASS, 30 October 1994.
6. Wendy Slater, 'The Russian Communist Party Today', *RFE/RL Research Report* 3 (12 August 1994): 1–6.
7. Thomas F. Remington and Steven S. Smith, 'The Development of Parliamentary Parties in Russia', *Legislative Studies Quarterly* 20 (November 1995): 457–89.

8. Timothy J. Colton, 'Economics and Voting in Russia', *Post Soviet Affairs* **12** (1996): 289-317.
9. *Kommersant-Daily*, 21 January 1995.
10. Alesky Kiva, 'Portrait of a Contender: Zyuganov is Not as Simple as He is Painted', *Rossiyskaya Gazeta*, 11 April 1996.
11. Gennady Zyuganov, 'Russia will be Great and Socialist: Political Report of the Central Committee to the Fourth Congress of the Communist Party of the Russian Federation', *Sovetskyaya Rossiya* (22 April 1997), in World News Connection, http://wnc.fedworld.gov.
12. Ibid.
13. *Pravda*, 13 January 1995.
14. *Kommersant Daily*, 21 January 1995.
15. *Sovetskaya Rossiya*, 24 January 1995.
16. *OMRI Special Report: Russian Election Survey* **11**, 5 (December 1995).
17. *Kommersant Daily*, 21 January 1995.
18. ITAR-TASS, 1 April 1994.
19. Zyuganov, *My Russia*, p. 141.
20. Sven Gunnar Simonsen, 'Still Favoring the Power of the Workers', *Transition* **1** (25 August 1995): 27–31.
21. Zyuganov, 'Russia will be Great and Socialist.'
22. Lenin, p. 429.
23. Interfax, 21 April 1997.
24. Roy Medvedev, 'Russia Today, the Socialist Left Center', *Svobodnaia mysl* (1994), reprinted in *Russian Politics and Law* **33** (March–April 1995): 457–89.
25. *Moscow News*, 26 January 1996.
26. ITAR-TASS, 7 January 1994.
27. *Glasnost*, 1–15 January 1995.
28. Robert W. Orttung, 'Rybkin Fails to Create a Viable Left-Center Bloc', *Transition* **1** (25 August 1995): 27–31.
29. ITAR-TASS, 28 January 1995.
30. ITAR-TASS, 28 January 1995.

3. Lithuania Beyond the Return of the Left

Terry D. Clark and Robin M. Tucker

The Lithuanian Democratic Labor Party victory in the 1992 elections to the national legislature ushered in the 'Return to the Left' in post-communist Europe. While the former communist party was soundly defeated just four years later in the parliamentary elections of 1996, the political left remains a significant force in Lithuanian politics. How is the left understood in Lithuania politics? What parties comprise the left and how do they differ from one another? How do we explain the success of Lithuania's left? What is the likely future for the country's left? We propose to explore these and other questions in this chapter. The first section defines the left in the country's political spectrum. The second section considers the differences between the two key parties of the left: the Lithuanian Democratic Labor Party and the Lithuanian Social Democratic Party. The chapter concludes with a consideration of the future of the left in Lithuania.

1 A HISTORY OF THE POLITICAL LEFT IN LITHUANIA

Lithuania's political left traces its origins to organizational activities by social democrats among ethnic Lithuanians at the end of the nineteenth century. While several social-democratic parties had been working to organize Jewish and Polish workers in Vilnius beginning in the latter half of the nineteenth century, the first organized efforts at agitation among workers of Lithuanian nationality did not appear until 1889. These efforts eventually led to the formation of the Social Democratic Party of Lithuania in 1895, the activities of which were almost exclusively centered in Vilnius.[1]

The party's leadership was decimated by the repression of political activity in the Russian Empire from 1897 to 1899. Nonetheless, the Social Democratic Party of Lithuania managed to resurface in 1900. The newly reconstituted party changed its focus from a primary concern with defending workers' interests to advocating independence from Russia. Reflecting the decision to de-emphasize economic matters in order to concentrate on issues of national independence, the party carried out organizational activities among rural peasants as well as urban workers until the Russian Revolution and subsequent independence of Lithuania.[2]

The Bolshevik seizure of power in Russia ultimately led to a split among social democrats in Lithuania. Those remaining in the Social Democratic Party of Lithuania argued that socialism could best be achieved incrementally and within an independent Lithuanian state. Others following the example of the Bolsheviks declared the necessity of a violent revolution, the elimination of private property and the creation of a workers' state uniting the peoples of the former Russian Empire. The disagreement ultimately ended in the formation of two parties, the pro-independence Lithuanian Social Democratic Party and the pro-Bolshevik Lithuanian Communist Party.[3] The former is the predecessor of today's Lithuanian Social Democratic Party (LSDP) while the latter is the predecessor of the present-day Lithuanian Democratic Labor Party (LDLP).

The Lithuanian Communist Party, which maintained close ties with the Bolshevik regime in Moscow, fared poorly in comparison to the Social Democratic Party in the first years of independence. While it managed to gain five seats in the elections to the first national legislature (the Seimas), it lost those seats in the next election. In contrast, the Lithuanian Social Democratic Party was a major political party gaining between 10 and 18 per cent of the vote in elections.[4] It reached its zenith in 1926, when it entered into a coalition government with the Populists. However, a military coup late in the same year forcibly dissolved the Seimas, introduced right-wing presidential rule and paralysed the Lithuanian left for the remainder of the inter-war period. The Lithuanian Communist Party was officially outlawed and the Social Democratic Party subjected to harassment and arrests.[5]

With the Soviet occupation, the Lithuanian Communist Party (LCP) became an arm of the Communist Party of the Soviet Union (CPSU), the only legal political party in Lithuania. Its membership staffed all social, economic and political positions of import. Other political parties were officially banned. The leadership of the inter-war Social Democratic Party was imprisoned or deported, or it managed to escape abroad where the party continued to operate as part of the Socialist International.

With the advent of perestroika, political organizing outside of the official structures of the Communist Party became possible. The process was initiated in Lithuania with the founding of Sajudis, in October 1998.[6] The LSDP re-emerged in Lithuanian politics in August 1989 when 150 delegates attended a founding congress. Four deputies elected to the new All-Union Congress of People's Deputies joined the party, which declared itself the heir of the inter-war Social Democratic Party. Soon thereafter it was admitted to the Socialist International. As the party had done at the turn of the century, the newly reconstituted LSDP placed as its primary goal the independence of the Lithuanian state. The party platform also called for the rejection of both the capitalist and socialist centrally planned economic models, calling instead for a mixed economy with a large state sector and a well-developed social welfare net.[7]

Such political activity outside of official party channels signaled the emergence of a de facto multiparty system and threw the LCP into crisis. Particularly troubling was the popular groundswell that formed behind Sajudis. Concerned that it would be decimated in the elections to the newly created republican-level Supreme Council of early 1990, the LCP held an extraordinary congress in December 1989, at which it debated whether to formally split from the CPSU. A majority voted for the split and formed an independent Lithuanian Communist Party. Those who opposed the split with Moscow formed their own party which retained formal ties with the CPSU, the LCP(CPSU).

Despite these efforts the independent LCP was dealt a severe blow in the 1990 elections to the Supreme Council. Sajudis candidates won an outright majority in the legislature. The newly elected assembly elected Vytautas Landsbergis, Sajudis's leader, as its chair and declared the formal restoration of independence, an act which launched an 18 month long struggle with Moscow (culminating with the collapse of the Soviet Union and international recognition of the country in September 1991). In spite of the electoral defeat, the independent LCP remained a major political player overshadowing all other parties on the political left in Lithuanian politics. While the independent LCP won 40 seats in the 1990 Supreme Council (17 with the endorsement of Sajudis), the LSDP won only nine and the LCP(CPSU) managed to gain only five.[8] More importantly, despite the party's minority status in the Supreme Council, an independent LCP government was installed by the legislature.

Renaming itself the Lithuanian Democratic Labor Party (LDLP) at its congress in December 1990, the former communists were not able to sustain their government for long. It was replaced in January 1991 following a series of confrontations with the legislative majority over negotiations with Moscow. After securing the concurrence of the Supreme Council for a moratorium on the act of the restoration of independence as a pre-condition to get the Soviets to the bargaining table, the LDLP government found itself subjected to attempts at micro-management by the legislative majority. The situation came to a head in January 1990, in the wake of public protests over proposed government increases on food prices. When Prime Minister Kazimiera Prunskiene flew to Moscow to hold talks with Mikhail Gorbachev, she was accused of plotting to re-establish Soviet rule. Upon her return, her government was displaced by a Sajudis government. A few days later an abortive effort to reassert Soviet rule in Lithuania left 14 dead and scores wounded.[9]

Lithuania's independence was formally recognized in September 1991 following the 'August Coup' in Moscow. The former communist party has continued as a major political party in the post-independence era. Following the adoption of a new constitution in the referendum of October 1992, the LDLP won 76 of 141 contested seats in elections to the new Seimas and the right to form the government. In early 1993, LDLP party leader Algirdas Brazauskas won election to the newly created office of President. LDLP governments and President Brazauskas ruled the country until the legislative elections of 1996 and the presidential elections of 1998.

While less successful than the LDLP, the LSDP has also been a significant party in the post-independence era, gaining eight seats in the 1992 elections to the Seimas and 12 in 1996. Nonetheless, the party has yet to govern. Further, the LSDP has thus far not been able to field candidates with sufficient national stature to make a serious challenge for the presidency. In the 1998 presidential elections, the party's candidate, Vytenis Andriukaitis, was defeated in the first round having received less than 6 per cent of the vote.

2   DEFINING THE LEFT IN LITHUANIA

Just what do we mean by the left in Lithuanian politics? The traditional understanding of the left–right political spectrum rests largely on class analysis. Parties on the political right represent the interests of the business classes while those on the left represent working-class interests, espousing egalitarian beliefs and championing government programs to reduce socioeconomic disparities between employers and employees. Many scholars argue that it is not possible to distinguish between political parties in much of East-Central and Eastern Europe using this traditional schema. There are a number of reasons offered for this. First, the class system is poorly articulated.[10] Communist regimes acted to suppress social differentiation thereby destroying the basis upon which classes might form. Hence, the newly emerging countries of post-communist Europe have been left without a class system. Second, while a nascent class system does exist, an inadequate passage of time has elapsed for parties to have developed clear identities with the interests of particular classes.[11] Third, the left–right continuum cannot be meaningfully employed as a typology in the post-communist state owing to the existence of a broad social consensus on maintenance of the welfare state.[12] Little debate exists within Eastern Europe about the economic structures the countries should adopt. Most parties believe in social welfare and strive for a small gap between rich and poor. Rather, debate centers around the pace of reform.

Given the lack of salience, which it is thought class politics possesses, and the relative consensus among political leaders about the economic structures of the country, many argue instead that value differences and the politics of identity have greater importance. As a result, it is easier to talk of the degree to which one party is more liberal or more conservative than another in relation to political issues revolving around conflicting value systems and identity politics. In essence an issue-voting model, rather than a class-based or socioeconomic model, is thought to best explain the differences among parties.[13] Markowski for instance contends that attitudes towards public issues are better predictors of (party) identification than class.[14] Among the relevant political issues on which it is argued political parties can be distinguished along a liberal–conservative continuum are those relating to the pace of economic reform, ethnicity, an East or West orientation in foreign policy, world views and religion.

Challenging this view, however, are those who contend that class and economic issues do indeed comprise a fundamental dimension along which political parties in East-Central Europe can be placed. While some argue that class politics existed during the communist era,[15] the more common view is that classes and class politics have emerged with the economic reforms of the post-communist era, marketization having produced the social differentiation necessary to their emergence.[16] In this same vein, others contend that the emergence of class-based political parties is associated with the transition from communism. Evans and Whitefield, for example, argue that those states that have experienced some degree of market success, possess greater ethnic homogeneity, and have not suffered the stresses of having had to secede from a previously existing state in order to achieve independence are more likely to develop class-based parties.[17] The most popular thesis, however, is that the pain of economic transformation together with increasing social differentiation, a by-product of the market reforms, have led to the emergence of both political parties representing class interests and class identity with political parties.[18]

In the Lithuanian case, the initial development of a party system arguably lacked any class basis. Indeed, until the formation of the Homeland Union (Conservatives of Lithuania) in spring 1993, the country had only one real political party, the former Lithuanian Communist Party, renamed the Democratic Labor Party.[19] The major issue in the years immediately following the parliamentary act restoring the country's independence in March 1990 was the achievement of independence. However, with the achievement of formal recognition as an independent state by the international community in September 1991, privatization and marketization began in earnest. Have these processes created the conditions necessary for the emergence of a class system and with it class politics? Can a left–right continuum be usefully employed in the Lithuanian case, or is the party system better defined by a liberal–conservative axis?

A number of observers of Lithuanian politics have asserted that the traditional left–right spectrum based on class politics can be applied to the Lithuanian case.[20] The results of a survey of 599 candidates to the national legislature (Seimas) in fall 1996,[21] provide evidence that such is indeed the case. When asked to place political parties on a scale from left to right (–10 being far left and +10 being far right),[22] the Lithuanian Socialist Party (LSP) was placed furthest to the left. The other two major parties located on the left were the Lithuanian Social Democratic Party (LSDP) and the Lithuanian Democratic Labor Party (LDLP). On the right were the Homeland Union (Conservatives of Lithuania) and the Lithuanian Christian Democratic Party (LCDP). The Center Union (CU) was located just to the right-of-center.

What is clearly evident from answers to subsequent questions, however, is that respondents placed parties on the left–right spectrum based largely on criteria related to class politics. When asked whether the representation of several specific classes was associated with the political left or right (see Table 3.1), there was a clear correlation between the left and representation of working-class interests (as well as those of the poor). There was also a noted correlation between the right and representation of the interests of the middle class and big business. What is even more evident, however, is the strong correlation between the left and traditional leftist values such as equality and a strong role for the state in social welfare.

However, there is an equally strong correlation between placement on the left–right continuum and two key issues in Lithuanian politics: nationalism and the foreign policy orientation of the state. The left is strongly associated with representation of the interests of national minorities (see Table 3.2), while the right champions the primacy of the Lithuanian nation. In our view this does not necessarily detract from the obvious association between left parties and the interests of the working class. Indeed, to the degree that representation of minority interests is congruent with leftist concerns with socially and economically disadvantaged groups we find no inconsistency. Nevertheless, we cannot exclude the salience of the issue dimension in Lithuanian politics.

This is all the more the case given the strong correlation in elite opinion between the left and a foreign policy favoring continued close ties with Eastern Europe and Russia. The right is associated with a foreign policy orientation toward The North Atlantic Treaty Organization (NATO) and the European Union. However, as we shall see when we discuss the respective party platforms of Lithuania's major political parties, they all pledge themselves to seek entry into the European Union and NATO. Indeed, there is such broad public consensus that the national legislature overwhelmingly

Table 3.1 Responses to questions on representation of class interests by candidates to the Seimas, 1996

Question	Response		
	Left	Right	Neither
Indicate which parties – those of the left or right – are most closely associated with these characteristics (question 12)			
Represent the interests of workers (question 12.10)	36.4	19.9	32.7
Represent the interests of the poor (question 12.1)	38.1	11.8	41.1
Represent the interests of the middle class (question 12.15)	19.2	36.3	32.7
Represent the interests of big capital (question 12.11)	23.8	53.0	8.1
Struggle for the increase of private capital in the economy (question 12.4)	7.3	74.0	6.6
Assert that state regulation is ineffective and limits human rights (question 12.13)	6.6	59.5	10.1
Assert that equal rights are only attainable when the state assures the satisfaction of the fundamental needs of humans (question 12.14)	40.6	15.9	18.0

Source: Survey conducted under the auspices of the Institute of International Relations and Political Science at Vilnius University during the period 20 September to 20 October, 1996.

passed a constitutional act on 8 April 1992, which prohibits formal membership in any multilateral organization on the territory of the former Soviet Union and explicitly bars entry in the Commonwealth of Independent States (CIS). Even though as a result of the act Lithuania has essentially been denied preferential prices on Russian oil, no major political party has contested the issue. Trying to avoid being labeled pro-Russian while at the same time recognizing the economic reality that Lithuania remains largely dependent on eastern markets, the political left has declared its intent to gain entry to the European Union and NATO while maintaining stable and mutually advantageous economic and political relations with Russia and Eastern Europe. Even this attempt at a realistic and balanced approach, however, has resulted in the left being identified as supporting an 'eastern' foreign policy.

Table 3.2 Responses to questions on issue positions by candidates to the Seimas, 1996

Question	Response		
	Left	Right	Neither
Indicate which parties – those of the left or right – are most closely associated with these characteristics (question 12)			
Represent the interest of national minorities (question 12.6)	46.2	11.6	21.2
Oriented to the East (question 12.7)	60.4	2.7	22.8
Oriented to the West (question 12.16)	5.1	69.8	8.9

Source: Survey conducted under the auspices of the Institute of International Relations and Political Science at Vilnius University during the period 20 September to 20 October, 1996.

What the data seem to argue is that the Lithuanian political party system is defined by the traditional left–right spectrum based on class politics. At the same time, the left has championed certain political issues that may or may not have a class or economic basis. In the Lithuanian case this includes the defense of the rights of national minorities and a more balanced approach to relations with Russia.

Analysis of the respective platforms of the five 'effective' parties in the Lithuanian political system confirms their ideological placing based on class politics. The Homeland Union (Conservatives of Lithuania) falls furthest right of the five parties. Indicative of the general consensus on the welfare state, the Conservatives call for a minimum wage law, pension insurance and medical insurance. However, the middle class interests of the party are reflected in an economic program that stresses a minimal role for the state in the economy and favors private ownership, protection of private property and free enterprise. Socially, the platform commits the party to the defense of the Lithuanian nation. In terms of foreign affairs, the party supports a policy line of integration into the European Union and NATO, arguing that economic relations with Russia should be maintained on friendly but equal terms.

Also on the right is the Lithuanian Christian Democratic Party (LCDP). Like Christian Democratic parties in the West, the party's platform reflects Christian morals and doctrine in this very Catholic country. Consequently, the LCDP has a greater commitment to the welfare state than the Conservatives. The party pledges to reduce poverty, guarantee minimal standards of living, implement a system of insurance for savings and reduce the unemployment rate. At the same time it is committed to decentralizing state power and reducing the size of the central government. The party's platform is far more supportive of small and medium-sized business than large corporations. While it calls for incentives and assistance to small businesses and farms, it pledges to end preferential tax treatment for large enterprises and foreign investors. Socially, the party states as its goal the eradication of the negative consequences to the Lithuanian nation resulting from the Soviet occupation. In foreign policy, the LCDP seeks integration with the West's economic and military organizations: the European Union, the Western European Union and NATO.

The Center Union (CU) is a right-of-center party. The party's economic policies are in some ways more rightist than those of the LCDP. For instance, the CU calls for reorganizing and further privatizing the state sector, stimulating competition, decentralizing government administrative control, enacting strict fiscal discipline and preventing government intervention in the economy. Nonetheless, the party platform also recognizes that the state must remain the provider of specific services for which it is best-suited, particularly social welfare and regulation of economic distortions such as monopolies and production of low quality goods and services. It also calls for state control of foreign loans and adapting social security and public health care to the needs of farmers. Like other parties on the political right, the CU calls for joining the European Union; however, its platform makes no mention of NATO.

Situated on the left of the political spectrum are the Democratic Labor Party (LDLP) and the Social Democratic Party (LSDP). Social welfare programs compose the core of the LDLP platform. The party promises to expand and decentralize welfare programs such as insurance of pension funds and support for families and disabled persons while enacting programs increasing the availability of adequate housing. While the LDLP's economic plank supports liberal economic policies and encourages competition and investment, it also seeks to subsidize agricultural production and to develop rural areas. In ethnic relations, the party affirms the importance of and state support to cultural and ethnic minorities in society. Like all major political parties in Lithuania, the LDLP supports a foreign policy of gaining membership in the Council of Europe, the Western European Union and NATO; however, it stresses that this must be done without disrupting important economic and political ties with Russia and Eastern Europe.

The LSDP platform declares that the party represents the ideals of political, social, economic and cultural democracy; and it calls for enacting principles of social justice. While the party declares itself wary of excessive management by the central government, it pledges to work to actively reduce the gap between rich and poor by instituting employment programs and protecting workers' rights. The LSDP platform calls for the central government to concern itself with the general welfare of the public through extensive programs, leaving the provision of services to local governments. It also promises to protect the rights of ethnic minorities and to gain entry into the European Union and NATO.

If the discussion thus far supports the thesis that Lithuania's political elites (political office seekers) view the country's party system in traditional left–right terms, what about the general public? Indeed, there are numerous studies demonstrating that there is little to no correlation between the political views of elites and masses in Eastern or East Central Europe.[23] The survey evidence from Lithuania suggests that the public has also developed a traditional left–right view of the country's political party system. Noted Lithuanian sociologist Rasa Alisauskiene's surveys demonstrate that the public ideologically locates the country's five major parties similarly to that of the elites (see Table 3.3). The LDLP is strongly connected in the public's mind with the political left. The LSDP on the other hand is seen as either a left or centrist party. The Center Union is situated by the general public in the center of the political spectrum while the LCDP and Conservatives are on the right.

The more important issue, however, is whether there is an emerging relationship between class identity and party affiliation. In other words, is the public's view of the political spectrum informed by class politics? That political elites have consciously undertaken to associate working class interests with the political left, in no way suggests that the public has done so as well. Nonetheless, we find the argument that the economic stresses visited on the working classes by the market reforms have given impetus to their identifying themselves with parties calling for the reversal or end of the 'hollowing out' of the state a compelling one. Indeed, the transfer of property into private hands as a result of privatization has radically reduced the ability of the state to protect the property-less from the vagaries of the new market. Worse still, in the Soviet era all labor unions were state institutions. Denied their patron, they have been left largely bewildered in the new market realities with neither the means nor the experience to defend labor interests in collective bargaining. None of this is to say that the public view of left and right in Lithuanian politics like that of the elites does not contain some issue dimensions. The tendency of pensioners, impoverished by the market reforms,

Table 3.3 General public ideological placement of Lithuania's political parties, 1992 and 1996

| Party | Percentage of Respondents | | | | | | |
| | 1992 | | | | 1996 | | |
	Left	Center	Right		Left	Center	Right
LDLP	63.0	6.7	3.0		63.0	1.7	5.6
LSDP	34.0	22.0	5.9		22.0	21.0	6.6
CU	6.5	53.0	2.3		2.3	61.0	3.5
LCDP	2.4	8.5	44.0		3.5	5.0	52.0
Homeland Union	2.5	4.7	68.0		6.1	3.6	56.0

Source: Rasa Alisauskiene, 'Attitudes and Values of Lithuanian Population, 1992-1996,' Baltic Surveys Ltd., unpublished paper.

to vote for right-wing parties because of their strong appeal to nationalism certainly argues against doing so. Our argument is that while mass political attitudes will lag behind those of elite attitudes, nevertheless, mass attitudes toward Lithuania's political parties based on class values are forming and that this is reflected in the public's perception of left and right in the Lithuanian political spectrum. The lag will be reflected in a stronger correlation between the traditional values of the political left and party leaders in Lithuania's two major parties of the left, the LDLP and the LSDP. Nonetheless, we believe there is substantial evidence to demonstrate that both the working classes and rural population identify with the political left more so than the right.

As early as 1992, public opinion surveys began noting differences in voting patterns based on class. Table 3.4 reports the results of a survey taken on the eve of the 1992 elections to the national legislature. While the business class is evenly divided (reflecting the Communist Party roots of many in the new business class) and the educated classes favor parties on the political right (reflecting the greater opportunities open to them by the market reforms), the working class and the peasantry decidedly favor the left. Lithuania's left also has the support of the country's ethnic minorities, in particular the Russian community which in addition to labor and the peasantry comprised key components of the LDLP legislative victory in the 1992 elections.

Not surprisingly given the LDLP's base in the largest social classes, the party's victory in 1992 was overwhelming as it gained an absolute majority in the national legislature and the right to elect the government. A few months later its candidate for President, party leader Algirdas Brazauskas won a resounding victory capturing over two-thirds of the national vote. In this light the left's defeat in the parliamentary elections of 1996 at first glance would appear to suggest that its identification with the working classes has significantly eroded. However, closer consideration of the 1996 vote reveals otherwise.

The LDLP deputy total in the Seimas went from 76 (its post-1992 election total) to 12 following the 1996 elections. Its primary opponent on the right, the Homeland Union (Conservatives of Lithuania), increased its share of seats from 29 to 70, one short of an absolute majority. However, it would be a mistake to conclude that the 1996 election results represent a voter shift toward the political right. Instead, the LDLP working class and rural base stayed home, a political phenomenon noted in several countries of post-communist Europe.[24] Reflecting this is the fact that while the LDLP achieved only 16 per cent of its 1992 vote in the 1996 elections, the victorious Conservatives experienced a gain of less than 10 per cent. Indeed, the LDLP received 650,000 fewer votes in 1996 than in 1992. This accounted for most of the decrease in overall voter turn-out from 1996 to 1992, about 75 per cent of registered voters going to the polls in 1992 compared to just over 50 per cent in 1996. Any doubts about the party's base were erased in the 1998 presidential elections when the LDLP-backed candidate, Arturas Paulauskas, was narrowly defeated with 49.29 per cent of the vote.

3   DISAGGREGATING LITHUANIA'S LEFT

If the left–right continuum can be employed usefully in the Lithuanian context, how do we distinguish among the parties on the left of the political spectrum? Using Giovanni Sartori's counting rules to determine the number of effective parties in the political system,[25] there are no more than five – the LSDP, the LDLP, the Conservatives, the LCDP and the CU.[26] The Lithuanian Socialist Party (LSP) is a small party which has demonstrated the capacity to win no more than one seat in the national legislature at any one time. Hence, there are only two parties on the political left which are capable of winning sufficient numbers of electoral seats that they conceivably could be of importance in forming a government, the Lithuanian Social Democratic Party and the Lithuanian Democratic Labor Party. The LSP – a Marxist–Leninist party with strong appeal in the country's agricultural north which has retained many of the Soviet era collective farms – won one seat in the 1996 elections to the Seimas. The Women's Party, headed by former Prime Minister Kazimiera Prunskiene, advocates strict government controls on the economy and the expansion of social programs benefitting women, children and families. The party has one seat in the current Seimas. The Peasants' Party represents the interests of former collective farm managers and has one seat in the Seimas while the Polish Electoral Action of Lithuania, an ethnically based party, currently has two seats. In contrast, the LDLP and LSDP occupy 12 seats each.

Not surprisingly, there are substantial differences between the two major Lithuanian parties of the left. These differences begin with their respective self-images. In order to overcome the electoral advantage that has thus far accrued to the LDLP, the LSDP has purposely adopted an image juxtaposed to that of the former communists. Party historians emphasize the LDLP's Bolshevik and Soviet past and point to the LSDP's historical stand in favor of national independence and against Russian dominance.[27] Charging that the LDLP is the party of the former *nomenklatura* and as such is concerned with the business interests of party members who have profited from privatization of state property, the LSDP declares itself the sole party that truly defends the interests of the working classes. To make this point with the voters, the LSDP refused to enter into a governing coalition with the LDLP following the latter's victory in the 1992 legislative elections. The LSDP has also succeeded in denying the LDLP entry into the Socialist International.

LDLP historians on the other hand, avoid discussing the party's historical roots. Indeed, party historians say little about either the Soviet or pre-war past.[28] Instead, they focus on the party having formally split from the Communist Party of the Soviet Union in December 1990 and the subsequent role it played in the restoration of the country's independence. While the LDLP celebrates these achievements, it nonetheless stresses that it represents all of Lithuania's citizens, not just the ethnic majority. More importantly, however, the party attempts to make the case with voters that it alone possesses the necessary competence to bring the country out of economic crisis in such a way as to lessen the pain for the working class and peasantry.

The views of party members as reflected in the political attitudes of their respective candidates to public office are notably different as well. The results of a survey of 599 candidates to the Seimas in fall 1996,[29] demonstrate this. Based on the results of the survey, LSDP candidates are markedly more supportive of working-class positions than are LDLP candidates. LSDP respondents were more supportive of the statement that 'the state must assure the social well-being of its citizens'.[30] Further, 97.5 per cent of LSDP respondents supported Swedish socialism as the best economic model for Lithuania. While 77.2 per cent of LDLP candidates did so, an additional 17.5 per cent supported the capitalist model.[31]

On the other hand, LDLP candidates are more likely to identify the political left with support for the rural sector, to support the interests of ethnic majorities and to favor a balanced position between the East and West in foreign policy matters. Some 84.2 per cent of LDLP candidates indicated that the political left represents the interests of peasants but only 57.5 per cent of LSDP respondents did so;[32] and 68.4 per cent of LDLP respondents identified the representation of the interests of national minorities with the political left compared to 55.0 per cent of LSDP respondents.[33] Finally, on a scale from '1' to '10' (with '1' being the first choice for a Lithuanian foreign policy position and '10' being the last choice) LDLP candidates ranked a treaty with both Russia and the United States near fourth with an average response of 3.769 while LSDP candidates ranked the choice near fifth with an average response of 4.794. (The Conservatives' average was 5.320, the LCDP average was 5.250, and that of the Center Union was 5.147.)[34]

None of this is to suggest that there are not notable differences of views within the two parties. Indeed, both suffer from the threat of fragmentation. This is most true for the LSDP. The fault line between the party's two main

Table 3.4 Political party preference by class and ethnicity, 1992

Political Party				
	a. Class* (percentage preference)			
	Intelligentsia	Business	Blue collar	Peasants
Political Left:				
LDLP	22.0	28.5	42.0	46.5
LSDP	11.0	8.0	7.0	4.0
Political Left,Total	33.0	36.5	49.0	50.5
Political Right: Sajudis (LS)**	33.0	23.5	22.0	21.0
LCDP	10.0	13.0	11.0	13.0
Political Right, Total	43.0	36.5	33.0	34.0

Table 3.4 continued

	b. Ethnicity (percentage preference)		
	Lithuanian	Russian	Polish
Political Left:			
LDLP	30.0	77.0	34.0
LSDP	7.0	8.0	6.0
LLS***		1.0	40.0
Political Left, Total	37.0	86.0	80.0
Political Right: Sajudis			
(LS)**	30.0	7.0	9.0
LCDP	16.0	2.0	4.0
Political Right, Total	46.0	9.0	13.0

Notes:
* Work categories used in the survey are those used during the Soviet era to classify employment sectors in the economy.
** Elements of Sajudis formed the Homeland Union (Conservatives of Lithuania) in 1993.
*** The Polish Union of Lithuania which later became the Polish Electoral Action of Lithuania.

Source: Infas-Bull Public Opinion Survey as reported in *Lietuvos Aidas*, 29 October 1992, p. 4.

factions centers on the model upon which to base the country's economy. One faction led by Vytenis Andriukaitis and Aloyzas Sakalas, argues in favor of adopting the Swedish model with broad-scale government support for large nationalized industries. While this faction has seemingly emerged as the dominant one judging by the party's decision to nominate Andriukaitis as its presidential candidate in 1997, a second faction led by Rimantas Dagys continues to challenge for the leadership role. This faction is more favorably disposed to government incentives to small businesses. Indeed, its economic development model is quite similar to that of the Christian Democratic Party.

The LDLP also suffers from factionalism. The 1992 Seimas was noted by the emergence of a three-way split among the LDLP deputies. One group largely argued for the maintenance of a Soviet-style economy. It was particularly concerned that large state enterprises and collective farms should not be privatized. Following the passage of the LDLP privatization legislation packages of 1993 and 1995, most of the members of this faction left the LDLP and joined either the Lithuanian Socialist Party or other smaller parties of the left. A second group led by Adolfas Slezevicius (Prime Minister from 1993 to 1996) was associated with the interests of the newly emerging business class, many of whom had been members of the communist *nomenklatura* and were well positioned to take advantage of the new opportunities afforded by the market reforms. The third group comprised party intellectuals, to include Justinas Karosas and Gediminas Kirkilas, who argued for moderate-paced, rational reform which would reduce the suffering endured by the lower classes by maintaining a large, well-developed welfare state. In the wake of the defeat suffered by the LDLP in the 1996 elections to the Seimas, the party intellectuals have assumed most of the leadership roles. However, business interests continue to be well represented, particularly those of large enterprises seeking state subsidies.

There are also substantial differences in the voter base between the two parties. As previously discussed, the LDLP draws support from the working class, the rural sector and ethnic minorities (particularly Russians). The defining characteristic of LDLP voters is their identification with the party. According to one recent survey, some 45 per cent of self-identified LDLP supporters vote for the party out of habit. The LDLP base is also quite stable. Only 3.8 per cent were prepared to abandon the party if it failed to fulfill its promises to the electorate, and an additional 3.8 per cent had been attracted to the party only recently.[35]

In contrast, the LSDP base is far less stable – 53.8 per cent were attracted to the party by its platform, 20.0 per cent were prepared to vote for another party if the LSDP fails to deliver on its promises, and 26.2 per cent were attracted to the LSDP only recently.[36] Probably most disturbing for the party's leadership, however, is that its base is largely confined to urban areas among more educated elements of the population. While it has actively pursued an alliance with labor unions, the party has largely failed to make any significant in-roads with the working class. Indeed, the LSDP has formal ties with most of the country's largest unions. Algirdas Sysas, the Chair of the Lithuanian Association of Trade Unions, one of the four largest labor unions in the country, was elected to the Seimas on the party list of the LSDP. However, these unions tend to be those having their roots in the Soviet era. Distrusting the unions, only 7 per cent of Lithuania's workers maintain formal membership. Even among those who do, there is very little understanding of collective bargaining. Instead, following Soviet era practice most citizens directly petition management or local government for redress of grievances.

4   EXPLAINING THE (MIS)FORTUNES OF THE LEFT

How do we explain the relatively greater success of the LDLP? As elsewhere in post-communist Europe, the former communist party seems to have made the case with voters that while it embraces democracy and the market, it is the legitimate defender of the welfare state.[37] As a consequence, the LDLP has remained a major political force in the country while the LSDP has yet to rule. Most troubling for the LSDP was that it was unable to pick up a significant number of disaffected LDLP voters in the 1996. As a consequence, the LSDP managed only to increase its deputy total from eight to 12 in the Seimas. The answer appears to lie in the LSDP's inability thus far to establish an identity with the voting population. The instability of its voter base is certainly adequate demonstration of this.

There appear to be at least three reasons for the LSDP's failure. First, it is not alone on the political left. It is one of two parties that claim to represent the interests of workers. Despite its best efforts, the LSDP has not been able to distinguish itself from the LDLP. When the LDLP invited the LSDP into the new government following its sweeping 1992 electoral victory, the latter refused, fearing that it would lose any hope of establishing a separate identity among the Lithuanian electorate. To make the case, the LSDP not only refused to join the LDLP government following the 1992 elections, it joined the opposition during the entire timeframe of LDLP rule from 1992 to 1996. The party was particularly critical of the LDLP privatization and marketization reforms, which it claimed hurt workers. LSDP leaders even declared that the LDLP was a right-wing party representing the interests of the business classes.[38]

Second, the LSDP has until recently been unable to develop a leadership with nationwide recognition. Its candidates have been relative unknowns. The LDLP on the other hand has benefitted greatly from the name recognition of President Algirdas Brazauskas. Just as importantly, having ruled from 1992 to 1996, many of the party's leaders have become household names in the country. It is only recently that Vytenis Andriukaitis, the LSDP candidate in the 1998 presidential elections, has given the party a leader with any notable degree of name recognition.

Third, the LSDP strategy to form a strategic alliance with labor unions in order to mobilize workers was predestined to fail. Having been stripped of their patrons in the Communist Party and state apparatus, labor unions are poorly prepared to engage in collective action in the new economic realities. Worse, unions enjoy little confidence among workers who have a poor understanding of collective bargaining. Hence, the unions are largely adrift, denied of access to the state which they formerly enjoyed and virtually devoid of any ability to mobilize workers.

To explain the LSDP's relative lack of success, however, is not to explain why the LDLP has emerged as a major player in the post-Soviet politics of Lithuania. It was the LDLP legislative victory of 1992 followed by its victory in the presidential contest of 1993 that ushered in the 'Return of the Left' in Eastern Europe. Scholars have focussed their attention on possible explanations for the resurgence of the former communist party, a phenomenon that has repeated itself in numerous countries of the region. Among the propositions offered are structural characteristics of the party system, intra-party factors and issues.

Those who have offered structural characteristics of the party system as a possible explanation for the success of former communist parties, have considered the degree of competition offered by both leftist and rightist parties. In the argument of some, the very presence of other leftist parties can reduce the potential for electoral success by ex-communists. With more parties to choose from that espouse similar beliefs, the more difficult it becomes to capture votes.[39] Related to this argument is the view that the choice to adopt proportional representation also reduces the likelihood that the former communists will achieve a strong competitive stance as such electoral systems lead to the formation of greater numbers of parties, to include competing parties on the left.[40] These propositions, however, hold little validity in the Lithuanian case where 70 of the 141 legislative seats are decided on the basis of proportional representation. While there are numerous small parties on the left, the LDLP as we have seen continues to dominate this part of the political spectrum, its only competitor being the LSDP.

Others contend that the former communists owe their victories to the poor organization of the opposition. Conversely, the more organized the opposition, the worse the ex-communists performed during the initial election.[41] Again, propositions focussing on the structure of the party system offer little explanation in the Lithuanian case. Political organizing began prior to independence. Indeed, Sajudis had already organized sufficiently to decisively defeat the former communists in the 1990 elections. While the Homeland Union was not organized until after the 1992 LDLP electoral victory, the LSDP and LCDP had effectively organized as political parties prior to those elections.

Better explanations for the strong showing of the former communists in post-independence Lithuania focus on the internal organization of the LDLP itself and the political issues dominating the agenda. As elsewhere in post-communist Europe, the LDLP enjoyed the advantages of being a former communist party, among them greater resources, an institutional base, and a politically experienced leadership. However, these factors would have been of little help if the party had failed to renew itself during the transition from communist rule. As John T. Ishiyama argues, those parties that tolerated dissent early in the process were better able to adapt to changing political situations. Just as importantly, they were able to renew their leadership and speedily adopt a reform image as a party that had embraced democracy and the market.[42] The successor party to the LDLP, the Lithuanian Communist Party (LCP), had begun the process starting in 1988 with the ascension of Algirdas Brazauskas to the post of party First Secretary in the wake of his predecessor's inability to deal with growing public loss of faith in the party. By the end of 1989, the LCP had separated from the Communist Party of the Soviet Union and by 1990 it had entered into a legislative coalition with Sajudis.

But what was equally important was the LDLP's ability to position itself as the party representing 'reform with a human face'. The pain associated with the marketization of the economy opened up great opportunities for the LDLP, as it did for other former communist parties in East Europe.[43] The very process of leadership renewal permitted the party to take advantage of the issue. As early as 1990, the party began to present itself to the public as the party best able to effect change at a moderate, more manageable pace. Supporting eventual independence for the country, the LDLP argued that economic dependence on the Soviet Union demanded that separation be accomplished in a rational manner, as opposed to a hasty and poorly prepared exit. As the right-wing government undertook radical reform of the economy from 1991 to 1992, the LDLP went into opposition, declaring itself dedicated to a market reform that would be less injurious to the public welfare. The 1992 legislative victory was the fruit of the LDLP's efforts.

5 THE FUTURE OF THE LEFT

Nonetheless, the crushing defeat suffered by the LDLP in the 1996 national legislative elections raises the question whether the LDLP will continue to be a major player in Lithuanian politics. And what about the LSDP and the political left in general? What is the likely future for the Lithuanian left? One possibility is that the left will wither away. Neither the LDLP nor the LSDP will succeed in capturing the loyalty of the country's lower classes. Instead the Christian Democrats will gain the support of the peasantry, and the parties of the right given their commitment to the welfare state will gain the loyalty of the working class. However, this is not a likely scenario. There is no evidence of a rightward shift in the voting population. Indeed, the 1996 election results are largely due to the decision of LDLP voters to stay home.

A second possibility is that the LDLP will collapse, leaving the LSDP as the sole contender on the left. The mere scale of the electoral defeat followed by obvious internal bickering within the party and Brazauskas's decision to retire from politics all point to this. However, the LDLP voter base did not 'leave' the party in 1996. It merely stayed at home. Indeed, much of that base returned to cast their ballots for Paulauskas, the LDLP-backed candidate, in the presidential race.

More likely scenarios focus on the internal politics of the LDLP and the LSDP. The major struggle within the LSDP pits the centrist Dagys faction against the leftist faction led by Andriukaitis. As discussed previously, the former supports state incentives to small business while the latter proposes the Swedish economic model for adoption in Lithuania. Within the LDLP, the power struggle revolves around the ongoing efforts of Ceslovas Jursenas, the current LDLP leader, to open the party to younger, more progressive elements. Jursenas's gift for compromise makes him a good bet to succeed, despite the opposition from the 'old guard'. He is assisted in the effort by the currently dominant group of intellectuals led by Kirkilas.

Depending upon the end game of the respective intra-party struggles, three possibilities suggest themselves. First, should Jursenas fail and Andriukaitis retain leadership, the younger more progressive elements of the LDLP together with the intellectuals would be likely to merge with the LSDP, leaving the LDLP as a small party representing the interests of the former *nomenklatura* now turned businessmen. Kirkilas had hinted of the possibility that he would leave the party in early 1998. While he has yet to do so, his decision will undoubtedly rest on Jursenas's efforts to revive the LDLP. Second, should Jursenas fail and Andriukaitis be ousted from the leadership, the LDLP progressives and intellectuals would be likely to form a new party with the Andriukaitis group. The new party would quickly come to dominate the Lithuanian left, leaving the LSDP and the LDLP with an uncertain future. Third, a successful Jursenas effort to renew the LDLP together with a victory by the more centrist Dagys faction within the LSDP would probably lead to a decision by the leftist faction to merge with the LDLP. In such a case, the rump LSDP would probably merge with either the Christian Democrats or the Centrist Union. A fourth and final possibility is that Jursenas will succeed in renewing the LDLP and Andriukaitis will continue to hold on to the leadership of the LSDP, a more likely possibility given the name recognition which Andriukaitis's presidential bid has given him. In such a case, the LDLP and the LSDP will continue as they are.

While the foregoing discussion argues that the left will survive in Lithuanian politics, it says nothing about how successful it is likely to be. This is likely to depend in large measure upon whether the parties of the left can successfully appeal to youth and adapt to changing economic realities. It is axiomatic that the future of any party depends on its ability to connect with youth. Those parties that can capture the imagination of younger generations will secure for themselves a strong base from which to recruit the most talented leaders and mobilize future voters. This fact has not been lost on either the LSDP or the LDLP. Indeed, the appeal of the left appears much stronger than that of the right among young people. This is all the more the case given the continued domination of pensioners in the Homeland Union, which serves to impede new ideas within the party.

Both the LSDP and the LDLP ran candidates in the 1998 presidential elections whose relative youth was in sharp contrast to the candidates of the right. The LDLP-backed candidate, Arturas Paulauskas, made the most direct appeals to young voters on this basis, portraying himself as the candidate of a new generation with new ideas. Indeed, one of his main campaign pledges was specifically targetted at young people. Paulauskas promised to revamp the country's system of higher education to make it more open for those wanting a university degree. Further, he called for a reassessment of the use of entrance exams as well as a radical increase in state financial aid to both students and universities.

Equally important to the future success of the left is the direction of economic change. Thus far economic change appears to have worked in the left's favor. The difficulties visited upon much of the population by the reforms have made them receptive to demands for a strong welfare state. Further consolidating the appeal of the left with large segments of the Lithuanian public is the continued domination of small and medium-sized industrial enterprises in the economy, as a result of which the left continues to receive substantial public support despite recent strong economic growth at 5.5 per cent per year.

All of this could change, however, if the structure of the Lithuanian economy were to be substantially altered. Indeed, Lithuania's recent entry into the global economy has made it increasingly difficult for the country to maintain a largely industrialized economy. There is increasing pressure to change to a service- oriented economy. As this occurs, the working-class jobs will decrease in numbers and be replaced by those not traditionally represented by the left. In the West, the left has responded by championing issues with appeal beyond its traditional labor base. The LSDP and the LDLP have shown little inclination in this direction thus far. Indeed, the transition to a post-industrial economy has received virtually no attention as yet. The LDLP platform calls for preserving old, efficient industry; stimulating investment and jobs in industry; improving relations between labor and management; and reviving labor unions. Its only mention of future economic change is a vague reference to the necessity to improve the conditions necessary to obtain and disseminate information more fully. While the LSDP is less focussed on larger industries, it makes no mention of the service sector or the integration of information and communications technologies.

Thus, while the Lithuanian left appears certain to survive, it is not altogether certain how successful it will be. The legacy of the communist past will ensure a commitment to the welfare state for generations to come. Continued distress caused by the economic reforms will only serve to assure the left against a right-wing usurpation of this commitment. But the strength of its electoral appeal will depend on continued success in attracting new generations of leaders as well as adapting to economic change. Of the two challenges, the latter appears more problematic. While the relative lack of attention given to the challenges which the transition to a post-industrial economy will present the left is not surprising given the continued economic crisis from which the country suffers, the left cannot continue to ignore the issue for long. Indeed, its continued appeal to youth will depend to a great extent on its ability to adapt to the changing demands brought about by globalization of the country's economy.

NOTES

1. Leonas Sabaliunas, *Lithuanian Social Democracy in Perspective 1893–1914* (Durham, NC: Duke University Press, 1990).
2. Ibid.
3. Ibid.
4. Ibid.; Alfonsas Eidintas, 'The Nation Creates Its State', in Edvardas Tuskenis, (ed.), *Lithuania in European Politics: The Years of the First Republic, 1918–1940* (New York: St. Martin's, 1997), pp. 33–58.
5. Alfonsas Eidintas, 'The Presidential Republic', in Tuskenis, (ed.), pp. 111–38.
6. Sajudis was the Lithuanian Movement for Perestroika, which emerged during the Gorbachev era. For a thorough examination of its founding and role in restoring Lithuania's independence, see Alfred Erich Senn, *Gorbachev's Failure in Lithuania* (New York: St. Martin's Press, 1995); and Alfred Erich Senn, *Lithuania Awakening* (Berkeley: University of California, 1990).
7. 'Obschestvenno-politicheskie organizatsii, partii I dvizheniia v Litve', *Izvestiia TsK KPSS* 3 (March 1991): 93–102.
8. V. Stanley Vardys and Judith B. Sedaitis, *Lithuania: The Rebel Nation* (Boulder: Westview, 1997), pp. 154–5.
9. Terry D. Clark, 'Coalition Realignment in the Supreme Council of the Republic of Lithuania and the Fall of the Vagnorius Government', *Journal of Baltic Studies* 25, 1 (1993): 53–66.
10. See, for example, Radoslaw Markowski, 'Political Parties and Ideological Spaces in East Central Europe', *Communist and Post-Communist Studies* 30, 3 (1997): 221–54.
11. See Michael G. Roskin, 'The Emerging Party Systems of Central and Eastern Europe', *East European Quarterly* 27, 1 (March 1993): 47–63.
12. See John T. Ishiyama, 'Structures, Leaders, and Processes of Democratization in Eastern Europe', *Comparative Politics* 27, 2 (1995): 147–66; Andrew Janos, 'Social Science, Communism, and the Dynamics of Political Change', *World Politics* 44 (1991): 81–112; Alison Mahr and John Nagle, 'Resurrection of the Successor Parties and Democratization in East-Central Europe', *Communist and Post-Communist Studies* 28, 4 (1995): 393–409.
13. Andras Korosenyi, 'Revival of the Past or New Beginning: The Nature of Post-Communist Politics', *Political Quarterly* 62, 1 (1991): 52–94.

14. Markowski, p. 238.
15. Kazimierz M. Slomczynski and Goldie Shabad, 'Systemic Transformation and the Salience of Class Structure in East Central Europe', *East European Politics and Societies* **11**, 1 (1997): 155–89.
16. H. Kitschelt, 'The Formation of Party Systems in East Central Europe', *Politics and Society* **20** (1992): 7–20.
17. Geoffrey Evans and Stephen Whitefield, 'Identifying the Bases of Party Competition in Eastern Europe', *British Journal of Political Science* **23**, 4 (1993): 521–48.
18. Jack Bielasiak, 'Substance and Process in the Development of Party Systems in East Central Europe', *Communist and Post-Communist Studies* **30**, 1 (1997): 23–44; Korosenyi; David S. Mason, 'Attitudes toward the Market and Political Participation in the Postcommunist States', *Slavic Review* **54**, 2 (1995): 385–406; Peter Mateju and Blanka Rehakova, 'Turning Left or Class Realignment? Analysis of the Changing Relationship Between Class and Party in the Czech Republic, 1992–1996, *East European Politics and Societies* **11**, 3 (1997): 501–42; Ivan Szelenyi, Eva Fodor, and Eric Hanley, 'Left Turn in Post-Communist Politics: Bringing Class Back in?', *East European Politics and Societies* **11**, 1 (1997): 190–224.
19. Alfred Erich Senn, 'Lietuvos partiness sistemos formavimasis', *Politologija* **2** (1996): 3–12.
20. Evans and Whitefield; Jurate Novagrockiene, '1996 m. Seimo rinkimai ir Lietuvos partines sistemos raida', *Politologija* **1**, 9 (1997): 118–32.
21. The survey was conducted by mail under the auspices of the Institute of International Relations and Political Science at Vilnius University during the period from 20 September to 20 October, 1996. The response rate was 46 per cent; 599 of the 1,280 questionnaires mailed were returned.
22. Question 11.
23. See, for example, William M. Reisinger, Andrei Yu. Melville, Arthur H. Miller and Vicki L. Hesli, 'Mass and Elite Political Outlooks in Post-Soviet Russia: How Congruent?', *Political Research Quarterly* **49**, 1 (1996): 77–101.
24. Alexander C. Pacek, 'Macroeconomic Conditions and Electoral Politics in East Central Europe', *American Journal of Political Science* **38**, 3 (1994): 723–44.
25. Giovanni Sartori, *Parties and Party Systems* (Cambridge: Cambridge University, 1976).
26. Using the formula developed by Rein Taagepera and Matthew Soberg Shugart (*Seats and Votes*, New Haven: Yale University, 1989), Jurate Novagrockiene obtains an index of 3.36 for the number of effective political parties in Lithuania. This represents an increase from previous years, therefore, the system is headed toward a four party system. See Novagrockiene, p. 125.
27. Vytenis Andriukaitis, Aloyzas Skalas and Rimantas Dagys, 'Lietuvos socialdemokratu partija', in Algis Krupavicius, Povilas Gaidys and Kestutis Masiulis, (eds.), *Politines partijos Lietuvoje: Atgiminas ir veikla* (Vilnius: Litterae Universitatis, 1996), pp. 233–43.
28. Gediminas Kirkilas, 'Lietuvos demokratine darbo partija', in Krupavicius, Gaidys, and Masiulis, (eds.), pp. 169–82.
29. The Institute of International Relations and Political Science conducted the survey at Vilnius University during the period 20 September to 20 October, 1996.
30. Ibid., question 3.2. Agreement with the statement was coded '1', disagreement was coded '3', and uncertainty was coded '2'. The LSDP average of 1,825 was closer to agreement ('1') than the LDLP average of 2.161. Further, in response to question 12.14, 65 per cent of LSDP candidates indicated that the political left was associated with the statement that 'equal rights are only attainable when the state satisfies the basic social needs of its citizens'. Only 45.6 per cent of LDLP respondents did so.
31. Ibid., question 15.
32. Ibid., question 12.9.
33. Ibid., question 12.6.
34. Ibid., question 14.3.

35. M. Degutis, 'Lietuvos tinkejai: partiju pasirinkimo motyvai', *Politologija* **1**, 9 (1997): 142–57.
36. Ibid.
37. Korosenyi; Mahr and Nagle.
38. LSDP leaders Vytenis Andriukaitis and Aloyzas Sakalas made this point during a round table with participants of the International Political Science Association Convention, Vilnius, Lithuania, 12 December 1996.
39. Mahr and Nagle; John T. Ishiyama, 'The Sickle or the Rose: Previous Regime Types and the Evolution of the Ex-Communist Parties in Post-Communist Politics', *Comparative Political Studies* **30**, 3 (1997): 299–330.
40. While there is widespread consensus on this score, see, for example, Maurice Duverger, *Political Parties: Their Organization and Activity in the Modern State* (London: Methuen, 1954); Douglas W. Rae, *The Political Consequences of Electoral Laws*, 2nd edn (New Haven: Yale University, 1971): Giovanni Sartori, *Comparative Constitutional Engineering* (London: Macmillan, 1994); Arend Lijphart, *Electoral Systems and Party Systems: A Study of Twenty–seven Democracies, 1945–1990* (Oxford: Oxford University, 1994) – there have been recent studies questioning the validity of the proposition, including Michael Coppedge, 'District Magnitude, Economic Performance, and Party-System Fragmentation in Five Latin American Countries', *Comparative Political Studies* **30**, 2 (1997): 156–87.
41. Bielasiak.
42. Mahr and Nagle; Ishiyama, 'Structures, Leaders, and Processes'; Ishiyama, 'The Sickle or the Rose?'.
43. Mahr and Nagle; Szelenyi, Fodo and Hanley; Mason.

4. Left Politics in Post-communist Hungary

Barnabas Racz

---

1 THE SYSTEMIC CHANGE AND THE CRISIS OF THE LEFT

The Background

While there were scattered antecedent violent clashes in Poland and the German Democratic Republic, the October 1956 Revolt in Hungary was the first major blow to de-Stalinizing communism everywhere. As Albert Camus observed: 'The Hungarians won and did more for human freedom and social justice than other nations in twenty years. Budapest showed the way'.[1] While more anti-communist than 'anti-left', the revolution indicated the possibility of shaking the totalitarian system from within. After the Soviet invasion and the initial suppression led by First Secretary Janos Kadar to re-establish communist party rule, the government moved toward gradual changes. Beginning in the late 1960s the Kadar reforms opened up the perspectives to economic decentralization, limited market orientation, Western contacts, increased living standards and reduced political tension. Hungary became a window-shop case generating rejection in the CMEA–WTO (Council for Mutual Economic Assistance–Warsaw Treaty Organization) countries and skirting the limits of possibilities in the constant shadow of Soviet intolerance. Reacting to the Polish Solidarity movement in the 1980s the winds of change began to flow progressively stronger and the by then popular Kadar and his immediate entourage were removed from the bastions of power in the party center in 1988. The fast-growing dissident movement, from within and from without the Hungarian Socialist Workers' Party (HSWP)[2] pressed for system replacement, while the party tottered only on the verge of 'system reforms' in the Gorbachevian sense. Events bypassed the stalling efforts of the party elite and the mass pressure and opposition groups forced the HSWP to negotiate a *modus vivendi*. The lengthy roundtable discussions in 1989 eventually led to

59

system replacement and the transformation of the ruling party into an (intended) social-democratic/socialist party: the 'newly' founded Hungarian Socialist Party (HSP).[3]

The sequence of events between 1956 and 1989 seem to indicate that the 'left' was rejected by society not only in its extreme form, but also the center-left variant. Western reports on the 1990 first pluralist elections were headlined by the media as 'the defeat of the left', and the victorious right-conservative parties in Hungary also thought that 'the left is basically dead' and has no future in the long run; it is the end of communism and all related left currents.[4] This perception was created by the euphoria understandably taking place over the collapse of one of the most suppressive systems in world history. Under the surface, however, the aforementioned assessment was contradicted both in society in general and in the political process in particular. Even though the HSP as the major force on the left had fewer seats in parliament than three other parties, with 10.9 per cent of the votes it remained a relatively viable opposition force. When taken together with the other left votes on the 1990 elections, the overall strength of the left was well over 20 per cent, and considering also the large bloc of non-voters, it was potentially stronger as turned out to be the case in 1994.

The objective of this volume is the fortunes of the left in the post-communist phase of the former Soviet bloc countries. The concept of the left for this purpose is defined here as the socialist left meaning those parties, movements which had Marxist ideological roots even if they moved away from them almost completely, but professed a prime interest in social justice. On the Hungarian scene in 1990 such parties were the Hungarian Socialist Party, the Social Democratic Party, the Hungarian Socialist Workers' Party (later renamed the Workers' Party), the Agrarian Alliance and support groups within other parties and especially the largest labor organization, the National Federation of Hungarian Unions (NFHU).[5] To assess properly the status of these left forces, they have to be viewed in the context of other major players on the political palette in 1990. Outside the HSP there were five parties entering parliament: two liberal and three conservative nationalist, while two leftist parties were on the top of the list of extra-parliamentary parties: the social democrats and the communists.[6]

The Main Actors: The Parties in 1990

It is impossible to provide here a detailed account of the parties' ideological profiles and organizational characteristics. Few had stable registered memberships and their programs often overlapped in vague generalizations. This was due to their relatively short existence and also because they often failed to build effective grassroot ties.[7] During the subsequent electoral campaigns more specific features began to emerge and they also underwent considerable mutations in organization and programs. We shall present here only a skeletal outline of the major parties as they entered the first pluralist election campaign and subsequent changes will unfold in later parts of the analysis.

The *Alliance of Free Democrats* (AFD) by its self-image was a social liberal force as well as the inheritor of the ideas of European social democracy. The party had taken an aggressive opposition stance against the government since 1988; it had an intellectual leadership including former communists. The 1990 program was based on a combination of liberalism and social democracy calling for a speedy transformation to a market economy; full integration with European institutions was also a key plank. The elitist nature of the party and the lack of mass support needed for such radical changes represented the most serious problems for the party both in 1990 and 1994.

The *Alliance of Young Democrats* (AYD or Fidesz) was born from the young intellectuals' opposition movement in the 1980s and stood on liberal principles, supporting a free market system with a minimal role for state redistribution, speedy privatization and limited attention to social policy.[8] The primary social role of the state should be the promotion of capital accumulation and only secondarily later income redistribution. The party defined itself in 1990 as left-center and support came primarily from urban-based intellectuals, with a weaker presence in the countryside and without an effective grassroot organization. As will be seen, similar to most other parties the AYD was forced to redefine itself for the 1994 election campaign.

The *Christian Democratic People's Party* (CDPP) program was based on Christian philosophy which was to be the guideline for the solution of all social problems. The three key principles of the party were the Christian state, which is the depository of public good, popular sovereignty and parliamentary democracy. The primacy of private property was fundamental, although the social policy of the government was also emphasized. Support came predominantly but not exclusively from the countryside, especially from the more Catholic Transdanubia.[9]

The winner of the 1990 elections and the oldest anti-communist opposition force was the *Hungarian Democratic Forum* (HDF). Its main objectives included systemic transformation 'without a catastrophe', adherence to 'historical tradition', opposition to extremism and development of a democratic political culture. It was a heterogeneous party including populist and liberal traditions as well as Christian democratic views. The Forum advocated a gradual approach to the agricultural question, a marked difference from the Smallholders' Party: this position, however, was abandoned in the property compensation legislation under the Smallholders' pressure. The party also held that an unlimited market economy is dangerous and a social market economy was needed.   In foreign policy the HDF pursued a confrontational stance regarding Hungarian minorities everywhere and integration into the European institutions was the central focus of diplomacy. The leadership included mostly intellectuals, senior figures in education, writers and philosophers.[10]

→   The *Hungarian Socialist Party* (HSP) originated in the October 1989 Hungarian Socialist Workers' Party Congress dissolving the party and founding the HSP. The separation from the former HSWP philosophical base, however, was not complete but the new party did have an experienced leadership and a developed organizational structure. The HSP claimed to be the heir of progressive thinking and reform communism with the objective of democratic socialism.   Thus the HSP stopped halfway between the former reform communism and a genuine Western social democracy and this affected the composition of its leadership as well as the party's changes on the elections.[11] Nonetheless, the HSP immediately applied for membership status in the Socialist International, but they had to wait years before full membership.

The *Independent Smallholders Party* (ISP) was one of the historical parties and it appealed to the small business, farmer and agricultural worker strata. The party program focussed on the primacy of private property while also recognizing community, and to a minor extent state property; in agriculture private farming ought to be the basis.   Ideologically the party also stressed 'traditional Hungarian values' and was closest to Christian democracy.[12] The support strata were mostly in the countryside and in the east, among the less-educated and the older voters. The party received relatively strong backing in the 1990 elections and entered the Antall coalition government, raising demands to 're-privatize', that is, the restitution of the original ownership conditions as of 1947 as well as the summary condemnation and rejection of the entire communist past.

The two strongest non-parliamentary parties were also important players of politics but fell short of the 4 per cent national vote threshold required by the electoral law to gain parliamentary mandate.   The *Hungarian Social Democratic Party* (HSDP) was a historical force in twentieth-century Hungarian politics. The party program in 1990 looked at the Western sister parties as models and, while accepting Marxism as the root of social democracy, it stepped over its dogmatism; it stood for a free market controlled by social policy in a balanced economic and political system. On the political map the social democrats defined themselves as left of center, open to all working elements in the society. In foreign policy European integration and cooperation with the Second Socialist International were stressed; the party had a chance to stage a comeback but internal struggles in the leadership, amateurish attitudes and organizational chaos reduced the party's backing in the elections.[13]

The *Hungarian Socialist Workers' Party* (HSWP), in 1991 renamed the Workers' Party (WP), originated in the splinter group of 272 delegates who did not go along with the transformation of the HSWP into a socialist party in 1989. Ideologically defined as a Marxist–Leninist party, it was rooted in leftist, left-social-democratic and reform-communist views. It recognized the positive contributions of the 40 post-war years including the period since the 1988 party conference ousting the Kadar leadership. The HSWP opposed 'right-wing capitalist forces' and saw future potential for the restoration of a predominantly collectively-based economy and pledged solidarity with other left-socialist, left-social-democratic and communist forces both at home and abroad.[14]

Loosely relating to the left-socialist parties the *Agrarian Alliance* (AA) was more a special interest group than a party. Its support came from the technocratic elements of the large-scale agricultural enterprises. Threatened by the Smallholders' attack advocating a 'return of the land' program, the Alliance's main objective was to prevent incompetent dismantling of the bases of agrarian production and to promote its democratic transformation.[15]

This short synopsis indicates that the parties were not crystallized yet in 1990 and later data indicate limited progress in this. They were all for pluralistic democracy and market economy but they were also backward looking and still psychologically getting even with the former one-party system, while future programs were lacking in specifics, especially on issues of economic transformation. The question arises whether these parties served the purpose of pure interest articulation by groups or were only umbrella organizations with a skeletal elite but without firm rank-and-file ties. The registered membership figures did not reflect the potential voting strength and the social composition of most parties was heterogeneous. Public opinion surveys indicated high numbers of voters in an uncertain state of mind before and during the campaign and potential non-voters represented a significant percentage immediately prior to the elections.

2 THE LEFT'S FIGHT FOR SURVIVAL: THE 1990 ELECTIONS

The above-named parties were the winners of the new pluralist elections and gained legislative representation, with the exception of the two smaller left parties: the social democrats and the communists, who remained outside of the parliament because they failed to reach the 4 per cent threshold of national votes prescribed by the Election Law. It appears that basically the same six parties continued to form the party structure in Hungarian politics for years to come: the 1994 elections showed a constancy of these parties unusual in other regional countries.

The 1989 Electoral Law[16] adopted perhaps the most complex electoral system in Europe: it created a three-tier system based partly on the West German and Austrian models.[17] Citizens have two votes: one for individual district candidates and one for the 20 territorial lists, each sending respectively, 176 and 152 representatives to the legislature. Parliament has 386 seats and the remaining 58 national list seats are derived from the so-called 'fragment votes' rechanneled to the winning parties on the basis of a complex mathematical formula. In the relevant literature the complexity is acknowledged but it is also generally accepted that the elections were fair and democratic, building the first firm legal foundation for the new pluralist system in the country.[18]

In virtually all post-communist states, socialist/social-democratic trends survived in the systemic transformation era and their political potential should not have been discounted. Leftist tendencies were clearly visible from Lithuania to Romania, including Hungary, with several left-of-center parties and factions even within the liberal parties. Public opinion surveys indicate that the political culture includes social values favoring the strong redistributive and protective role(s) of the state. Nonetheless the system-changing elections resulted in the predominant victory of the right-of-center parties (Table 4.1), which after the election formed the Jozsef Antall-led coalition government in power in 1990–94: the Hungarian Democratic Forum was the pluralist winner of the elections, followed in the right-of-center group by the Independent Smallholders' and Citizens' Party and the smaller Christian Democratic People's Party.

The election results clearly show that the nationalist–conservative parties combined had the decisive edge, but also that no party won a clear majority position. Furthermore the parliamentary seat distribution and also the territorial list votes indicate the 'one-thirder' political culture in the country which by and large prevails even today and is likely to survive in 1998 and beyond. The left-voter support was weaker: the Western and Hungarian media buried them and saw them as defeated, however this was a serious case of misjudgment. A closer analysis of the election data shows that the combined left vote was approximately 26 per cent (Table 4.2), a relatively powerful potential for staging a comeback.

As the data show, the socialists won only limited representation in parliament – only 33 of 386 seats. However, the left's limited legislative presence was not a realistic measure of the voter preferences because the 4 per cent rule excluded smaller parties below this threshold. From among several such parties, the most significant ones were the reform-communist Hungarian

Table 4.1   Summarized final returns for the six major parties, 1990

Party	Vote (%)	Individual district seats	Territorial seats	National seats	total
HDF	24.73	115	40	10	165
AFD	23.83	34	34	23	91
ISP	11.40	11	16	23	44
HSP	8.55	1	14	18	33
AYD	5.44	1	8	12	21
CDPP	6.46	3	8	10	21
Agrarian Alliance	1.00	1	–	–	1
Independent	n.a.	6	–	–	6
Joint Candidate	n.a.	4	–	–	4
Total					386

Sources: Tamas Moldovan et al. (eds.), *Szabadon Választott—Parliamenti Almanach* (Budapest, Idegenforgalmi Propaganda Kiado, 1990), p. 44; *Magyar Közlöny* (Official Gazette), 13 May 1990, pp. 1082–3.

Table 4.2   Socialist-left votes, 1990 (territorial lists)

Party	%	Votes
HSP	10.89	535,064
SWP	3.86	180,964
SDP	3.55	174,434
Agrarian Alliance	3.13	154,004
Total	21.25	1,044,466
Abstainers	+5 (estimate)	
Total Socialist Left	26.25	

Note: Based on 35 per cent non-voters, the estimated 5 per cent is a conservative figure.
Source: Compiled by author, see Table 4.1.

Socialist Workers' Party and the Hungarian Social Democratic Party; the picture was also blurred by the large number of non-voters whose political preferences remained uncertain (35 per cent in the first round and 55 per cent in the runoffs).

The socialists became the fourth largest force in the legislature,[19] but, without effective cooperation with other opposition parties, their role was severely curtailed. Nonetheless the party was the best-organized left force, led by an experienced and politically sophisticated leadership; it was likely that it would retain its prominent role among the left forces before and after the 1994 elections.[20]

The figures for the more representative first round indicate that the left votes comprise about one quarter of the total, more than it would appear in the light of the parliamentary seats only. The low performance in individual districts was partly due to competition among the leftist parties. The three parties combined show an impressive force: united they could have made a difference, fragmented they lost. Both in individual districts and on the territorial lists the combined totals of the three left parties were more impressive than the separate outcome for the Socialists. On the territorial lists, all the left votes combined would have resulted in the left forces taking three out of 20 counties and such an alliance was the second choice in six other counties.[21]

It is noteworthy that the highest percentage of votes for the left emerged in the north and/or on the plainland but not in Transdanubia, and there also was a difference in participation between the west (Transdanubia) and east (plainland); the former's involvement was generally more intense and produced more liberal (AFD) victories[22] both on the territorial lists and in individual districts.[23] Perceptions about geographical differences and their meaning vary and factual differences are palpable between the two regions and were recognized by outstanding historians.[24] The eastern part of the country generally produced more leftist votes and the data seem to go in tandem with today's economic (unemployment) figures: in the northern hard-hit industrial areas the leftist support was the highest both in 1990 and 1994. The picture of the political landscape emerging from the elections is not a realistic mirror of a cross-section of the voters. The distortions in the electoral system and voter passivity resulted in significant deviation. While the HDF was the strongest party, it had only a plurality position, controlling 43 per cent of the parliamentary seats and was forced to enter into coalition raising the specter of an uncertain future. The partnership with the ISP and CDPP foreshadowed the Forum's eventual drift from a right-of-center to a strongly conservative–nationalist–populist position. There were several vital issues which eventually decided the future of this coalition: foremost among these were the questions of agricultural policy including the land ownership problem[25] and all painful privatization measures causing severe hardship for the working classes. The ever-growing foreign indebtedness threatened economic collapse and in foreign policy the Western orientation and the Hungarian minority problems abroad also raised vital questions as did the entire institutional–constitutional reconstruction. It was clear that the new government needed wide societal support across the national spectrum for the solution of these tasks and that any of these issues might have broken the new coalition's ability to govern effectively, causing further harm to the economy already then teetering on the edge of collapse.

The left won the fight for survival but naturally lost its primacy at this historical juncture; however, the often-stated perception that socialism was defeated was an error in judgment. The socialists emerged as the fourth largest party in parliament and the other left components were excluded. Yet, this did not render them non-existent in the democratic process and contingent upon circumstances they could have been expected to become important players in politics. After the 1990 elections the HSP remained the strongest left party and the potential leading nucleus of all left-of-center forces. Such cooperation later failed to materialize for a number of reasons as the subsequent discussion will show.

The second-largest left force was the HSWP with a reform-communist agenda and former *apparatchiki* support, gaining 3.68 per cent of the national vote with the status of being the seventh-largest party and remaining the lead force of all non-parliamentary parties up to 1998. The Social Democratic Party showed the weakest support with a national vote of 3.55 per cent. The party was marred by internal dissent and power struggles, undermining its appeal to the voters and almost fading away in 1994.

The election outcome triggered a mood of victory over the 'defeat of socialism' (of any kind) simultaneously with a declining sensitivity by the new governing coalition to human hardships caused by plant closures and the threat of dismantling the large-scale agro-enterprises. The elections resulted in a weakened left position representing one-quarter of the electorate but it was far from being defeated. In view of the given economic, social and psychological factors, it had a potential far beyond the numbers of parliamentary representation. This generally was not widely recognized but some analyses proposed that the left could exercise more influence in the future, their contemporary dismissal by the victorious parties notwithstanding. It was also understood that to a large extent an expanding political role would also depend on cooperation between labor unions, workers' councils and parties.

The dormant strength of the Hungarian left should not have surprised any objective analyst, foreign or domestic. There are usually no quantum leaps in human development and such attempts by force generally backfire. There was a 40-year continuity of the party-state system and it had its powerful influence which could not be broken overnight. There were undoubtedly some aspects of communism's legacy which, rightly or wrongly, were positive in many people's minds and combined with left traditions in the political culture of the twentieth century created a considerable support for socialism and solidarity. Fear from the drastic changes economically and familiarity with the former ruling party and their leading figures, elite and group interests combined gave strong backing to the HSP and bolstered its survival. It also has to be kept in mind that neither in 1956 nor in 1989 was there an unequivocal rejection of socialism/social democracy in Hungary: in both cases significant support existed for a mixed economic system. Last, but not least, the former ruling party became an important promoter of change; considering all of these factors, it is understandable that the left supporters opted for gradual or even only partial change.

3 THE ROAD TO VICTORY

Gathering Strength

While acknowledging with satisfaction the success in survival, the HSP at the same time realized its relatively weak position. The reconstruction of the party and rebuilding the political base was an enormous task amidst the atmosphere of political quarantine and ostracization by all other parliamentary parties. To succeed, the HSP had to erect all three sides of a triangle: rebuild the party organization; secure the voter support in the society at large; and convince the electorate about the failures of the conservative coalition.

The party did not waste time and right after the elections in May 1990 held its second congress, carefully weighing the lessons of the elections. Acknowledging that the HSP did not separate convincingly from its parent organization, this congress settled the identity of the party by distancing itself from the old HSWP ideology.[26] From now on the focus was on a social-democratic orientation which opened the way later to potential cooperation with the liberal parties then in opposition. The HSP became increasingly self-confident in its major role and began to stress that it was the only viable counterweight to a right-wing alternative; in doing so the party began to reach out to the latent passive elements in society.

In 1991 and 1992 the grassroot party-building process unfolded impressively and frequent meetings were held by top party leaders and parliamentary representatives everywhere in the countryside. Internal disagreements between various 'platforms' or factions in the party did not result in a party split.[27]

Given the limited and isolated status of the socialist group in parliament, the question of legislative strategy was not an easy one. In the first phase the socialist caucus was almost dormant under the direction of Imre Pozsgay but after his withdrawal from the party at the 10 November 1990 Congress, Zoltan Gal led the faction successfully to the end of the parliamentary cycle in 1994 opting for a cautious but more articulate legislative policy. The performance of the socialist caucus in this phase was nothing short of remarkable: from among all parliamentary parties they were the only ones free from demagogy, from personal intrigues and attacks, and the group acted in a sophisticated professional manner becoming well-informed mature politicians with previous experience.[28]

While the party was never able to influence the dominant majority in the legislative process – the coalition voting machinery made it an absolute principle to vote down even the smallest socialist amendment proposals[29] – the HSP caucus can claim a respectable record in presenting moderate leftist alternative positions. Critically active behavior was observable on most key issues of domestic policy (for example, the constitutional modification and the fiscal autonomy of self-governing units), while in the economic sphere social concern for workers and the lower socioeconomic strata was forcefully pursued. Particularly strong opposition was exhibited regarding the most controversial legislative proposals by the conservative coalition, especially the land compensation and reprivatization issues which critically affected the future of agriculture and property relations in the coming years.[30] The socialist caucus was also concerned with the right-wing restoration drift of the Antall coalition, the weakness of the HDF *vis-à-vis* the radical conservative pressures from the Smallholders' Party, and the unrealistic confrontational stance toward the surrounding countries with large Hungarian minorities.

The HSP contacts with other left-socialists were minimal after the elections: cooperative efforts remained mostly unsuccessful. The Social Democratic Party was involved in self-destructive internal disagreements and ties with the reform-communist HSWP would have been too risky politically, since the HSP itself was still quarantined as ex-communist by all parliamentary parties. Alliance with the labor unions also came very slowly but in 1992 the strongest, the NFHU, and the socialists declared their intention to cooperate including in future election campaigns. Public opinion polls taken between 1990 and 1992 show some fluctuation in the still low HSP popularity but there appeared a sustained backing which grew progressively. By the end of 1992, polling data indicated 10 per cent voting and 30 per cent support for a future coalition partnership with other parties.

At the end of the second year after the system-changing elections the HSP began to break out of isolation. With the deepening economic crisis and skyrocketing unemployment reaching more than 700,000, socialist-left policies were accepted by not only those who were nostalgic for the late Kadar era's job security and/or welfare policies, but also by new supporters who became alienated from the Antall coalition's socially indifferent and restoration-oriented tendencies and saw social democracy as a viable alternative. The legitimacy and credentials of the HSP also were enhanced by ← the international recognition by Western sister parties: the Socialist

International Congress in Berlin extended observer status to the party by a vote of 42 to 4 in 1992.[31]

On the domestic theatre the first successes began to show in a series of by-elections: in 1991–92 out of five parliamentary by-elections the socialists won three and were second in one, indicating shifting voter sympathies. The left base in the electorate was expanding under economic pressures, simultaneous to the acceleration of right-wing drift at the end of 1992. This was also manifested by HDF Vice-President Istvan Csurka's political pamphlet, from which the Forum's leadership did not distance itself unequivocally.[32] In this context, these events left scope for the HSP and the AFD, the two modernization parties, to move closer in the future, forecasting the image of a possible alliance. Within the broad mosaic of these different political factors, the single bloc of the Hungarian left and at its core the Socialist Party, all things considered, acquired a reasonable but limited chance to play a larger role, including some coalition alliance with other opposition forces. The realization of this potential eventually went even beyond the HSP expectations in the landslide victory for the left in 1994.

The conservative right-of-center coalition approached the 1994 election campaign in a deteriorating condition and declining popularity. The 1992–93 polls indicated a drop in HDF support and the party also had a serious setback because of the crisis created by Vice-President Csurka and his followers, who eventually separated from the Forum. Prime Minister Antall's death further weakened the party and his successor Peter Boross did not have the stature and charisma of his predecessor. The other parties were in equally weak condition: the AYD–Fidesz peaked at 38 per cent popular support in mid-1993 but was plagued by internal dissent; without effective grassroot organization this appeared to be only a protest sign short of electoral commitment as the party shrank gradually to its 7.02 per cent level on the 1994 elections. The ISP also disintegrated on the parliamentary caucus level, where the majority repudiated Jozsef Torgyan's radical and demagogic attitudes, but the small CDPP remained by and large constant, faithfully following the Forum's lead.

None of these parties – save the HSP – had a crystallized organization and all were catch-all parties[33] with a fluctuating electoral support. The six-party political system appeared to be suitable enough to survive two elections, indicating perhaps a developing tradition in post-communist political culture, but there were tidal waves of voter movements back and forth on the political spectrum.[34] Former abstainers moved toward the socialists and then moved away from them in 1996–97 toward the Smallholders and AYD; many Forum voters shifted also to the HSP as they abandoned it later. The organizational structures of parties with the exception of the socialists were generally so deficient and transient that they would defy systematic study.[35] Party leaders frequently manifested only their own views, with little or no reference to rank-and-file opinions. The support groups were like shifting sand and voter preferences showed wide fluctuations; it was already clear that this would be repeated in the post-1994 era too.

The gradual rise in the success of the HSP was to a large extent due to their ← excellent organization, inherited from the past. While there were and still are coordination problems among the leadership, the parliamentary caucus and the rank and file, overall the hierarchical organization of the party proved to be reasonably efficient, facilitating the election campaign work and generally keeping close links between the central and local layers of the organization. Staffed mostly by experienced professionals in the early 1990s and establishing intra-party democratic procedures, the socialists were second to none in this respect.[36]

By early 1994 the conservative coalition exhausted its political capital; and the opposition crystallized on the left side of the equation. Two converging lines met in focus: the rising rejection of the Forum coalition and the pendulum swinging back in the direction of the left. All parties were in some kind of disarray on the coalition side, and the AYD–Fidesz became momentarily irrelevant. The spreading discontent was palpable in the society which this time opted for cautious social-democratic policies against the unknown risks of the discredited right. The political center being vacuous a center-left policy seemed to be attractive; a policy which professed solidarity and which promised a market economy with social responsibility.[37] The Antall government's economic policy procrastinated and showed timidity in facing the crisis of the skyrocketing foreign debt and inflation; the damaging corruption in the hands of party elites; economic stabilization; unrealistic wage levels and welfare institutions; unemployment crisis and loss of former markets; the crippling of agricultural production through the land-return policy dismantling the large-scale production units and reverting to nineteenth-century small farming.[38] Philosophically the government looked backward, creating the impression of restoration of some aspects of inter-war political culture and in foreign policy pursued a path of confrontation without real power toward the surrounding states' Hungarian minority problems. These critical assessments were not shared unanimously in the society: Hungary remained a 'one-thirder' country and even after 1994 it was clear that the right-center and right retained somewhat less than one-third support, still a powerful base, which came back to haunt the left in 1998.

In all objectivity the conservative coalition wrote history by establishing the *Rechtstaat*, the constitutional structure, operated the democratic institutions by and large smoothly, and generally presided over the systemic transformation in a politically mature way – outstanding in the post-communist region. Yet, the electorate turned against it in a heavy critical way and passed – perhaps too harsh – judgment. History will render the final verdict.

The country went to the polls in May 1994 and held the second-generation democratic elections amidst growing signs of a socialist plurality gain. However, even the socialists were surprised at the political earthquake in the form of a landslide socialist victory, resulting in a 54 per cent absolute majority in parliamentary seats. It was observable in the post-Iron Curtain region since 1992 that left-of-center forces gradually reinforced themselves and Hungary was no exception.[39] The left came back with unexpected strength, not even foreseen by the most optimistic socialists. The reasons for this are complex and discussed in detail elsewhere;[40] however, there seems to be a consensus that the economic transformation, frustration with unemployment, the lost status of the worker strata and psycho-political nostalgia for past security played the major roles.

The socialists won the strongest position with a 32.99 per cent score on the territorial lists and also swept into victory in 149 (85.6 per cent) of the individual districts. With the input by the national list and re-channeled fragment votes, the socialists took control of 209 (54.14 per cent) of the parliamentary seats, while their later coalition partner AFD took 28 (19.74 per cent) seats on the territorial lists and 16 (9.1 per cent) individual seats, which combined with the national list gains (25) translated into 69 (17.87 per cent) parliamentary seats; thus the socialist–liberal coalition controlled a total of 278 (71.97 per cent) seats in the legislature. All other opposition parties together have only 106 (27.46 per cent) seats in parliament, (see Table 4.3).

Table 4.3 Correlation between territorial list votes and parliamentary seats, 1994

Party	Vote	%	Number of Seats	%
HSP	1,781,504	32.99	209	54.14
AFD	1,065,889	19.74	69	17.87
HDF	633,770	11.74	38	9.84
ISP	476,272	8.82	26	6.74
CDPP	379,523	7.03	22	5.70
AYD	379,344	7.02	20	5.18

Source: Report of the National Election Committee, Magyar Közlöny, 70, 28 June 1994.

Looking at the breakdown of the votes between the three left-socialist parties, the correlation of political strength changed decidedly among them and other left parties once again remained outside parliament on account of not exceeding the modified 5 per cent national threshold rule. The Workers' Party performed somewhat more weakly than in 1990 but still remained on the top of the extra-parliamentary parties. The overall election results reinforced the former finding showing that the society basically retained its three-way structure: left-socialist, liberal and right-of-center. However within the left component the relative strength of the parties underwent significant mutation: the Workers' Party position shrank, and the HSDP virtually disappeared. The territorial list returns indicate the picture of the three parties combined, as shown in Table 4.4.

Table 4.4   Territorial list votes for the three left-socialist parties, 1994

Party	Territorial list votes
HSP	32.99
WP	3.19
HSDP	0.95
(%)	37.13

Source: Report of the National Election Bureau, Ministry of the Interior.

Not counting here the estimate of non-voters, it is obvious that the left component grew meaningfully compared to 1990. The regional trends in the country were similar to the previous election data: the strongest left votes were cast in the northeast and east mirroring the historical precedents in 1985 and 1990.

Assessment: Left Defeat Turned to Triumph

As stated above, the perceived demise of the left in 1990 was in error. Both Western and post-communist analyses misjudged the relevant political–economic–social factors under the influence of euphoria. On the Hungarian scene the election data indicated the strength of the socialist left: the socialists, the reform communists and the social democrats. The socialists ←
became the most significant leftist force in 1990 and built the basis for the resurgence of the left in 1994.

The Social Democratic Party received the weakest support in 1990 with a national vote of 3.5 per cent or 174,434 votes, with no wins in individual districts. The party's record was characterized by often trivial internal conflicts: not finding its ideological identity, lacking in competent leadership, backed by an older membership without support from youth, historical social-democratic traditions did not balance the party's weakness. In the early 1990s the HSDP gradually declined and paid a heavy price for their failure to emerge as a viable force: in 1994 the national vote ratio fell to 0.95 per cent and the party ranked only eleventh nationally and fifth in the extra-parliamentary group of parties. The dimensions of the socialist victory further overshadowed the Workers' Party which, however, retained its firm position as the strongest non-parliamentary party but declined both in absolute number of votes and also in relation to the socialists – the gap between the two became wider. The national vote ratio declined from 3.68 per cent to 3.19 per cent, while the overall left component grew from 26.25 per cent to 37.13 per cent (see Table 4.4). A careful assessment therefore would indicate that the WP has a small but solid base.[41]

With the defeat of the right-conservative coalition the left took back the political power and the mastery of governance. Those who were surprised disregarded underlying currents in the Hungarian society: they forgot the remaining strong leftist components tied to twentieth-century historical roots. The collective memories of the society included left currents ranging from the 1919 events to the continued social-democratic traditions surviving in the inter-war years; the influence of the populist writers, the support to the communist–social-democrat leftist bloc after the Second World War and last, but not least, what many Hungarians rightly or wrongly held as positive achievements of the 40 years of communism, irrespective of the rejection of the party-state in 1956 and 1989. In none of these instances was there an unequivocal repudiation of the social redistributive role of the state and étatism was not alien to this thinking. The views held by the post-communist society made the possibility of a leftist turn seem likely. Major Western and Hungarian studies indicated relatively high preference for leftist social values as compared to all measured post-communist and Western countries; also the belief in materialist values in Hungary was higher than elsewhere.[42] The psychological shock of transformation from reform communism to market economy also played a role. Generally radical socialeconomic transformations do not happen successfully unless they are forced; it is understandable that the political pendulum swung back to the left in anticipation of a slower gradual transition.

On the 25 May 1994 election night, HSP President Gyula Horn appeared in the packed auditorium of the party headquarters. In the presence of the domestic and international media, he gave a short speech: 'We won. From within the walls of the parliament, politics will again be carried into the worker settlements and the countryside'.[43] Horn talked about reconciliation and offered a coalition to the free democrats amidst thunderous applause. He can take a large share of the credit for having engineered the comeback of the socialists and the left. It was a heady night and a spectacular victory. What followed later during the socialist governance was less spectacular and more torturous – by 1997 Horn became the least popular political leader in the country.

4 FROM THE PEAK OF POWER TO THE DECLINE OF THE LEFT?

In his election night speech, party president Horn stressed that the victory at the polls did not mean a socialist majority support in the electorate and that not all voters supporting the HSP were socialists or would become so, thus social reconciliation and rapprochement were essential. The winning party with an absolute majority of 54.14 per cent in parliament exercised prudent self-restraint by building a political alliance to carry out the expectedly bitter task of economic stabilization and to strengthen the legitimation of the HSP power, still often labeled both in Hungary and in the West as 'ex-communist'.[44] It appears that while the winner deserved credit for political astuteness, proper reading of the political map showed not only the left success and the right loss, but more importantly that society was still divided between three major forces approximately evenly: the list votes show the left with 37.13 per cent, the liberal parties with 26.76 per cent and the right-of-center conservatives with 27.59 per cent of electoral support and the center remained vacuous.[45] Considering these aspects realistically, the socialists turned directly to the Alliance of Free Democrats (and others) to join them in the governance. Only the liberals accepted the challenge and after long and arduous debate decided for coalition with the socialists.[46]

The coalition formation was dubbed as significant and historic by some, because it was not an absolute necessity.[47] The ensuing difficult negotiations between the partners led in a relatively short time to a detailed agreement setting up the conflict resolution mechanism and the basic tenets of the coalition programme: the government would turn to the future instead of the past and would work for European integration. The key issues were specified as economic transition, privatization and concomitant social problems. While the former government procrastinated with the economic stabilization program, the new socialist–liberal government faced this task amidst some electoral expectations which were quite different from what had been presented, and which for many voters appeared not in tandem with the former campaign thrust of the coalition parties.[48]

In terms of typology of coalitions, the socialist–liberal alliance was a combination of government and political coalitions, the former aiming at the distribution of power and the latter at political objectives as well.[49] The partners' maneuvering space was more circumscribed in this formation, because effective governance requires both legislative and administrative cooperation. This coalition therefore qualifies as the highest type; it aims at parliamentary and government cooperation and joint governance.[50] Thus in theoretical perspectives the somewhat unique socialist–liberal coalition took shape between two relatively different, but partly similar (solidarity) parties on the political scale. Both are markedly far from political extremities and are characterized by a pragmatic approach toward policy processes.

The new pact relied on a wide popular support based on the positive assessment of the skill and flexibility of the partners. Both factors were present in the second half of 1994 but voter confidence began to decline by the end of the year and plummeted in the early months of 1995,[51] especially after the announcement of the economic stabilization program. From its inception the durability of this coalition depended on its ability to manage the likely breaking points: the collapse of the agreement between the parties, the substantial weakening of the parties from within, the breaking-down of leadership, the dramatic shifting in public opinion precipitating a government crisis and premature new elections. While the threatening shadows of these scenarios could not be excluded in 1994 there was reasonable hope for the continuation of the socialist–liberal alliance in the future, providing governance stability and economic stabilization. However, it was also seen by some observers that if this minimum scenario did not materialize, a resurgence of the conservative or even radical forces could not be excluded assuming they could find a unifying nucleus still missing in 1994–95. Indeed, later events by 1996–97 show that this assessment was not without foundation.[52]

The relationship between the coalition parties had a shaky start: competition for influence and positions and the implementation of policy programs were the key issues. However, the partners succeeded in muddling through the first few critical months. After staring in the abyss of the collapse of their pact, they realized that a more orderly and open relationship was needed. There was restlessness in the 209-member socialist parliamentary caucus because of the lack of consultation with them, and the triangular relationship among the faction, the party and the government became controversial; representatives felt they were marginalized. The issue was hotly debated in Panel No. 3 of the Fourth HSP Congress, where conflicting views were aired without a resolution of the problem, which continued to exist in subsequent years. While undoubtedly the relationship between these actors remained less than smooth, there appeared to be no major undemocratic feature present and coordination among the three sides of the triangle was managed on a pragmatic basis.[53]

While both parties had reasonable success on the local elections at the end of 1994, the key issues of national economic policy were postponed and no decision was forthcoming. Personal and policy conflicts between Finance Minister Laszlo Bekesi, and the Prime Minister led to the resignation of the former in January 1995. Panic reaction to this created the impression that the coalition would fall apart, together with the Bekesi-stamped economic plan, triggering the ascendancy of the left-labor forces within the HSP.[54] However, with the appointment of Lajos Bokros to the finance minister post, and his announcement of the severe stabilization program on 12 March 1995, the coalition survived the pressures but quickly began to lose public support. This possibility, foreseen by the 'solidarity' committed socialist leadership, played an important role in the hesitation and postponement of the harsh measures: since the elections approximately 10 months of valuable time had been wasted to undertake the crucial surgery needed to prevent the collapse of the economy.

The real test for the success of the left (and the coalition) began with the belated launch of the economic stabilization package which was a breakthrough: the government abandoned its self-imposed passivity, which it had adopted since the elections. The program sent shock waves through society and opposition against it started immediately on a wide scale of the spectrum. The feared identity crisis now suddenly became a reality: the social-democratic left which rejected the conservative-right policies of four years appeared to abandon solidarity and, instead, forcefully restrained income and welfare by limiting wage increases and benefits. Opposition critics were quick to exploit the cul-de-sac stressing the anti-social nature of the policies, stemming from past communist experiences. However, it was obvious that no matter what government would have been in power, it would have to bite the bullet because the Hungarian economy had reached the breaking point and financial insolvency was on the horizon.[55]

The gist of the policy package called for radical steps in four major areas: a reduction in huge government spending, including the social distribution systems; the acceleration of the privatization and growth-stimulating measures; the reform of the treasury and the administrative apparatus, effective measures against corruption and the black economy; and, finally, a devaluation of the forint on an ongoing basis.[56] The net result of the Bokros package for the average wage earner was a stagnation and/or reduction of living standards. Thus it was not surprising that after the introduction of this plan to parliament, it was met by an immediate rebuttal by the labor unions and most organized and invisible interest groups within and without the political structure. A compromise-seeking process was launched resulting in serious concessions by the government, yet not making the economic package impotent. The coalition's survival depended on the success or failure of this policy and after an expanded debate and many modifications, in May 1995 parliament finally voted in favor of the amended proposal: the vote was 231 for, 91 against with three abstentions. It is noteworthy that the AFD faction voted unanimously for the passage and in the HSP caucus there were only a few line-breakers. With this accomplished, the government embarked on a long and arduous road. Western reaction and IMF response was generally favorable but everything depended on subsequent legislation and effective implementation.

The smooth sailing of this plan was doomed from its inception. A central feature of the stabilization plan was restriction on consumer spending as related to the wage/inflation ratio. Real wages began to decline immediately, setting off further protests in a society whose expectations were unrealistically high.[57] The Constitutional Court in several decisions also added fuel to the fire and declared parts of the package unconstitutional, stating that several provisos had a retroactive affect on previously acquired individual entitlements.[58]   The rejection of the society at large was expressed simultaneously by many interest groups, yet by 1996 there emerged a grudging acceptance amidst signs of some economic recovery which, however, could not be translated (yet) to the individual level. The coalition government was also targetted by the heavy artillery of the concentrated fire of the opposition, which now claimed to be the real socially conscientious forces. By the end of 1997 some key objectives of this plan still stood unimplemented, including the huge entitlement redistribution systems.

As mentioned elsewhere the Hungarian government, beginning with Kadar, spent many years attempting to buy off the public tolerance with economic concessions. The vicious circle of foreign loans accelerated even after 1990. The stabilization plan attempted to break this cycle of appeasement to redistributive demands. However justified this was, the plan was presented too harshly and without adequate public discussion; this was the government's fault, but in this writer's experience economic realities often fall on deaf ears in contemporary Hungarian society. No group and/or individual, many of them quite well off even by Western standards, wanted to accept the hard facts rooted in the devastation of the Second World War and 40 years of communist failures of the economy. It appeared indeed that society at large, including restless interest groups, were unwilling and/or unable to make concessions, leading to potential political instability and further destabilization of the economy.[59]

It is obvious that the government followed social-democratic tendencies in the long run, but the opposition and the extra-parliamentary extremist forces look only at the current short-range picture, thereby endangering the even limited achievements of the economic stabilization and creating skepticism in the international financial and political circles toward Hungary's political and economic stability in the coming years.

In the winter of 1996–97 the signs of some decline of the left were unmistakably visible and the index of the political clock began to move backward toward where it had been four years previously. The economic reforms and society's reaction seriously eroded the original voter support for the left coalition, similar to other regional countries, for example, Lithuania and Poland. Nonetheless the socialists held the line and succeeded in keeping the party together; under the surface, however, widening cracks were observable. A major corruption scandal erupting in 1996 served as convenient ammunition for the right opposition, the extremists and the discontented to demand ever more loudly the resignation of the government and to take politics onto the streets.

Increasing segments of public opinion saw the stagnating and declining living standards not as consequences of the long-term economic status of the country but as faults or even ill will of the ruling coalition. This psychological rationalization and extrapolation of frustration was exploited fully by the opposition, making demagogic and unfounded accusations against the government as well as unsubstantiated promises for a better future solution.[60]

It is paradoxical that the right and left extremists appear to hold similar or even identical views advocating manipulation of Hungary's international loan commitments, projecting a policy of unilateral termination of contractual agreements and moratoria on payments. These are key points both in the ISP and Workers' Party proposals.[61] The socialists and free democrats appeared to have lost their self-confidence and even worse their ability to address people effectively on the grassroot level. The leader of the social-democratic platform within the HSP, Ivan Vitanyi, and other party leaders commented in 1997 that the party had lost contact with the common citizen, which was their great advantage in the pre-election campaign phase in 1993–94. It was not unlikely that the left coalition might yet overcome this loss of confidence; by late 1997 there was no strengthening of the far left Workers' Party and the Leftist Platform within the HSP and the trends ran in favor of the right-wing opposition lead by the ISP.

Disenchanted socialists and supporter votes did not move toward the far-left but to the far right ISP. The late 1996 and early 1997 trends, as mirrored in voter surveys, show a voter realignment toward the ISP which was neck-and-neck with the Socialists and the formerly liberal Fidesz–Citizens' Party now leaning to center-right. In late November 1996 the HSP still led with 26 per cent of those choosing a party as compared to the AYD, (22 per cent) and the ISP, (20 per cent). In the total survey population of those not yet choosing parties, the three parties were dead even 15 per cent at that time.[62] Beyond this, however, the left was on a downward trend: several early 1997 surveys showed the ISP on top with 26 per cent, followed by the AYD, (25 per cent), and the socialists sank to third place with 22 per cent.[63] Understanding that such opinion survey sympathies are subject to mercurial changes and that there was one more year to go before elections, the decline of the left strength indicated the tenuousness of electoral support for the future.

The past came back to haunt the leftist forces in Hungary, on the other hand prudent observers foresaw this possibility. It was established earlier in this chapter that it would be a serious error to disregard other important signals from the elections won by the left in 1994. The voting returns indicated not only the relative strength of the left but also that of the liberals and right-of-center nationalists and conservatives. It was plausible to expect that the right-of-center parties would work for reconstruction of their political base and the socialist–liberal coalition might burn out during the following four years with the less than promising economic outlook, shifting the main thrust of voter support in favor of a center-right nationalist–populist–conservative combination. It appeared that events in 1996–97, for better or worse, moved in this direction, but subsequently the left started a steady recovery.

5   ALTERNATIVES BEYOND THE LEFT

In early 1997 serious political trouble surfaced for the left coalition and their support strata in society. Nonetheless, while the left lost significant ground, a recovery was not excluded as there still was a solid voter base for socialist-left parties.

The pre-election year started with the still unresolved questions of the major corruption scandal of 1996 in which the coalition parties had not been directly implicated but the media played on public suspicions.[64] The opposition used these issues as convenient causes to corner the government, to force its resignation or at least to 'force them to the wall'.[65] Furthermore an increasing crescendo of criticism and resistance by some agrarian interest groups against tighter legal rules regarding taxation and social insurance contributions almost paralysed the government. Beginning in February 1997, various farmer groups began to stage demonstrations and transport blockades to press for the withdrawal of proposed legislation and full exemption from social insurance contributions and even taxation records; the government avoided confrontation and met almost all demands. However, the drive against the government intensified and it soon became clear that the real motive went far beyond the original grievances and political action was undertaken with the aid and support of the opposition parties, notably the ISP, the CDPP and the HJLP (Hungarian Justice and Life Party) extremist group; the latter had been able to move tens of thousands of demonstrators on the national holiday on 15 March. The movement spread and, stimulated by the agrarians, other groups and various organizations across the spectrum also began to air their demands irrespective of the threatening financial consequences to the budget and in the final analysis to the hard-earned financial status of the country in the international community. As Prime Minister Horn expressed in parliament 'if the government would satisfy all these demands, several years' total budget would have to be spent on them. We do not have the means to do this'. He also pledged to continue the objectives set and followed by the coalition government.[66]

Amidst the negative public atmosphere, the open defiance of law and public order (attempted shut-downs of border crossing points and the capital city), the government's utmost caution was viewed as weakness. Events soon reached the danger point of potential disturbance or even social explosion and undermined the strength of the left. What was feared only as a phantom in 1994 became a reality by 1997: the trust capital of the coalition was nearly burnt out. In opinion polls in the first half of 1997 the socialists sank to third place: among those who selected a party the ISP led the pack with 29 per cent, followed by the AYD–Fidesz, (24 per cent), and trailed by the HSP, (22 per cent). The AFD also declined to 8 per cent and the coalition support groups' composition was also negative: in the younger categories (18–22 years of age) the AYD had 26 per cent and the HSP only 6 per cent, while in the 65 and older groups the HSP had 16 per cent and the AYD, 6 per cent.[67] Provided that the younger voters went to the polls, a serious socialist loss could be seen; the non-committed/passive strata consisted of 40 per cent of the voting population. The voters with higher education proportionately favored more the Fidesz and the HSP, while the lower educational strata tended to support the ISP which was also more prominent in the countryside. If these trends had continued, the top contenders would probably have been the ISP and the Fidesz – and the left would have remained behind. The Workers' Party did not improve their standing (2 per cent) and the social democrats did not feature in the statistics.

The fate of the left is fateful indeed: it could not deliver on 'solidarity' nor could it credibly uphold the hope for miraculous quantum leaps. Thus it became an easy target to the opposition and the extremists who argued that the socialists sold out the people and the country. Undoubtedly there were serious mistakes of policy: the economic stabilization plan was introduced without previous social debate, some blunders occurred legally/constitutionally and serious corruption and questionable dealings did not help. Policy implementation was less than satisfactory and often timid. On the positive side the socialist–liberal coalition could claim notable successes in key areas: the smooth and democratic operation of the administration; the basic goals of stabilization; and the beginning of real modernization attracting Western capital investment. Overall, public order and the rule of law prevailed and in foreign policy Hungary made excellent progress in the direction of European Union and NATO integration as well as financial solvency. The sensitive issues of the Hungarians abroad were handled in a qualitatively new way as compared to the former regime: a historical reconciliation advocated by the government was partly successful, and Romania, but not Slovakia, responded favorably.

While coalition leaders stressed these achievements repeatedly, public assessment became increasingly more negative before the mercurial electorate changed direction again as the elections came closer. By late 1997 several factors moved the political seismograph back to the left: the patient maneuvering of the coalition helped to derail the provocative confrontations; the completion of the basic treaty with Romania and the new Constantinescu reform era[68] in tandem with the Madrid conference inviting the three Central European 'lead-states' to join NATO.[69] The modest but steady improvement of the economy[70] opened the door to gradual improvements in living standards for pensioners, educators, public service employees and other key interest groups which lent support for the left in 1994 but were critical of the economic stabilization. After a series of conflicts the HSP also closed ranks again with the major labor union NFHU re-establishing the electoral alliance for 1998, and even business groups felt more trust in a coalition-led stability than with the uncertainties projected by the opposition.[71] Last, but not least, the overwhelming chaos and infighting in all parliamentary and extra-parliamentary right opposition parties/groups shed an increasingly favorable light on the governing coalition. The fight to the hilt approach of the opposition over the NATO and land referenda eventually also backfired and exposed the obstinacy and disarray of the opposition,[72] projecting the image of a nostalgic, backward looking force without a minimum common platform and future image – a contrast with the socialist–liberal objectives moving toward European integration, market economy and modernization.

The socialist primacy has been reconquered by the early fall of 1997, commanding 34 per cent support, followed by the ISP, (22 per cent), and sending Fidesz back to third place (21 per cent), but there were also 40 per cent 'uncertain' and/or passive (non)voters, a significant unknown in future elections. There is a lamentable lack of realism in these changing negative perceptions, because from among all surrounding regional post-communist states, overall the Hungarians fared quite well, but the average citizen was reluctant to make these comparisons. It is a bitter truth, however, that irrespective of who will run the government and with what economic program, the real GDP growth potential of the Hungarian economy will be limited for some time to come. Failure to come to grips with this fact will remain the most central issue of Hungarian politics.

The recovery of the left from a perilous decline was completed with the socialist–liberal coalition's near victory in the elections on 10 May 1998. The mentioned economic issue was one of the key points in the disagreements between the HSP and its challenger the AYD–CP: the coalition projected a modest 4–4.5 per cent sustainable GDP growth, while the opposition promised an ambitious 7 per cent and tax relief – an obviously unrealistic stance. On the territorial lists reflecting popular support more accurately the HSP led with 32.92 per cent and the AFD 7.58 per cent, while the strongest opposition AYD–CP trailed with 29.47 per cent and the ISP had 13.15 per cent.

At this juncture at the last minute, a right-of-center electoral alliance materialized: the AYD–CP became a right catch-all party and the conservative-nationalist HDF and ISP threw their support behind them, winning a significant number of the individual contests and taking more seats than the HSP–AFD combined. On the 24 May run-offs deciding the 176 individual districts, the HSP took 54 and the AFD 2 seats (totaling 56), against the 90 AYD–CP and 17 HDF, (totaling 107). Because of the electoral law mathematical rules these territorial and individual district voting returns translated into 158 seats for the socialist–liberal coalition against 165 for the AYD–CP/HDF and with 48 ISP seats the right opposition controls a total of 213 seats. This is a comfortable absolute majority but short of the two-third votes needed for constitutionally ordered important issues. Thus these elections ended the socialist–liberal governance but also underscored our previous findings about the sustained strength of the left in Hungarian politics.

Since the winner Fidesz was short of the 194 votes needed for legislative decisions, a new coalition was needed for executive and legislative governance. At the end of May 1998, negotiations indicated the forming of an AYD–CP/Forum/ISP combination while a grand coalition between the Fidesz and the HSP seemed unlikely. The stability of such a government is a crucial question: within the Fidesz proper a number of heterogeneous groups/programs are housed and the same is true of the other parties, which all in turn are in serious conflict with the core AYD–CP. In the absence of a two-thirds majority in parliament, the longevity of the new governance remains to be seen: new government combinations and/or premature elections cannot be excluded.

6 THE LEFT IN PERSPECTIVE

The Status of Democratization

The changing fortunes of the left on the Hungarian political palette reflect the turbulent years of post-communist transition. Different in some respects from other countries the Hungarian party structure in the 1990–98 era was characterized by relative stability: the six parliamentary parties in 1990 also dominated the 1994 electoral campaign but major mutations took place by 1998 and fermentation is likely to continue.[73] This party structure closely mirrors the main trends in the political culture, but there are meaningful parties/groups outside the perimeters of the legislature.[74] While there was apparent stability in the six parties, none was capable of mastering a popular majority or even coming close to it in the elections. The parties' heterogeneous composition and their catch-all nature interrelated with voter instability and large segments of the population were in the uncommitted/passive category. For the same reasons intra-party struggles led to intra-party divisions with the exception of the HSP which, however, also struggled with internal tensions and possible fractures. The left in general was already relatively strong in 1990 but divided they lost, while in 1994 the socialists were able to put together a winning team. Other parts of the left-of-center barely survived: the Workers' Party is still consistently visible but the social democrats have almost disappeared as viable players. The radical far-left reform communists have no grip on significant voter blocs and in this respect the picture is different from other post-communist countries. The party has a centralized orthodox organization with serious democracy deficiencies; its members and supporters are former *nomenklatura* figures and HSWP members, and they tend to vote in the run-offs for the HSP.[75]

In the broader perspective the status of intra-party democracy in the largest left party is of paramount significance. The picture is by and large positive and the HSP's credentials are also strengthened by its full membership in the Socialist International since 1996, where Gyula Horn fulfills a vice-presidential function. The party by-laws provide a democratic but sometimes vague organization.[76] Local organs are independent units which formulate their own structure(s) but the method(s) of procedure are not clearly defined (By-Laws, Para. 11); likewise the territorial units (counties–*megye*) make decisions about political and personnel questions but no specifics are given (Para. 12). A party congress is held regularly at least every second year or under certain circumstances more frequently. The Congress is the main policy-making body which elects the highest organ, the Presidency consisting of 9–15 members (Paras. 12–14). Between party congresses a National Committee (*Valasztmany*) fulfills important advisory and guiding roles but the Presidency is not formally bound by them. The Committee's composition is too large to be effective and two-thirds of its members are delegated by the lower party organizations and approximately one-third are delegated or invited from other social/political organs (Paras. 17–19).[77]

The Presidency is the center of action coordinating the respective roles of the party, the legislative caucus and the government if it is a governing party (Paras. 20–22). The body includes an executive vice-president, three other vice-presidents elected by the Congress and also *ex officio* the parliamentary caucus leader. The main operational functions of the Presidency are defined in the by-laws as: (a) the relations to society at large; (b) communications and propaganda; (c) international relations; (d) youth affairs; and (e) affairs of local self-government units. The respective presidency members responsible for these functions are selected by the body on a consensus basis (Para. 21 k). While majority rule is standard in intra-party elections, vagueness and lack of secret votes in some instances blur the party proceedings. In nominating procedures, only open votes are provided and the required percentage of votes is not always defined.[78] Party elections can be held from the lowest to the highest level if 10 per cent of the members so request (By-Laws, Appendix 2, III).

There seem to be conflicting perceptions about the real functions of the National Committee. Some party functionaries suggest that the Committee has only limited input in policy-making decisions which are lodged in the hands of the highest organ(s).[79] However, other party spokesmen question this and stress that the Committee's functions are clearly defined and the Presidency could not disregard the Committee which forms a direct tie to and is a product of the lower (local) party organizations and the mass of membership.[80] The difference may be more apparent than real: the Committee is inserted between the Congress and Presidency and has to respond to the transmitted input coming from the membership at large. Bypassing this reality would soon make the party elite into the peak of a pyramid without a foundation.

The HSP is a somewhat loose alliance of different groups/views. The formulation of various platforms is not only tolerated but encouraged and this seems to be one way to prevent a more serious party fracture.[81] Intra-party critiques question the selection of congressional delegates favoring those groups fulfilling party/government functions but do not doubt the democratic nature of party proceedings: 'Reservations against the leadership have to be subordinated to the strategic goals of the party', that is, to prevent the recapture of power by the right opposition.[82] Generally criticism and dissent is free: for example, there were open attacks of Horn's 'strong arm tactics' but with the approach of the 1998 elections both critiques and opponents acknowledged that at the present there is no one who could successfully succeed Horn.[83] On a comparative scale, while the socialists are less than perfect they would win the democracy contest against all other parliamentary parties, many of them plagued by power-driven leaders, expelling their own members and parliamentary representatives or simply dissolving themselves.

The convulsive political arena is only an outward manifestation of the individual citizen's everyday life on a micro-scale and the status of the national economy on the macro-level. The collapse of the party-state in 1989 was nothing more and nothing less than a shocking quantum leap from a predominantly state-controlled economy to a predominantly market-defined one. The Antall government's economic non-policy was essentially a massive denial of realities and postponement of inevitable harsh measures. Neither society at large nor the elites could absorb the devastating results of the Second World War and the 40 years of a command economy plus accumulating foreign loans with ever-increasing interest payments. Societal reaction to these facts shows a frantic desire for material well-being *and* the continuation of the protecting institutions of the entitlement programs created by the redistributing role of the former party-state. This tendency contributed to the ascendancy of the left in the early 1990s and subsequently to the resentment of the economic stabilization, and painful reforms, by reducing real wage levels and purchasing power. These policies were branded by the opposition as neo-liberal and resulted in an alienation from the left, which increasingly was perceived as abandoning the solidarity principle.

Critiques across the spectrum claim that the return of the left was due to the surviving communist elites, who remained in key (economic) positions in the early 1990s and who often defy party identifications: their congruence was definitive in the left comeback, after which they solidified their political–economic bastions. However appealing this perception sounds, it appears lacking in hard evidence. While the late Kadar technocracy is still an important group in the elite,[84] analyses indicate that this is steadily changing. Two-thirds of the HSP support originated in 1994 from blue-collar strata and 90 per cent of these never were communist party members; two-fifths of the former HSWP membership also voted for other parties, mostly the AYD and the AFD.[85] Thus the concept that former party membership equals articulate group identity and defines HSP party profile is at least controversial.

It is argued here that the disintegration and/or dissolution of the HSWP (both in 1956 and 1989) shows that hard-core Marxism–Leninism did not captivate the elite summarily. Many of these elements never were truly communists and may not even have been moderate social democrats. The older *nomenklatura* began to fade away gradually and are being replaced by a younger reform generation who were still largely educated under the party-state but show remarkable ability and flexibility. Between 1990 and 1994, right conservative intelligentsia, who were older or had ties to the pre-communist right of center, also entered the new elite especially on the political and/or public service level and a new entrepreneur class emerged in increasing numbers as well. Finally the youth and the generational cycle have already diluted the former elite and this will continue to accelerate in the future. However, the fermentation of the elite does not mean that the HSP today is not the relatively largest home for former *nomenklatura*/party members, but it does suggest that this may not retroactively prove their past ideological stance – the late Kadar elite was more career-oriented technocrat than ideologically zealous.

While the slow elite fluctuation contributed to the return of the left, this *per se* would be insufficient to cause the breakdown of the left sympathies in society, in which grassroot forces survive which are indifferent to the elite's alleged entrenched interests: the political culture in the 1990s carries a long history of progressive traditions and social responsibility from the early part of the century. The 1994 electoral landslide catapulting the left back into power was an expression of hope for a change *cum* solidarity, pluralist democracy combined with existential security. When the economic situation forced the socialist–liberal coalition to confront the country with reality and sacrifices, the frustrated expectations triggered the downward trajectory of the left. The increasingly materialist contemporary Hungarian society was not willing and able to identify with Finance Minister Bokros's statement: 'The country lives beyond its means'.[86]

Bitter memories of the party-state are intertwined with ideological slogans few truly believed, but which still penetrated the political culture: 'worker power', 'the country is yours, you build it for yourself'.[87] While revolting in 1956 and 1989 against what they thought to be a travesty, these images were absorbed by the psyche of workers/employees, who now found themselves out in the cold, swelling the ranks of the unemployed with a loss of security and a decline in living standards. The HSP–AFD coalition was not able to lead into the promised land – and had difficulty channeling this disaffection into positive energies. Thus losers of the transition, including many formerly privileged worker-cadres and their descendants, felt they deserved better but instead were deserted by the left. They rejected the former power but not themselves, and many took some of these frustrated left values into non-leftist parties/movements or became non-political cynics.

The influence of other than purely economic factors on the voting trends cannot be disregarded. Future elections may show abandonment of past patterns and parties rooted in the ideological categories of early post-communism. The HSP and the WP both have crucial problems with the absence of youth support and a 1997 spring socialist survey shows them leaning more heavily toward the right.[88] However, the youth also became less nationalist and more cosmopolitan with a Euro-Atlantic orientation.[89]

In balance, then, tomorrow's voting preferences may tilt more toward the right-of-center provided that such a truly centrist party alliance will finally appear. The runaway technological/information revolution, the galloping market globalization and massive infusion of Western capital and concomitant culture may accelerate this trend. With the substantial expansion of the number of students in higher education and the snowballing effects of eletronic communications, European integration may cause a meaningful ferment in the post-communist party system as we know it today. This could affect the left in ways unforeseeable at the present: the modernization of the economy with negative social effects may have an impact on the future party alignment with presently uncertain variants.

A Glimpse into the Future

In 1998 the Hungarian left lost its parliamentary dominance but retained its strong position in the political landscape. For all practical purposes the left became synonymous with the HSP: neither the WP (3.95 per cent) nor the HSDP (0.80 per cent) was able to get into parliament and their future re-emergence is even less likely now. Based on the territorial lists, the three left parties together represent 36.95 per cent of the voters, approximately the same ratio achieved in 1994 (Table 4.4). The HSP has a reliable core of firm membership and supporters who backed the party in three elections: 1990, 1994 and 1998. Although the labor organizations lost a lot of influence in the privatization process, their alliance remains an important factor for the left.

Given the existence of simmering intra-party conflicts in the HSP, skilled political maneuvering will be required to hold the party together under the pressures of post-election adjustment and oppositional strategy regarding decisions yet to be made in the transition process. Since it is uncertain that after the next four-year cycle the HSP would govern again, internal conflicts could resurface at the highest level, including the controversial Horn leadership of the past eight years.

The AYD–CP became the strongest challenger of the socialist–liberal coalition in 1998: in the campaign they emerged as a catch-all right-conservative alternative to the left attempting to project an image of a new center force but campaigning partly on left values. The next four years will be crucial for them: if they can consolidate the heterogeneous right-of-center support coming from the ISP, the CDPP and the HDF with their liberal core and capture some of the social policy agenda, they could provide a credible counterweight to the left. The outlook for this is doubtful and if this attempt fails, the socialists would still have a chance to retake the governance provided they will be able to cope with the needed generational change in the leadership and project a fresh image drawing the vital younger support. The left, however, in or out of the government is likely to remain an important player in Hungarian politics for some time to come. Political culture and demographic trends reflecting the aging of the population as well as current and future stresses of the new global economic realities appear to ensure this, but the left will inevitably remain in a schizoid situation with the economically limited potential to deliver on the socialist agenda.

The resentment of the economic transformation and the downsizing of welfare institutions breeds strengthening leftist trends in the West where there were no communist parties in power.[90] In the east the left is at least partly tied to the images of the former ruling communists and thus austerity measures undermine the left and reinforce other (populist) forces. Unless balanced by compromises, such a drift could become ominous in post-communist East Europe. If the left were to have a strong presence in at least some of the regional countries and could prove itself to be successful, this could have an effect elsewhere; conversely, spectacular failures could have some impact in other countries including Hungary.

In addition to the problems of the new market economy and privatization, post-communist societies including Hungary will be faced with accelerating pressures created by technomodernization, adding to the tenuousness of social peace – and the long-term consequences cannot be specifically foreseen. Amidst this turmoil the crux of the left philosophy – solidarity and social justice – is very likely to survive. However, if the left is to play a significant or dominant role, it has to be infused with a new life-saving identity – a new 'New Left' which would be able to be effective in charting a novel strategy to which the young generations could relate.

The post-party-state transition generally does not proceed with quantum leaps and it progresses gradually; shock treatments proved to have their own limits defined by social-resistance. The predominant role played by social democratic/socialist governments in the European Union may have a serious impact on post-Soviet countries which depend heavily on capital investments.

There seems to be no simple answer to the left's dilemma in Hungary and/or elsewhere. The factors at play overlap and their admixture varies over time and place. In the cyberspace era, dissatisfaction with problems of capital globalization set in motion critical and opposing forces.[91] In this process, the socialist left may play a crucial balancing role.

NOTES

1. Albert Camus, *Resistance, Rebellion and Death* (New York: Vintage, 1974), pp. 147–64.
2. In Hungarian, Magyar Szocialista Punkaspart (MSZMP).
3. In Hungarian, Magyar Szocialista Part (MSZP); see Mihaly Bihari, 'Ket Kongresszus Magyarorszagon' ['Two Congresses in Hungary'], *Tarsadalmi Szemle* (1990), pp. 1, 19–30; also Rudolf Tokes, *Hungary's Negotiated Revolution* (Cambridge University Press, 1996), pp. 347–56.
4. For example, *Magyar Nemzet*, 10 April 1990; *RFE Research*, 6 April 1990, pp. 24–5; *The Ann Arbor News*, 9 April 1990; *New York Times*, 9 April 1990, p. 23.
5. In Hungarian, Magyar Szakservezetek Orazagos Szovetsege (MSZOSZ).
6. The following is only a brief synopsis; for more information, see Barnabas Racz and Istvan Kukorelli, 'The Second Generation: Post-communist Elections in Hungary in 1994', *Europe-Asia Studies* **47**, 2 (1995): 251–79.
7. Although the parties became more crystallized by 1994, they are still fluid and 'catch-all' parties, that is, they have weak ties to the electorate under conditions of modernization, see Alan Ware, (ed.), *Political Parties, Electoral Changes and Structural Response* (New York: Basil Blackwell, 1987), p. 22.
8. Program of the Second Congress, in Sandor Kurtan, et al. (eds.), *Magyarorszag Politikai Evkonyve 1990* (Budapest: Aula Kiado, 1990), pp. 494–500.

90   *The Return of the Left in Post-communist States*

9. CDPP Program, in ibid., pp. 511–19.
10. *RFE Research*, 15 September 1989, pp. 1–11; 16 March 1990, pp. 23–36.
11. Bihari, pp. 1, 19–30; HSP Election Program, *Nepszabadsag*, 3 February, 1990, pp. 23–36.
12. ISP Program, in Kurtan, et al. (eds.), *Magyarorszag Politikai Evkonyve 1990*, pp. 501–5.
13. Otto Angyal and Alpar Toth, *A Magyarorszagi Szocialdemokrata Part Programm-tervezete* [MSZDP Program], (Budapest: MSZDP, 1990), pp. 1–201.
14. Documents of the MSZMP Fourteenth Congress, in Kurtan, et al. (eds.), *Magyaroszag Politikai Evkonyve 1990*, pp. 568–75.
15. *Nepszabadsag*, 19 May 1990.
16. '1989: XXXIV Law on the Parliamentary Elections', *Magyar Kozlony* [Official Gazette] **77**, 30 October 1989, 1305–28.
17. Marta Dezso, 'Valasztasi Rendszerek Nyugat-Europaban' [Electoral Systems in Western Europe], *Jogtudomanyi Kozlony* **7** (1989): 258–62.
18. Barnabas Racz, 'Political Pluralization in Hungary: the 1990 Elections', *Soviet Studies* **43**, 1 (1991): 109; also Marta Dezso, 'Bonyolult is vitatott is', in Tamas Moldovan et al. (eds.), *Szabadon Választott-Parlamenti Almanach* (Budapest: Idegenforgalmi Propaganda Kiado, 1990), pp. 5–12.
19. Imre Hanyecz and Janos Perger, 'A tobbparti parlament szamokban', in Sandor Kurtan, Peter Sandor and Laszlo Vass (eds.), *Magyarorszag Politikai Evkonyve 1991* (Budapest: Okonomia Alapitvany-Economix Rt, 1991), pp. 135–48.
20. Imre Hanyecz and Janos Perger, 'A Magyar parlament tevekenysage szamokban', in Kurtan et al. (eds.), *Magyarorszag Politikai Evkonyve 1992* (Budapest: Demokracia Kutatasok Magyar Kozpontja Alapitvany-Economix Rt, 1991), pp. 104; see also *Orszaggyulesi Jegyzokonyv* [Parliamentary Minutes] vol. 10, December 1991, p. 4325.
21. See Table 4 in Barnabas Racz, 'The Socialist-left Opposition in Post-communist Hungary', *Europe-Asia Studies* **45**, 4 (1993): 650.
22. Territorial list voting was highest (66%+) in four counties and Budapest, all in the west; lowest (64%–) in nine counties including only two in the west. There is a wide spread: the highest ratio was in Vas county, 76.71 per cent, lowest in Szabolcs-Szatmar, 53.62 per cent. Individual district returns show similar patterns in both rounds. Data computed on basis of official figures in *Magyar Kozlony* **44**, 13 May 1990, pp. 1013–82.
23. In the nine Transdanubian counties the AFD won 15 districts; in the other 10 counties it won only 10 districts and in Budapest it won 9 out of 32; see *Moldovon et al. (eds.), Szabadon Választott*, pp. 42–3; also *Magyar Hirlap*, 10 April 1990.
24. Mihaly Vajda, the philosopher, referred to this on election night on TV Budapest, generating an interesting debate in the media; see *Heti Vilaggazdasag*, 6 April 1990, pp. 72–4.
25. The ISP advocated a return to the land ownership status of 1945–47.
26. Party Communiqué, *Nepszabadsag*, 26 April 1990; see also press reports in *Magyar Nemzet*, 26 April and 21 May 1990; for a theoretical discussion of the left and socialism, see *Nepszabadsag*, 26 May 1990.
27. The more important factions were the social-democratic and the leftist platforms. The latter criticized sharply the leadership for its compromising/weak stance. Racz, 'The Socialist-left Opposition', p. 657.
28. See Ibid. see also Note 34.
29. Racz, 'The Socialist-left Opposition', 651–54; *Nepszabadsag*, 18 November 1991.
30. Part of the agricultural crisis in 1997 was traceable back to the re-establishment of property relations to the pre-1947 status quo.
31. *Nepszabadsag*, 18 September 1992.
32. The Csurka pamphlet clearly includes chauvinistic and racist views; see Ernest Beck, 'Hungary Fears Right-Wing Violence', *The Wall Street Journal*, 29 December 1992, A/4.
33. The concept of 'catch-all' parties refers to weak ties to the electorate under conditions of modernization; see Ware (ed.), p. 22.

34. See Gabor Toka, 'Parties and their Voters in 1990 and 1994' in Bela Kiraly (ed.), *Lawful Revolution in Hungary* (New York: Columbia University Press, 1995), pp. 131–57.
35. Such study should include the analysis of party organization, elite–member relations, voter relations and financing; for an excellent study of ten constitutional democracies, see Ware, (ed.), especially pp. 1–23.
36. Racz, 'The Socialist-left Opposition', pp. 660–63.
37. Ivan Szelenyi, 'Van-e szavazobazis a kozepbalon'? [Is there a voter-base on the Centre-Left?], *Nepszabadsag*, 19 January 1992. For a sociological survey of social values in Hungary, see the excellent analysis by Gyorgy Csepeli and Antal Orkeny, *Ideology and Political Beliefs in Hungary – The Twilight of State Socialism* (London & New York: Pinter, 1992); and also Gy. Csepeli and A. Orkeny, 'Trends in Perceptions of Social Injustice in Hungary 1989–1995,' paper presented at the American Association for the Advancement of Slavic Studies Convention, Boston, 16 November 1996.
38. See Zoltan Farkas, 'The Antall Government's Economic Policy', in Cs. Gombar, E. Hankiss, L. Lengyel and Gy. Varnai, (eds.), *Balance – The Hungarian Government 1990–1994* (Budapest: Korridor, Centre for Political Research, 1994), p. 178.
39. For example, especially in Lithuania and Poland.
40. See Cs. Gombar et al. (eds.); also Barnabas Racz and Istvan Kukorelli, 'The Second-generation Post-communist Elections in Hungary in 1994,' *Europe-Asia Studies* **47**, 2 (1995): 251–79.
41. For a full study of the Workers' Party, see Barnabas Racz, *The Far Left in Post-communist Hungary: The Workers' Party* (Pittsburgh: The Carl Beck Papers in Russian and East European Studies, University of Pittsburgh, 1998).
42. David S. Mason, 'Justice, Socialism and Participation in the Post-Communist States', in James R. Klugel, David S. Mason and Bernd Wegener, *Social Justice and Political Change* (New York: Aldine de Gruyter, 1995), pp. 49–80.
43. *Ket Het* (Budapest) no. 102–3, June 1994.
44. Two assessments appear to be centered around the defense of the Antall coalition and the summary criticism of the HSP as 'former communists'. See E. Oltay, 'Former Communists Win the First Round of Hungarian Elections', *RFE/RL Research*, 27 May 1994, pp. 1–5; and also E. Oltay, 'The Former Communists' Election Victory in Hungary', RFE/RL Research, 24 June 1994, pp. 1–6.
45. This is a total of 91.48 per cent, the remaining points were gained by parties below 5 per cent; on the top of this list is the Workers' Party with 3.19 per cent.
46. The AFD Congress voted for the coalition with 562 votes for and 187 against, *Nepszabadsag*, 6 June 1994.
47. For the discussion of the Coalition Agreement, see Racz and Kukorelli, pp. 272–74; for text of documents, see *Nepszabadsag*, 25 and 27 June 1994.
48. The preliminary HSP political document stressed the intactness of entitlement programs and promised the defense of welfare institutions, 'A modern demokratikus Magyarorszagart' [For the Modern Democratic Hungary], *Ket Het* no. 24, December 1993, pp. 8–9.
49. See Michael Laven and Norman Schofield, *Multi-party Government: The Politics of Coalition in Europe* (Oxford University Press, 1990), and Ian Budge and Hans Keman, *Parties and Democracy: Coalition Formation and Government Functioning in Twenty States* (Oxford University Press, 1990).
50. It surpasses the 'proto-coalition' for preliminary election cooperation as well as the 'electoral alliance' type; see Attila Agh, 'Koalicios kormany – Europai tapasztalatok' [Coalition Government – European Experiences], *Tarsadalmi Szemle*, 1994, pp. 6, 19–31.
51. By June 1995 the HSP tied even with the ISP with 24 per cent and the AFD shrank to 16 per cent, Szonda–Ipsos Survey, *Nepszabadsag*, 10 June 1995.
52. Barnabas Racz, *Beyond the 1994 Hungarian Socialist–Liberal Coalition* (Toronto: Hungarian Studies Association of Canada, 1995), pp. 6–7.

53. The Fourth HSP Congress at Miskolc City, on 24–26 November 1995, devoted a separate panel no. 3 to this issue. Imre Szekeres, parliamentary faction leader, proposed a new committee for coordination but the motion was not adopted. (Information based on author's presence at the meeting.)
54. Bekesi's plan was endorsed by the AFD coalition partner and was opposed by the left wing of the HSP.
55. Janos Kornai, 'The Dilemmas of Hungarian Economic Policy', in Bela K. Kiraly (ed.), *Lawful Revolution in Hungary 1989–94* (New York: Atlantic Research and Publications Columbia University Press, 1995), pp. 323–50.
56. For the full text of the Bokros program see *Nepszabadsag*, 17 February 1995.
57. See Finance Minister Bokros's and Horn's statements regarding Hungarians living beyond their means, *Nepszabadsag*, 16 March 1995 and 2 May 1995.
58. Especially targetted by the Constitutional Court were new restrictive rules regarding supplementary benefits for children, *Nepszabadsag*, 1 July 1995.
59. See Kornai, 'The Dilemmas of Hungarian Economic Policy,' p. 340.
60. For example, see ISP Economic Program, *Nepszabadsag*, 4 November 1995; for Workers' Party economic proposals, see the Seventeenth Congress document, 'With the Workers' Party into the 21st Century', Supplement, *Szabadsag*, December 1996.
61. Ibid.
62. Szonda–Ipsos survey, *Nepszabadsag*, 25 November 1996.
63. Public opinion data by Szonda–Ipsos reported in *Nepszabadsag*, 8 February 1997.
64. The so-called 'Tocsik affair' involved alleged illegal financial payments by the Privatization Agency (APV), *Nepszabadsag*, 24 January 1997.
65. Istvan Csurka HLJP (MIEP), President's statement, Nepszabadsag, 24 March 1997.
66. For Horn's statement, see Nepszabadsag, 1 April 1997. For anti-government offensives of various agricultural groups see press reports, especially *Nepszabadsag, Magyar Nemzet, Szabadsag,* February, March, April 1997.
67. Szonda–Ipsos poll, *Nepszabadsag*, March 1997.
68. Full text of the Romanian–Hungarian Basic Treaty, *Nepszabadsag*, 2 September 1997.
69. The NATO Madrid Conference in July 1997 extended invitations to the Czech Republic, Hungary and Poland.
70. *The Wall Street Journal*, 16 July 1997.
71. HSP announcement regarding an alliance with the National Federation of Hungarian Unions (NFHU), *Nepszabadsag*, 1 February 1997.
72. All parliamentary parties supported NATO membership; the referendum vote in November 1997 was 85.33 per cent in favor with a 49.24 per cent participation (see Communiqué of the National Election Committee (OVB), 18 November 1997). The most vocal opposition was led by the Workers' Party.
73. Laszlo Lengyel, 'Tigris a fan' [Tiger on the Tree], *Nepszabadsag*, 1 November 1997. The HDF split into two parties and the seceders (Hungarian Democratic People's Party– HDPP) were present in parliament in 1997; the CDPP, having expelled most parliamentary representatives from the party, faces an uncertain future and is likely to become a satellite of the ISP.
74. Szonda–Ipsos, *Nepszabadag*, 10 October 1997. The successful capturing of the 'uncommitted' voters could hold the key to the prospective realignment of the parliamentary forces. On the top of the extra-parliamentary parties is the Workers' Party; the labor organizations, especially the NFHU, have important left links; for a list of non-parliamentary parties, see Racz and Kukorelli, p. 257 and note 22.
75. See Racz, *The Far Left in Post-communist Hungary,* pp. 5–33.
76. A Magyar Szocialista Part Alapszabalya [The By-Laws of the Hungarian Socialist Party], published by the HSP (Budapest: Mediant, 1996), hereafter referred to as 'By-Laws'.
77. In 1997 there were 154 members from the territorial units and 72 invited, making a total of 226 members; information by HSP parliamentary advisors, October 1997.

78. See By-Laws, Appendix 3, III, 4 and 5, 22–3.
79. Interview with parliamentary staff members, October 1997.
80. Interview with Dr Zoltan Gal, President of Parliament, October 1997.
81. The main identifiable intra-party factions in 1997 were the Social Democratic Alliance, the Socialist Faction, the Leftist Platform, and the Left Youth Association (BIT). On party proceedings these factions operate openly and they also exert internal pressures. (Personal observations by the writer at the 1995 Miskolc City Fourth Party Congress.)
82. Statement by HSP Left Platform leader Sandor Balogh, *Nepszabadsag*, 14 October 1997.
83. See Lengyel.
84. See interview with sociologist Erzsebet Szalai, 'Erdekeinkert is felelosek vagyunk' [We Are Responsible for Our Interests], *Kritika*, (Budapest), October 1997, 27–9.
85. Ferenc Gazso, 'Voltegyszer egy allampart' [There was Once a State Party], *Tarsadalmi Szemle*, 1996, pp. 3–13.
86. See note 57, above.
87. See Ivan Volgyes, *Politics in Eastern Europe*, (Chicago: Dorsey Press, 1986), pp. 112, 285–307.
88. A joint study by the Academy of Sciences and the Left Youth Association (BIT) shows political indifference in the young population and somewhat more preference to the (far) right; see Domjan Katalin, 'The Future Image of the Youth', *Nepszabadsag*, 4 March 1997, p. 8.
89. The Author's extensive guest teaching experience since 1988 at various Hungarian universities corroborates the changing attitude of the students.
90. For example Germany, France, Italy, and the United Kingdom.
91. George Soros, 'The Capitalist Threat', *Atlantic Monthly*, no. 279, February 1997, pp. 45–8; also Thomas Vietorisz, 'The Global Information Economy, Privatization and the Future of Socialism', in *The First International Conference of Social Critical Reviews* (Budapest, Eszmelet Foundation, 1991), pp. 35–58; and Serge Latouche, 'A Megagepezet es a tarsadalmi kapcsolatok szetzuzasa' [The Mega-machinery and the Destruction of Societal Connections], in *Eszmelet* **27**, 2 (1994): 73–89; Jacques Attali, 'The Crash of Western Civilization: The Limits of Market and Democracy', *Foreign Policy*, no. 2 (1997): 54–64.

5. Young, Westernized, Moderate: The Polish Left after Communism

Janusz Wrobel*

My friend Bartek is a communist. He's not a reformed communist, either. He's an old-fashioned, honest-to-goodness, unrepentant Marxist who yearns for the good old days in his homeland, Poland. To the consternation and dismay of the West, Bartek and millions of his compatriots voted to return the communists to power in Poland's last election.[1] (Jon Paul Sydnor, US Peace Corps volunteer)

1 INTRODUCTION

The day 4 June 1989 will be remembered as the beginning of the end of communism in East-Central Europe. On that day, the first semi-free elections to the bicameral Polish parliament took place. The state was still communist, and the way in which balloting was organized guaranteed a majority of 173 seats in the lower house (Sejm) for the communist Polish United Workers' Party (PZPR). Nevertheless, the non-communist Solidarity Citizens' Committee (OKP) won all 161 possible seats in the Sejm and 99 of the 100 seats in the Senate. An independent candidate took one seat.[2] The spectacular defeat of the communists brought a dramatic shift of power in Poland. Tadeusz Mazowiecki, Solidarity activist and Catholic intellectual, was designated to form the first non-communist government in the Soviet bloc. Most importantly, the new events were accepted as precedent. President of the USSR, Mikhail Gorbachev, assured the world that the 'Brezhnev Doctrine' was dead and that the Soviet Union would not intervene in the satellite countries.

A domino effect had begun behind the Iron Curtain, and it soon reached its peak in Berlin when the Wall was transformed into the Gate, proving again that nothing is unthinkable in politics. The mono-party system went into hibernation, the spirit of freedom took over, and for a while, hope for a bright future overshadowed the problems that would not disappear with the end of the totalitarian system. The euphoria did not last long. The Poles, as well as those in other post-communist nations, quickly learned that the price of freedom would be high too, and that liberty itself is demanding. One indicator of the changing mood of the newly liberated Polish society was that a sense of 'happiness' was reported by only 11 per cent of the respondents to a poll conducted by J. Kurczewski in 1990.[3] The same questions asked in 1988 revealed 13 per cent of the respondents declaring that they were 'happy'.[4]

The diminishing enthusiasm for the merciless capitalism that replaced the socialist welfare state found its dramatic expression in the results of the 19 September 1993 parliamentary elections that were won in Poland by the Democratic Alliance of the Left (SLD), the umbrella organization of the former communists. The SLD won 171 of the 460 seats in the Sejm and 37 in the Senate.[5] The Polish right, rooted in Solidarity, the first non-communist trade union established in 1980 within the Soviet bloc, and supported by the Roman Catholic Church, was shocked and seemingly unable to grasp the reasons for its defeat. Misfortunes never come singly and two years later, the right had another shock: Aleksander Kwasniewski, the leader of the SLD, won the November 1995 presidential election over the incumbent, Solidarity leader Lech Walesa.

What is the origin of Polish left? How different is the present-day SLD from the PZPR of the communist era? Are the SLD members really ex-communists? How could the left successfully attract voters only four years after the fall of state communism? How does the left appeal to the habits of the heart of post-communist Polish society? What is the future of the left in democratic Poland? These are questions which will be addressed in this chapter.

2 THE ORIGIN OF THE POLISH LEFT

In 1948 the PZPR was established as a merger of two parties: the Polish Socialist Party and the Polish Workers' Party. From the very beginning, the PZPR operated as the tool of the Soviet army occupying Poland. As in other communist countries, the PZPR was a criminal organization that was responsible for countless atrocities against the Polish nation. As Radek Sikorski stated:

> Communist terror in Poland may have been a pale reflection of what had transpired in the Soviet Union, but it still managed to claim the lives of several hundred thousand people. Political murders occurred as late as the 1980s. Such crimes should be punished where possible. Justice should be seen to be done, or else new scoundrels might think that they can always get away with it.[6]

The criminal aspect of the PZPR activities is widely recognized and described also by Western historians, for example:

> Polish communism had brought neither truth nor bread. It was spiritually bankrupt, economically incompetent, repressive, intolerant and grotesque in its distortion of fact. Counting the Soviet as well, communism was also murderous on a scale Hitler could only dream of.[7]

These were the basic similarities between the PZPR and the communist parties of the other countries in the Soviet bloc. Let us focus now on several differences. From its beginning, the Polish Communist Party struggled with significant resentment among the Poles. By contrast, the communist parties of Bulgaria, Hungary, Romania and Yugoslavia had won a certain popular appeal thanks to their anti-Nazi activities. The contribution of the Polish communists to the anti-German resistance movement was of a marginal character. For the Poles the popular Second World War heroes were the underground Home Army soldiers who did not differentiate between the Nazi and the communist enemies.

The traditional Polish resentment toward the Soviet Union was the result of a painful past. Russia had partitioned Poland three times, and together with Nazi Germany invaded Polish soil in September of 1939. The Polish communists were of course aware of the popular animosity toward the Soviets and in the post-war years tried to present themselves not as obedient puppets of the Russians, but as Polish patriots. The subsequent party first secretaries –Wladyslaw Gomulka, Edward Gierek and General Wojciech Jaruzelski– continually stressed to the people their primary commitment to Polish interests. Jaruzelski, who himself imposed martial law in 1981, made many efforts to present himself to the Poles not as 'a Russian general in Polish uniform', but as a rescuer of Poland who prevented a Soviet invasion.

Poland and the Polish communists were indeed fortunate and smart enough to avoid the direct Soviet intervention that took place in Hungary in 1956 and in Czechoslovakia in 1968. As a result of those events, the Hungarian Communist Party of Janos Kadar and the Czechoslovak Party of Gustav Husak were marked with the stigma of traitors. Consequently, the image of them among their compatriots was unambiguously pejorative and nobody in Hungary had discussed possible patriotic motivations of 'the butcher of Budapest'.

Another unique feature of Polish communism was its relation to the Church. As in other socialist countries, the Church in Poland was persecuted. But in no other socialist country did the Church have such influence. Only the Polish communist leaders had to deal regularly with the Church hierarchy and, from time to time, they sought its support. Gomulka asked for help from Cardinal Stefan Wyszynski. Gierek was received by Pope Paul VI. As a result, the people for the first time in socialist Poland heard the words 'God bless Poland' broadcast by state radio. It was General Jaruzelski who tried to improve his image through John Paul II's visit to Poland in 1984. Mieczyslaw Rakowski, the last first secretary of the dying PZPR, stated that a party member might attend Church services and still be a good communist. Finally, Kwasniewski, when president, went to the Polish National Shrine in Czestochowa to seek a blessing.

The role of the Church in Polish politics as well as Polish society throughout and beyond the communist period was as important as it was complex. The Church contributed tremendously to the collapse of communism by creating the only recognized, independent shelter for oppressed Poles, including those who were atheists. Only in this country were there 'non-believers' who were 'church-goers'. These were mainly political dissidents who did not believe in God but attended mass in a symbolic act of opposing communism. Paradoxically, the same Church, after the collapse of the party regime, through its vigorous political involvement on the side of the right (to the point of calling an act of voting for the left 'a mortal sin') inadvertently and ironically pushed many outraged voters into the arms of the left.

The Polish communists who sought to pursue their political aims in this complex and often hostile environment were inevitably affected by the realities which shaped their approach and which they subsequently created. In the end, their orthodox tendencies were weakened, an inner conflict of loyalty appeared, and the result prepared the ground for their transformation and modernization.

3   THE PZPR AND THE SLD – HOW FAR, HOW CLOSE?

Despite its name, the Polish United Workers' Party was never united. From the very beginning of its existence the party was a mixture of true believers and cynical opportunists, modest ideologists and smart thieves, the nationalists and internationalists, the anti-Westerners and Westernized technocrats, pro-Russian traitors and agents and defenders of the 'Polish' way in 'building socialism', conservatives and reformers. This coalition of divergent political inclinations could rarely concentrate enough power to fight both its own internal dissidents and the anti-communist opposition. The very fact that leading dissidents like Leszek Kolakowski, Jacek Kuron and Adam Michnik had started their political journey as party members reveals something of the internal diversity of this self-appointed 'leading force of the nation'.

The major crisis within the PZPR was connected with the birth of Solidarity. This first independent trade union within the Soviet bloc was a hybrid that grew from two very different (at least at the surface) roots: Christianity and utopian socialism. For example, the 21 demands of the August 1980 strike in Gdansk included one for a weekly broadcast of a live mass by the state radio and also, 'Demand no.14: Reduction of retirement age for women to fifty and for men to fifty-five', 'Demand no. 18: Establishment of three-year paid maternity leaves for raising children'.[8] There are at least three possible explanations why such unrealistic social demands were formulated: either the authors of them did not know how catastrophic was the state of the Polish economy, they believed that the creation of the 'workers' paradise' was actually possible, or the demands were formulated in a way that excluded the possibility of fulfilling them, therefore creating a pretext for further strikes that would ultimately lead to the collapse of the entire system. One political reality is clear: Solidarity's attempt to improve the standard of living of the workers was appealing to those communist party members who wanted their party to provide for the workers. As a result, those members of the communist party joined the new, non-communist union. At first, the PZPR did not react to the double membership of their reform-oriented members. When in 1981 the tensions between the government and Solidarity became serious, the party demanded that its members leave Solidarity, creating for some a conflict of loyalty.

The imposition of martial law on 13 December 1981 by General Jaruzelski, the first secretary of the party, was the deciding stage in the split within the PZPR. The party reformers and the party members who had also previously belonged to Solidarity felt betrayed, and many of them decided to leave the PZPR. The 1980s marked the stage of agony of the party. Its inability to reform the economy, internal fights and mutual accusations contributed to the further demoralization of the membership.

In January 1990 the PZPR was dissolved and a new party was formed, called the Party of Social Democracy of the Republic of Poland (SdRP). In its founding declaration, it referred to the tradition of the socialist parties of Western Europe, thus trying to distance itself from the PZPR and its unpopular past. Before the first parliamentary elections to take place in post-communist Poland on 27 October 1991, the recycled communist party had created an alliance with the All Poland Trade Union Alliance (OPZZ), the umbrella organization of the former communist trade unions. The association of the SdRP and the OPZZ was named the Democratic Alliance of the Left (SLD). The new left coalition obtained its first popular success in the 1991 elections by winning 11.98 per cent of the vote and 60 seats in the Sejm.[9] Among the 29 parties that participated in this election, only one other party garnered similar support – the Democratic Union (UD) led by T. Mazowiecki which obtained 12.31 per cent of the vote resulting in 60 seats in the Sejm as well.

In the next parliamentary elections, on 19 September 1993, the SLD won over the UD and formed the government. The SLD received 20.41 per cent of the vote with 171 seats in the Sejm while the UD obtained 10.59 per cent and 74 seats in the Sejm.[10]

In November 1995 the Poles voted in their second presidential election since the collapse of communism. The first round was contested by 13 candidates. Aleksander Kwasniewski obtained 35.1 per cent of the vote; Lech Walesa received 33.1 per cent.[11]   Because no candidate received more than 50 per cent of the vote, a run-off election took place. The SLD leader, Kwasniewski, defeated Walesa, the candidate of the right, obtaining 51.7 per cent of the vote,[12] and in this way the left became the leading force on the Polish political scene. Walesa supporters tried unsuccessfully to challenge the results of the elections, contending that Kwasniewski had misled the electorate by falsely claiming that he held a graduate degree as well as not being entirely forthcoming about his wife's financial status.[13]

So, within half a decade, the SdRP/SLD was able to transform its image and almost cleanse itself of the stigma of the old, oppressive, infamous PZPR. The Polish left accomplished this transformation in response to forces which were external as well as internal to Polish politics.

4   HOW THE IMF, JEFFREY SACHS, SOLIDARITY AND THE POLISH RIGHT HELPED THE POLISH ECONOMY AND THE POLISH LEFT TO SUCCEED

On 19 August 1989, the Polish parliament formally endorsed Tadeusz Mazowiecki as the first non-communist prime minister in the Soviet bloc. The Solidarity members who won their elections turned almost overnight from conspirators of the banned underground trade union into legitimate representatives of the government. Unfortunately, the euphoria of the election faded quickly. The Polish economy was in ruins: inflation had reached 2,000 per cent, production had dropped 25 per cent below earlier declines and the Polish government owed the West and the Soviet Union over $45 billion.[14] The new government obtained financial help from the World Bank and the International Monetary Fund as well as the restructuring of Polish debts under the condition of drastic cuts in the state budget including the termination of price subsidies and controls. The Polish government turned to Jeffrey Sachs among others for advice, and the Poles were introduced to 'shock therapy'. It was the Solidarity government which took on the task of readjustment.

From the very beginning, the Mazowiecki government was bogged down by the dilemma rooted in the basic conflict of interests in which Solidarity was embroiled. As a trade union it was supposed to defend the workers' interests; as the government in what was still a socialist state, it also represented the biggest employer. Grazyna Staniszewska, a member of parliament, expressed the problem clearly:

> I feel very badly in this role, and I am obliged to support the government which was formed by us, a government which now must take such unpopular measures. Obviously I was not prepared for this. I was prepared to be in opposition. We thought that, for one year at least, the communists would have the government, and we Solidarity would be in opposition, and we could go on defending the workers. But everything happened so fast. We had to form a government, and we must support this government in these tough measures. And I feel very bad about it.[15]

Another demand that came from the West was privatization. At the beginning it went rather quickly and smoothly. However, the irony was that the ex-communists were in managerial positions, had money and were ready to become capitalists. Always stereotyped collectively as thieves, this time they could steal in compliance with the law. The common people, whose economic conditions worsened at first, reacted to this rapidly widening gap between rich and poor with resentment and anger.

Solidarity was perceived by its many supporters as an organization that betrayed its ideals. It was supposed to restore truth, dignity, and society's well-being. It promised that economic prosperity would come with political change, and was widely viewed as failing to fulfill its promise. Not many Poles understood that Solidarity's leaders had little choice. Rather, what the electorate saw appeared more like some form of duplicity.

As fledgling private businesses grew, they soon offered new job opportunities. But to secure them, prospective employees were often required to sign a declaration waiving their right to join a trade union. The former members of Solidarity viewed this as a betrayal of the Poland that they had fought for.

With the social discontent gathering momentum, Solidarity, at least for the time being, lost its credibility as the defender of the workers. It was accused of creating a bonanza for the *nomenklatura* and was damaged by financial scandals involving members of the new government. So there was a new opportunity for the return of the left to the political scene, but it was a new left which appeared with a fresh face and an image of moderation. Its goal was not to restore communism, but to continue democratic and economic changes at a slower pace, with respect for the social costs of economic reform. What the new left offered was in fact capitalism with a human face.

The political parties of the right were not able to mount a coherent challenge to the rapidly rising voices of moderation. A lot of energy was lost in the course of mutual accusations and power struggles. Their attitude based on belief in historical justice (in terms of profiting from being a part of the establishment) was in an apt way pronounced by the prominent leader of the right, Jaroslaw Kaczynski, who stated that the strongest party within the umbrella organization Solidarity Election Action Party (AWS) was FINU – the abbreviation of 'Fuck It – Now Us!' (in Polish TKM – '*Teraz Kurwa My*').[16] It was a joke but it illustrated well the approach of the right. They expected that now it was their turn, and it was understood by them as a given. They were veterans of the fight for independence, they suffered political oppression that included imprisonment, and they were the only alternative to the ex-communists (who, it seemed to many, would be hated by the Poles forever). But paradoxically, the politicians of the right also carried the legacy of the governmental style of their predecessors. This reality was perhaps unavoidable, since the communist style of governing had been, for almost half a century, the only way in Poland. The dissidents had not been exposed to different patterns; they were raised in political kitsch, and it left its mark on them. The misfortunes of the Polish right before the September 1997 parliamentary elections that were won by the AWS may be aptly summarized by the words of George Bernard Shaw: 'There are two tragedies in life. One is not to get your heart's desire. The other is to get it'.

What were these sins of the communist rulers that the right repeated? Let us bring here the seven of them in alphabetical order: arrogance, greed, ignorance, populism, provincialism, ugliness and underestimation of the enemy. When, before the 1995 presidential election, at the beginning of the television debate of the two major contestants, Lech Walesa refused to shake the hand of Aleksander Kwasniewski and added the comment 'I would not even offer you my leg', many Poles were infuriated. Although many believed that they should vote for Walesa, he seemed by this time to embody the bad taste and poor judgment of the loser. They would regret voting for him as much as voting against him.

Kwasniewski won. Many Poles and the free world were shocked. Kwasniewski was a *real* ex-communist: he had been a minister of sport and physical education in the communist government after the imposition of martial law, the government widely viewed as consisting of hypo-cynics and hypo-opportunists. And Kwasniewski had not turned into an angel over night. He lied about his university degree; and when it was revealed that his wife did not pay taxes on a huge amount of money, he stated that he was not aware that they, the Kwasniewskis, earned so much in a given year.[17]

Polish politics of all denominations as well as the other post-communist states and even the highly developed democratic countries such as the US suffer from the lack of political culture, mediocrity and kitsch. It seems that all the features mentioned are rooted in one general illness, namely: the deprivation of good taste.

Not many people are qualified to speak about good taste, especially in the world of politics, but there is one man who came to the dominion of politics from the sphere of aesthetics. This man is Vaclav Havel, who proved by his presidency that the saying 'power demoralizes and the absolute power demoralizes absolutely' did not refer to him. The following are Havel's reflections on the world of politics experienced by him:

> Of course in politics, as elsewhere in life, it is impossible and pointless to say everything, all at once, to just anyone. But that does not mean having to lie. What you need is tact, the proper instincts, and good taste. One surprising experience from 'high politics' is this: I have discovered that good taste is more important than a postgraduate degree in political science. It is essentially a matter of form: knowing how long to speak, when to begin and when to finish, how to say something politely that your opposite number might not want to hear, how to say, always, what is most essential in a given moment, and not to speak of what is not essential or uninteresting, how to insist on your own position without offending, how to create the kind of friendly atmosphere that makes complex negotiations easier, how to keep a conversation going without prying or, on the contrary, without being aloof, how to balance serious political themes with lighter, more relaxing topics, how to plan one's journeys judiciously and how to know when it is more appropriate not to go somewhere, when to be open and reticent, and to what degree.[18]

Havel's description refers clearly to the very characteristics that Polish politicians of the left and right have seemed to lack. Of course, what for the more sophisticated part of society might be a negative trait may be perceived in a positive way by others.

Between November 1995 and September 1997, democratic Poland was ruled by an ex-communist majority in parliament and by an ex-communist president. Most of the voters elected them because of the hardship of life in a post-communist country in transition. The younger generation and a more liberally oriented part of the intelligentsia voted for them because they ran a dignified campaign in which they promised to continue democratic reforms. In addition, they were rather young and rather handsome, were intelligent and had a sense of humor, were moderate in their opinions, were Westernized and knew foreign languages. Simply, they were the incarnated contradiction of the stereotype of the communists of the old era.

How did they do? Not so badly, taking into consideration the annual economic growth rate of 6 per cent, the highest one among the emerging democracies, the low rate of unemployment that is now below two digits, and the strong and stable exchange rate of the Polish currency. Regarding foreign policy, the ex-communists successfully pursued the Polish aspirations toward membership in NATO. Certain progress was also achieved regarding prospective Polish participation in the European Union. Good relationships with neighboring countries were carefully maintained. Those successful events proved that the SLD was committed to democratic reforms and did not plot to turn Poland back into a mono-party system with a centrally planned economy.

All the achievements mentioned did not secure for the SLD a victory in the ← parliamentary elections that took place on 21 September 1997, in which the Alliance of the Left lost to the Solidarity Election Action Party. The AWS received 33.8 per cent of the vote compared to the SLD's 27.1 per cent.[19] Yet the SLD's total was 6.7 per cent higher than its share in the September 1993 elections. The results show that the SLD electorate is solid, stable and even growing. Still, the modernized and moderate image created by the SLD was not enough when it came to the matter of the social costs of the economic reform. In his report from Poland, Jon Paul Sydnor, the American Peace Corps volunteer, wrote about Bartek, a young man who voted for the ex-communists in the September 1993 parliamentary elections.[20] In September 1997, the same Bartek probably voted for the AWS because the left had promised a less aggressive program of social protection than the AWS. Firmly rooted in the trade union tradition, the AWS has learned to promise the material benefits of better living standards so desired by the Poles. Like many, Bartek likely still believes in campaign promises and can hardly recognize the cynicism embodied in the principle: 'Nobody will give you as much as I shall promise you'. The confusion of the Polish voter is evident in the speed of Polish political shifts. One does not change the habits of the heart or one's political intuitions as quickly as the shifts in Polish political support.

5 THE HABITS OF THE POLISH HEART AND THE FUTURE OF THE POLISH LEFT

It was Georg Wilhelm Friedrich Hegel who said that we have the sort of statesmen we deserve. His words were not intended for the years of the communist oppression when the Polish citizenry lacked influence on the choice of their statesmen. After 1989, Hegel's words regained their powerful meaning. Jose Ortega y Gasset's unsophisticated, rather primitive and populist 'mass-man'[21] entered politics and placed his representatives on its scene. The socialist slogan 'power for the masses' experienced a renaissance. Looking at many Polish politicians of right and left, one has an impression that indeed – according to a popular Polish maxim – 'Power lies on the streets', and everybody skilled enough to bend over can pick it up. In this way, power reached the masses with all its consequences. Progress in building a state run by the rule of law was slowed by common and open corruption, bribery and graft, and many fraudulent and shady businesses involving the highest members of state administration.

The insolence of certain fraudulent and unqualified politicians carries us back to Ortega y Gasset's psychological profile of the so-called self-satisfied mass-man:

> If from the view-point of what concerns public life, the psychological structure of this new type of mass-man be studied, what we find is as follows: (1) An inborn, root-impression that life is easy, plentiful, without any grave limitations; consequently, each average man finds within himself a sensation of power and triumph which, (2) invites him to stand up for himself as he is, to look upon his moral and intellectual endowment as excellent, complete. This contentment with himself leads him to shut himself off from any external court of appeal; not to listen, not to submit his opinions to judgment, not to consider others' existence. His intimate feeling of power urges him always to exercise predominance. He will act then as if he and his like were the only beings existing in the world; and, consequently (3) will intervene in all matters, imposing his own vulgar views without respect or regard for others, without limit or reserve, that is to say, in accordance with a system of 'direct action'.

It was this series of aspects which made us think of certain defective types of humanity, such as the spoiled child, and the primitive in revolt, that is, the barbarian.[22]

Almost ten years after the collapse of the mono-party system, dominant in the post-communist societies is still confusion born of the conflict between the communist legacy that is haunting people's minds and their capitalist expectations. The predominant hope was for the development of a 'third system' (neither infamous socialism nor merciless capitalism) which merged the good from both. From communism would come free medical care, free education and subsidized family vacations; from capitalism would come decent salaries, a high standard of living and medical care of high quality. The idea is simple: combine Swedish social protectionism with low American taxes. Unfortunately, like all simple ideas in a complex world, attempts to make it real deprive it of its simplicity. And the resultant new complexity is neither as familiar nor as attractive as the original idea.

On the other hand, the habits of the heart formed under the old communist welfare state have not ceased to exist in post-communist Poland. Some of the tendencies of the Polish population which influence the ongoing evolution and often stand as impediments to the development of democracy and prosperity are as follows:

1. *The perception of authority as separate from the people* The widespread sense of power over elected representatives is largely restricted to the power to install and remove them. 'Them', or those who govern are still seen as distant from the common people, vulnerable to criticism and removal, but not as 'one of us'. Nor is the government seen widely as an extension of the

society from which it arises. It is seen, rather, as something over and above society and daily life, in a sense untouchable and as a power to make and fulfill promises of 'us', the society.

2. *Lack of self-organization on the local level* The citizens show a lack of initiative in taking problems into their own hands and beginning 'grass roots' politics and movements. This reluctance results in part from a past in which those who tried to change something were accused of challenging the party and its authority and consequently punished.

3. *Dishonesty and double morality* Socialism created the cult of cunning, according to the slogans 'They pretend that they pay, therefore we pretend that we work' and 'Since the state uses all means to cheat its citizenry, the citizens must use any means to survive'. In addition, what belonged to the socialist state did not belong to anybody, and so was either not respected or whenever possible stolen for private use. The old cat and mouse game of communist society has not been forgotten, and this memory expresses itself in a resistance to taxes and no strong inclination to act out in business the maxim 'Honesty is the best policy'.

4. *To rule means first of all to provide for yourself* The Polish word '*koryto*' (trough) functioned as a synonym of power; the expression '*dorwac sie do koryta*' (to hug the trough) meant to become part of the establishment and to steal as much as possible. For the left, acting according to this rule is the continuation of historical tradition. For the right, doing the same is being reimbursed for historical injustice.

5. *The doctrine of social equality* A view once spouted by all but liked by none, this meant that in practice all would be equal in misery. Today, the gap between the very rich and the majority brings increasing resentment. A sense of envy has become common and powerful, and it is at times masked and expressed as a nostalgic longing for social equality. The rigid restrictions of a society committed to that principle are too often forgotten, and so less attention is devoted to finding ways to increase liberty for all and encouraging self-reliance.

Without losing sight of the complexities caused by the above tendencies, one should watch certain basic trends closely as the next century unfolds in Poland. One can expect that a more developed capitalism will not erase the social differences of wealth or class distinctions. Creation of a prosperous, stable and well-established middle class will require perhaps the next half century. In the meantime, the overriding reality of Polish society will continue to be the lack of a successful decommunization of the hearts and minds of the population. And to this extent, most of the workers, the young people, the pensioners and the liberal intelligentsia will continue to look to the left as the representatives of their interests. This sector of the population can be expected to be the source of a mostly stable electorate for the left. The Solidarity movement will undergo further transformation with more radical and vindicatory factions oscillating toward the left. The right will continue to become less and less able to embarrass the left by reference to Stalinist crimes as the latter become as historical as the Nazi occupation of the Second World War.

Overall, the prospects for the left are good. The Polish left is not a radical left, but a moderate one striving to stake out political territory with a style compatible with the spirit of parliamentary democracy and still standing for some individual protections for the population. The major task of the right is to reshape its way of thinking about the left, by shifting from dreams of removing it from the Polish political scene, to strategies for coping with a persistent even if not fully clear and stable opposition.

NOTES

*I wish to thank Dr. Raymond Pfeiffer for his time, comments and suggestions that have improved my text significantly.

1. Jon Paul Sydnor, 'Bartek is a Communist', Polish American Journal **2** (1996): 8.
2. *The Europa World Year Book 1990*, Vol. II (London: Europa Publications, 1990), p. 2108.
3. Janusz Wrobel, 'Capitalist Aspirations and the Communist Legacy in Poland', *Journal of Interdisciplinary Studies,* **1/2** (1992): 139-57.
4. Ibid., p. 153.
5. The Europa World Year Book 1994, Vol. II (London: Europa Publications, 1994), p. 2417.
6. Radek Sikorski, *Full Circle: A Homecoming to Free Poland* (New York: Simon & Schuster, 1997), p. 232.
7. Tina Rosenberg, *The Haunted Land. Facing Europe's Ghosts after Communism* (New York: Vintage Books, 1996), p. 168.
8. Wrobel, p. 147.
9. *The Europa World Year Book 1992*, Vol. II (London: Europa Publications, 1992), p. 2259.
10. *The Europa World Year Book 1994*, p. 2417.
11. *The Europa World Year Book 1998*, Vol. II (Europa Publications, 1998), p. 2671.
12. Ibid.
13. Ibid.
14. Minton Goldman, *Russia, the Eurasian Republics, and Central/Eastern Europe* (Sluice Dock, CT: Dushkin/McGraw-Hill, 1998), p.156.
15. Ofa Bikel, 'Poland: The Morning After' [Transcript of the program, 'Frontline', No. 808, aired 27 March 1990, PBS], p. 4.
16. Mariusz Urbanek, 'Brzydkie wyrazy', *Polityka* **33** (15 August 1998): 44–5.
17. *The Europa World Year Book 1998*, p. 2671.
18. Vaclav Havel, 'Paradise Lost' *The New York Review of Books* **4** (1992).
19. *Encyclopaedia Universalis* (France S.A., 1998), p. 63.
20. Sydnor, p. 8.
21. Jose Ortega y Gasset, *The Revolt of Masses* (New York: W.W.Norton & Co., 1932).
22. Ibid., pp. 97–8.

6. The Left in Slovenia

Danica Fink-Hafner

1 INTRODUCTION

Neither right nor left are absolute concepts.[1] It also is not true that the end of the Cold War and most communist regimes meant the death of leftist concepts and ideas. Over the last two decades they have in fact been revised and been attributed with new meanings in both the East and West.[2] Since the left today is devoid of a singular identity and any clear definition, we first need to define the left for the purposes of this chapter. Traditionally, in Europe the left has been defined in two ways, as the extreme left (communist parties) and in the sense of social democracy. There are some typical common issues among the two party families[3] such as support for social equality, public ownership, welfare state and ideas of participation in decision-making in the economy and the political system (various concepts of self-management concerning workers' participation and self-government in local communities). Besides that, there have also been clear differences, especially with regard to the strategy of pursuing their goals (communist revolutions and social-democratic reforms) as well as religious tolerance in the case of social democracy and communist intolerance toward religion and the Church.

Recent research[4] shows that the pluralization theory on left–right is supported by empirical evidence. Knutsen stresses that left–right semantics reflect first and foremost the economic values and interests (and religious/secular according to the broader version) in society, and these interests will remain the key to left–right identification since such values and interests will continue to be the central conflicts in society.[5] We are going to base our definition of the left on Knutsen's findings about the persistent impact of left–right materialist orientations and on his thesis that left–right semantics have an impressive absorptive power – the new meanings of the left and right are being added to the old meanings in various contexts and historical periods.

In this chapter, we define the left as a set of values, an ideology and a group of political players supporting social equality as a value, social equality as a goal of public policies (the welfare state concept) and ideas of ordinary people's participation in the fields of economic and political democracy.

In order to at least partly answer the question of the historical fortunes and possible future of the left in Slovenia, we shall analyse several factors directly or indirectly influencing the faith of the left in the 1990s. Accordingly, we are going to present the history of the left on Slovenian territory, the ideological structure of the Slovenian party arena in the process of democratic transition, the spread of leftist values in Slovenian society and party ideologies, ideological shifts in coalition governments and political preferences of voters and the upper class. Our thesis is that social democratic values are widespread in society, although the existence of conflicting values allows the acceptance of more (in the European sense) liberal[6] concepts of the state and its role in securing the welfare of its citizens. Political parties of all the main party families in Slovenia have incorporated these kinds of values and statements in their party manifestos and activities. Political developments in the 1990s have shown that broad support for some classical left values and public policies among voters is translated into electoral support neither for the only party in Slovenia which declares itself to be left (the United List of Social Democrats – the reformed former communist party) nor for the anticommunist social-democratic party. Therefore, we cannot fully define the left in Slovenia in terms of specific, existing political parties.

2 HISTORICAL OVERVIEW OF THE LEFT'S FORTUNES IN SLOVENIA

The United List of Social Democrats (ULSD) is the oldest (reformed) party in the new Slovenian party arena. It is one of the successors of the Communist Party of Yugoslavia formed after the First World War and also a successor of the Communist Party of Slovenia, later renamed the League of Communists of Slovenia. From their organization in 1920 through to the 1980s, Slovenian communists were closely linked to the Yugoslav Communist Party. It is interesting that Slovenians did not attend and were even critical of the founding congress of the Yugoslav Communist Party in 1919 held by the left-wing factions of social-democratic parties during the existence of the First Yugoslavia.

After the formal split between the left (revolutionaries) and the right (reformists) in the Slovenian Social Democratic Party in 1920, the left wing dropped out of the Second International and joined the revolution-oriented Yugoslav Communist Party. A separate Communist Party of Slovenia was founded in 1937, but remained subordinated to the Yugoslav communist organization. Between the First and Second World Wars, the Communist Party was illegal for most of the time.

The Slovenian wing of the Yugoslav Communist Party organized the People's Front to fight against fascism in 1934, and the Yugoslav Communist Party did the same in 1935. During the Italian and German occupations in the Second World War, the People's Front of Slovenia developed into the Liberation Front (*Osvobodilna fronta*). Under the leadership of the Communist Party, a very small party cadre proved to be the only force capable of organizing mass resistance immediately after the German attack in the spring of 1941. The Liberation Front soon started replacing the collapsed old political system by creating so-called institutions of people's power. The system was so well developed by 1944 that the first Slovenian parliament and government could be established.

These successes and the leading role of communists in organizing resistance forces gave the communists important popular legitimacy. However, in the course of building the new Slovenian state's institutions in the free territories, they took over the power and excluded other ideological groups (especially Christian socialist groups). Communists used force and even performed executions in constructing a new socialist political regime after the Second World War which, by the end of the 1980s, had become a key factor in the crucial split between the successor parties to the socio-political organizations of the socialist system on the one hand, and the newly-created political parties in the context of democratic transition (especially the Christian Democrats and the Slovenian Social Democratic Party) on the other hand.

Historically, the ULSD emerged from the group of revolutionary Bolshevik workers' parties which gained and maintained a dominant role in the socialist political systems for more than forty years after the Second World War, despite the Yugoslav Communist Party's ideological and political split with Stalin in 1948. Under the pressure of economic, social and nationalist developments within the former Yugoslavia, the socialist political system gradually evolved to adapt to decentralization, introduction of different forms of workers' and citizens' participation in the workplace as well as in managing local communities and different social sectors such as social services (for example, education, health, social security). These practical steps were founded in the ideology of self-management, idiosyncratic to the Socialist Federal Republic of Yugoslavia. However, none of these innovations seriously questioned the authoritarian characteristics of the political system.[7] Specifically, the leading role of communists in all sectors in managing the state and society remained intact. Other political parties or any other opposition organizations were not allowed. There were some socio-political organizations (such as the Socialist League of Working People, the League of Trade Unions, the League of Socialist Youth and the League of Veterans'

Associations) which acted as 'transmission belts' of the leading Communist Party and had fixed numbers of seats in assemblies at the local level and at the level of the republics of the former Yugoslavia as well as at the Yugoslav federal level.

The Slovenian League of Communists was the most emphatic about introducing the changes partly because of growing oppositional pressures in Slovenia during the 1980s. Criticism of the communist political system, recognition of multipartism, protection of human rights, the market economy and the rule of law were preconditions for maintaining party legitimacy in Slovenia at the end of the 1980s. Moreover, they were also preconditions for the Slovenian League of Communists' successful and relatively smooth introduction of a multiparty system in Slovenia. The Slovenian League of Communists was able to adapt to the new circumstances and gained the highest percentage of votes compared to other parties in the first democratic elections of 1990 (Table 6.1).

Because of its electoral support, The League of Communists – Party of Democratic Renewal (the ULSD's predecessor's name in 1990) was able to gain a position in the government in 1990, even though it was an opposition party. It was also officially included in three of the six governing coalitions (Table 6.2) so far (1990–98).

The first (at least formal) exclusion of the reformed communists was the first government formed by Demos – a bloc of newly-formed opposition parties – in 1990, and the second exception was the formation of the current government formed after the November 1996 elections (the ULSD left the former government deliberately in January 1996). Integrated with several other small, newly-established socialist parties it had been one of the most successful parties in the transitional period (1989–92). Despite the 1996 election loss of an important share of votes when the party of pensioners (DeSUS) decided to compete on its own, it received up to 9 per cent of the votes, proving it has a stable core of electoral support.

In the new political context, the ULSD declared itself to be one of the two social-democratic parties in Slovenia (the Slovenian Social Democratic Party being the other one) having roots in the first Slovenian Social Democratic Party formed at the end of the nineteenth century, although the communists split off from the social democrats in 1919. The ULSD claims ideological sources in several philosophies and historical experiences such as Christianity, humanistic philosophy, enlightenment, the tradition of a critical theory of society, experiences of the workers' and resistance movements in the world and especially experiences of the workers' and resistance movements inSlovenia including those in the 1980s and early 1990s. After declaring itself to be a party of the left in 1990, the reformed communist party shifted ideologically twice more. A more temporary orientation toward the political

Table 6.1 Percentage of votes for parties gaining parliamentary seats in 1990, 1992 and 1996

Party	1990*	1992**	1996**
United List of Social Democrats	17.3	13.6	9.0
Liberal Democracy of Slovenia	14.5	23.5	27.0
Slovenian Christian Democrats	13.0	14.5	9.6
Slovenian People's Party	12.6	8.7	19.3
Social Democratic Party of Slovenia	7.4	3.3	16.1
Socialist Alliance	5.4	+	++
Liberal Party	3.5	+	+
Slovenian National Party	++	10.0	3.2
DeSUS	+++	+++	4.3
The Greens of Slovenia	8.8	3.7	+
Democratic Party	9.5	5.0	+

Notes:
* Parliamentary Elections in April 1990, Socio-political Chamber, proportional system, no. of seats: 80 (78 for parties and 2 for representatives of national minorities).
** Parliamentary Elections in December 1992 and November 1996, National Assembly, proportional system (d'Hondt's System), no. of seats: 90 (88 for parties and 2 for representatives of national minorities).
+ Not in parliament
++ Did not compete
+++ Did not compete separately

Source: National Election Commission, Republic of Slovenia.

center was replaced by a left orientation after 1994.[8] It currently appears that the party is in decline, but preserves its core supporters.[9]

We could summarize that the historical fortunes of the communist/reformed communist left in Slovenian territory have been going up and down. The Communist Party shifted from a marginal, even illegal, political force to a dominant, governing authoritarian political force of the socialist regime. After

Table 6.2   Party composition of governments in Slovenia (May 1990 to August 1997)

Period	Party of Prime Minister	Other Parties	Status
16.5.1990–14.4.1992	SCD	SDA, SFP–PP, SDPS, GS, LP	Majority
14.5.1992–12.1.1993	LDP	DP, SDPS, GS, ULSD	Majority
25.1.1993–29.3.1994	LDP	SCD, SDPS*, ULSD	Majority
29.3.1994–26.1.1996	LDP	SCD, ULSD*	Majority
26.1.1996–10.11.1996	LDP	SCD	Minority
27.2.1997	LDP	SPP, DeSUS**	Majority

Notes: For a list of abbreviations, see Appendix 6A.
*   The SDPS left the government on 29 March 1994 and the ULSD left the government on 26 January 1996.
**   The key structure of this coalition government is bipolar. At the time of the forming of the government, the number of ministries was split into two equal clusters, DeSUS had a minister without portfolio, LDP had the position of PM and, for the SPP, a new position of Vice-Prime Minister was politically invented, despite not being formalized by the new Law on Government.

Source: Office for Personnel, Government of the Republic of Slovenia.

democratization at the end of the 1980s, it became a relatively successful actor of 'transplacement'[10] in Slovenia. It was rewarded for its adaptive behavior at the first free elections. At the moment, it seems to be a party in decline. So, while democratic transition (a change of political system) was favorable to the party, the consolidation stage is not. Looking at historical trends, this political group on Slovenian territory seems to have been gaining legitimacy and broad popular support in times when its political struggle was combined with a struggle for Slovenian national prosperity or even survival (for example, in the case of the anti-fascist struggle or in making the political and legal foundations for an independent Slovenia in 1990–91), but has not been very successful when building primarily on its own leftist social and political goals.

3 IDEOLOGICAL STRUCTURE OF THE SLOVENIAN PARTY ARENA DURING DEMOCRATIC TRANSITION

In the study of party system development in the Central and Eastern European post-socialist countries, the most popular hypothesis seems to be linked to the characteristics and actors of democratic transition. Recently, the idea of (dis)continuity gained a special place due to interest in the fate of former communist parties in the context of young democracies. Golosov[11] has shown that the emerging party systems tend to be shaped by the modes of communist rule and by the modes of democratic transition contingent upon them. Huntington stresses that a consensual, less violent transition provides a better basis for consolidating democracy than do conflict and violence.[12] This is why he considers negotiated transplacements as being the most supportive of consolidation. Cotta believes that a continuous transition enabling the old ruling party to control, at least to some extent, the turn of events, would seem to provide the most favorable conditions for some degree of survival of that party in its original version, or more probably with a refurbished image (a new name, new leaders and so on).[13]

The Slovenian experience has so far shown that transplacement (defined by a strong role of the opposition as well as the adaptive role of the reformist party of the old regime) could open good prospects for a relatively intense process of consolidation of the party arena. We believe this is also true for the core group of the successfully transformed former party-satellite and newly-established parties, although the process of selection of 'survivors' is cruel. The Slovenian experience has also revealed that the idea of continuity and gradualism does not mean a lack of deeper change over a longer period of time, although Slovenia has not experienced the clear-cut ideological and political shifts seen in certain other post-socialist countries. In particular, the results of the 1996 parliamentary elections and the ensuing party struggles involved in the creation of a coalition government have shown that the party system structure, the dominant ideological clusters and the relationships between the parties can change radically even in the consolidation stage of transplacement (Table 6.2).

Party system development in Slovenia is idiosyncratic, although it does share certain similarities with developments in other East-Central European post-socialist countries experiencing the transplacement mode of transition. There are some similarities, for example, with the Hungarian and Polish experiences in relation to the gradual mode of democratic transition, the existence of a pretransition liberalization stage, the development of a relatively strong opposition within the old regime, the adaptive behavior of the old political elite (especially in Hungary) and the persistence of the communist/anti-communist cleavage.

Still, the ideological characteristics of the party arena in Slovenia (such as the historical tradition of the liberal/conservative–clerical cleavage and a weak social-democratic ideological segment) seem to be quite specific when compared to the domination of the liberal/nationalist cleavage in other Central and Eastern European post-socialist countries.[14] Unlike other Central and Eastern European reformed communist parties, the communist successor party in Slovenia entered the new parliamentary arena after the first free elections as the strongest individual party and, even as an opposition party, gained a ministerial position. In addition its former 'liberal' leader, Milan Kucan, gained great support when elected President of Slovenia. Interestingly, after the 1990 election success, its support for the party has been shrinking noticeably toward its share of 'natural' supporters. It seems that the success of former communists is determined not only by the mode of transition but also by certain other factors, especially the strategies and abilities of other parties in the new party arena.

The Slovenian case shows that the continuous mode of transition could be less painful, but it does not necessarily bring long-term rewards to the key actors in the transition stage. Probably, the story thus far of the success and fading away of the reformed successor to the Slovenian League of Communists cannot be understood without taking into account the Slovenian League of Communists' role in the Yugoslav context of the 1980s. We believe it was the national question on which the Slovenian League of Communists gained an important part of its fresh legitimacy at a time when the (Yugoslav) socialist system was losing it.[15] Within the Slovenian political context, its legitimacy was also re-created in the process of adopting liberal and democratic ideas born in the opposition circles. In a way, the reforming League of Communists played two cards – the nationalist one in the external (former Yugoslav) political arena and the liberal one (allowing more freedom for opposition activities) in the domestic (Slovenian) political arena. After the transition stage, another reformed party has been dominating the liberal orientation within the party arena (the reformed League of Socialist Youth – now the Liberal Democracy of Slovenia), and the nationalist orientation has mostly become the domain of the parties on the right. The third, social-democratic orientation (as in Slovenian historical tradition and like other Central European post-socialist parties in the 1990s) has become relatively weak after the success of socially democratized former communists at the first free elections. It is also because the other, anti-communist, social-democratic party only won greater electoral support when it introduced more elements of the ideology of the right. Social democracy in classical European terms lacks political sources in Slovenia due to a long-running privatization process,[16] the slow creation of the two social groups in conflict and the subordination of the labor/capital cleavage to other key social and political cleavages.

During the 1990s, the key cleavage in the party arena seems resistant to change. It is the cleavage between the newly-formed, anti-communist political parties on the one hand, and two primary former socio-political organizations, the United List of Social Democrats (former communists) and the Liberal Democracy of Slovenia, on the other. The latter party developed out of the coalition between the reformed Socialist Youth League, the newly-emerging business strata and Janez Drnovsek, an influential politician from the transitional period. There are also other ideological and political cleavages which are becoming increasingly similar to those known in older Western European democracies, and are expressed in the party affiliation to different ideological party families and in their support for typical policy alternatives. We can say that the following party families have had representatives in the Slovenian political arena during the 1990s: Christian democrats (recently in decline), liberal party (recently rising), social-democratic parties (unstable, mixed fortunes), agricultural parties (recently on the up), parties of pensioners (recently increasing, but not very strongly), extreme right parties (in sharp decline over the last few years), and green parties (falling sharply during the last few years). The dominant ideological structure in the Slovenian parliamentary arena measured by 1996 election support and based on expert and public opinions on the positioning of parties along the left–right continuum (starting on the left and moving toward the right) would be something like: reformed communists (left) 9 per cent, pensioners' party (left) 4.3 per cent, liberal (center/center-left) 27 per cent, agricultural – Slovenian Peoples' Party (center-right) 19.3 per cent, Christian democrats (center-right) 9.6 per cent, anti-communist social-democratic party (right and center-left)[17] 16.1 per cent, and the national party (right and left),[18] 3.2 per cent. Obviously, center-left and center-right parties are altogether supported by about half of all voters. There is no extreme left or clearly relevant extreme right party, although some authors[19] warn that some ideas and acts are shaping the radical right in Slovenia – including (according to Rizman, the most powerful political personality of the radical right in Slovenia) the leader of the anti-communist social democracy movement, Janez Jansa.

During the process of the democratic transition from socialist to post-socialist democratic systems, there have been some shifts in the macro-ideological structure of the party arena. Whereas in the period just after the first free elections, the key macro picture of the party arena was bipolar defined along the communist/anti-communist cleavage, in the following period a tripolar macro picture emerged composed of the liberal, social-democratic (United List) and conservative/clerical cluster of parties (also including the anti-Communist Social Democratic Party). After the 1996 parliamentary elections, a new bipolar macro-structure appeared which could be described as a fragile equilibrium between the center-left and center-right clusters of parties which reminds one of the historical liberal/conservative (clerical) cleavage. To a great extent, this bipolarism interferes with the communist/anti-communist cleavage (the cleavage between the successor parties historically linked to political organizations from the old regime and the newly-established anti-communist parties).   There are some other cleavages   within   the   party   arena   (such   as   center/periphery, traditionalism/modernism, rural/urban, church/state), but the two key cleavages mentioned above seem to dominate over the others. In the case of certain key issues (such as denationalization of forests and giving them over to the Catholic Church in Slovenia), the two key cleavages also include other cleavages (especially the church/state cleavage and the cleavage between traditionalism and modernism).

4 WHAT IS THE LEFT IN CONTEMPORARY SLOVENIAN POLITICS?

The United List of Social Democrats is the only party in Slovenia to currently declare itself as a party on the left side of the left–right ideological continuum. Despite that, we argue that the question of what is the left in contemporary Slovenian politics still lacks a full answer. It is possible to answer that question from at least three viewpoints, such as: (1) the narrowest one focussing on the existence of communist or social-democratic parties; (2) a slightly broader view presupposing that all the successor parties of former socio-political organizations existing in the old regime are in the post-communist political context defined as the left; and (3) the broadest view of the left focussing on the presence of left values among voters and in party ideology regardless of voters' affiliation to specific parties or the affiliation of specific parties to party families.

   With regard to the first viewpoint, our thesis is that (even the reformed) communist party and ideology is in decline while the newly-established (anti-communist) social-democratic party has been gaining electoral support in the last few years by its movement toward certain traditional social bases of the center-right or even right politics. Election results in the 1990s (Table 6.1) favor the proposition that whenever a certain party builds explicitly on its left orientation, it loses electoral support and whenever it builds its electoral appeal on (for the left) 'non-typical' orientations it gains more support. For the former communists, these kinds of political orientations would be in agreement with gradual regime change without using violent repression and putting stress on the national question (autonomy of Slovenia within the former Yugoslavia, independence of the Slovenian state). As to the social democratic party, it would be inclined to cooperate with the Catholic Church, targetting the religious and those living in the more traditionally-oriented countryside as a possible party-social basis, and taking rightist positions in the case of 'national' questions (for example, defining state borders with Croatia, criticizing the government for accepting 'too many' refugees from Bosnia and evaluating the role of the *domobranci* who collaborated with the occupational forces during Second World War). When the United List exhausted its popularity from the time of transition (1989–92), and after its phase of a center-left social-democratic orientation, it returned more to the left and started to lose its electoral support. In contrast, the Social Democratic Party, which under its new leader Jansa has turned further to the right, has started to gain electoral support. This is why we assert that in Slovenia the left seen in the classical terms of communist or social-democratic political organization is in decline.

From the second point of view, one presupposes that all the successor parties to former socio-political organizations existing in the old regime are, in the post-communist political context, defined as being on the left. Here we argue that the two remaining successor parties in the parliamentary arena cannot easily be defined as left. The Liberal Democracy of Slovenia has emerged ideologically out of the gradual transformation of the League of Socialist Youth of Slovenia from a communist ideology toward a liberal ideology in the European sense with a center-left connotation. Former communists evolved from the left to the center-left and then back to the left again.[20] It is interesting that the development of the former communist transmission belt into an autonomous political party with a liberal orientation has proved to be much more successful than the reformed communist party's building upon center-left or primarily left values.

Consistent with Cotta's hypothesis on the support for a ruling party of a former regime in ongoing democratic transition,[21] we could expect the following causal relations: the stronger the support basis of the ruling party of the non-democratic regime, and the more continuous the transition, the greater the probability of maintaining the support for those of a left (although transformed) orientation and for such a party surviving as a significant political actor within the democratic regime. We believe that gradual democratic transition in which the former ruling party did play an active role has so far favored the maintenance of a relatively strong center-left orientation among voters, but this has not been translated directly into support for the transformed communist party. It has been the opposition from within the old system (the successor of the Socialist League of Youth), that has gained the most. With the consolidation of the newly-established parties, the center-right orientation is gaining even in the situation where the two parties having roots in the old regime are still jointly attracting the same electoral support as during the transition stage (Table 6.3).

Table 6.3   Selected features of the party arena at the 1990, 1992 and 1996 elections

Party arena	1990	1992	1996
No. of competing parties at elections	17	33	18
No. of parliamentary parties	9	8	7
Percentage of valid votes for old (successor) parties entering parliament	37.1	37.0	36.0
Percentage of valid votes for new parties entering parliament	54.8	45.3	52.7
Percentage of 'lost' votes (not represented in parliament)	8.1	17.7	10.6
No. of parties in the governing coalition	6	4(3)(2)*	3**

Notes:
* The SDPS left the government in April 1994, and the United List in January 1996 leaving only two parties in the coalition.
** The new coalition government, composed of the Liberal Democracy of Slovenia (Prime Minister Drnovsek), the Slovenian People's Party and the Democratic Party of Pensioners, gained the support of parliament on 27 February 1997.

Source: National Electoral Commission, Republic of Slovenia.

Paradoxically, while the center-left parties have been keeping their 'joint' electoral support, they are losing their position in relation to the center-right cluster of parties. This is because no simple zero-sum game is involved where the right gains at the left's expense. It is also about the struggle for those votes not yet represented in the parliamentary arena (Table 6.3).

From the third point of view, it seems that the moderate elements of social democracy are maintaining its vitality, especially in terms of support of the ideas of social equality and the welfare state in Slovenian society. Malnar[22] has established that Slovenia's normative environment is much more supportive of the Central European 'social market economy' model of capitalism than the more liberal models of capitalism ('liberal' defined in European terms), where market principles dominate welfare distribution. Intolerance toward large social inequalities is widespread in Slovenia. But this is an insufficient indicator of social-democratic orientations. On the basis of comparative research, Malnar[23] discovered that the average support for reducing inequalities is very high in such different countries as Slovenia, Germany, Norway and the USA. Here, what really makes a difference between countries is the way of reducing inequalities according to the majority opinion. Basically, it is a question of acceptance of state intervention. While in

Slovenia and Norway, the average voters would fully support the idea of reducing social inequalities and the idea of state intervention, Germany's citizens are more cautious about state intervention and in the USA state interventionism has the least support.

In Slovenia, government intervention in welfare matters is not perceived as limiting an individual's personal (economic) autonomy, but rather in a very positive way as a form of enlarging an individual's (economic) security. At the same time, research[24] revealed that while Slovenia's adult population strongly supports the values of social equality and the welfare state in the health sector, a significant part of society was then already adapting to falling welfare standards in the health insurance field by buying additional individual health coverage. Hence, one can conclude that social-democratic values are quite dominant in Slovenia, but an important segment of society is accepting reductions to the level of their implementation in the framework of social policies and are taking more responsibility for their own social security.

Taking into account Slovenia's dominant social values and the way of adapting Slovenian society (especially the middle class) to the processes of cutting down the size of the welfare state for economic reasons, it is not surprising that similar values (or rather a mixture of values) can be found in the party platforms of diverse Slovenian parliamentary parties such as the Social Democrats, the United List, the Christian Democrats, the People's Party, or the Liberal Democracy. This is why our second thesis is that the left as a specific segment of social-democratic values and ideology has survived within otherwise extremely diverse ideological party milieus. This phenomenon could be described by the quite common idea that Slovenia should develop in the direction of the Scandinavian type of welfare state.[25]

Liberal Democracy of Slovenia[26] seems to be the most cautious party in the field of welfare policies. It supports human rights, the rule of law, freedom of choice and equal opportunity in all spheres of social life, the market economy, democratic organization of the political system, the liberal notion of the state in society and social policy only having the role of correcting the failures of the market economy, separation of the Church from the state (especially in the context of public education, although it did make some concessions in this area during the 1992–96 term) and ecological issues.

The Slovenian People's Party is originally from the realm of agricultural parties, but can also be seen as a conservative party, highly respecting traditional values such as work, family, home, homeland as well as the Christian ethos. It has also accepted modern ideas of the market economy, the rule of law and 'values of Western civilization.'[27] Besides the farming community and inhabitants of rural regions in general, the party manifesto and party activities also target some other social groups such as workers, entrepreneurs, the educated (especially technical experts), youth, women and the retired. The idea of a polycentric pattern of development of Slovenia goes hand in hand with the party's demands for decentralization, development of the regional level of local self-management and an increased role of civil society in policy-making. The party supports the development of neo-corporatism in the form of a social partnership. The SPP is in favor of a welfare state, especially of a nationally guaranteed minimal level of economic and social security, health care and retirement for all. Its general proposals for active social policies in the field of health care, education and solving the problems of unemployment are sometimes complemented by specific proposals on how to solve problems of marginal groups, especially high school and university students, young families and the disabled. The need for equal representation in politics with regard to gender is also stressed.

The anti-communist Social Democratic Party stresses that its key goals are achieving 'a social state' and the rule of law, appealing to all 'who live on the basis of their honest work, good and honest economic management and honestly earned pensions' as well as to the youth in the process of education, and they express an enormous ideological distance from the other social-democratic party. The United List of Social Democrats stresses similar elements in its party manifesto (such as the need for social solidarity, concern for social policies, worker participation in decision-making at the workplace, a healthy environment, care for marginal social groups, support for the idea of collective bargaining and co-determination at the workplace). Social-democratic parties are characterized by extremely similar voting behavior in parliament when deciding on typical social-democratic issues.[28] We can conclude that both social democratic parties support traditional social-democratic policies, although Jansa's social democrats seem to be a bit more restrictive at least at the normative level of the party platform.

Slovenian Christian Democrats stress that their activity is based on the Christian ethos, Christian social doctrine and heritage of Slovenian Christian social thought. Their main programmatic goal is moral social renewal, which means renewal of social values like diligence, honesty, reliability, responsibility and development of new characteristics of 'our human being' such as creativity and culture. The party manifesto stresses respect for human individuality, social justice, mutuality and solidarity, and the principle of subsidiarity in the relationship between civil society and the state (the state should not interfere in the functions which civil society actors perform as well as the state). It considers the family a fundamental unit of society, and endorses the notions of the equality of men and women, youth policies enabling the young to take an active part in solving their social problems, social care for the elderly, creation of 'multi-generational' communities, free public education at all levels with a stress on special education for 'social responsibility'. The SCD idea of a welfare state is a combination of personal responsibility for social security with the role of the state in the field of social policies, concern for national culture, care for the natural environment and respect for ethical criteria in the field of science and technology. The SCD supports the concept of a 'social-market economy', where the market economy is adjusted by concerns for the environment and social security. Like some other parties, they support the (neo)corporatist idea of social partnership and local self-management.

We can conclude that each of the five biggest parliamentary parties in Slovenia includes an important amount of social-democratic (left) elements in their party ideologies. Elements which are relatively common include: respect for social equality, taking care of marginal social groups, support for redistributive social policies and the relatively strong role of the state in that field (welfare state) as well as support for corporatist arrangements. Still, there are also important differences, especially with regard to evaluation of the socialist system (the United List tends to be more selective and also stresses the good aspects of the old regime) and the question of Church/state relations (clearly leftist orientations are obvious here in the case of the United List and the Slovenian National Party, Liberal Democracy is compromising, while anti-communist social democracy, the People's Party and Christian Democrats tend to develop close relations with the Catholic Church and support its political demands).

5 ASPECTS OF THE CURRENT AND FUTURE FORTUNES OF THE LEFT IN SLOVENIA

The following aspects and factors of the current and future fortunes of the left in Slovenia seem to be very important: voters' preferences and electoral support, upper-class support and party capacity for coalition-building.

Voters' Preferences and Electoral Support

From the voters' preferences point of view, we could say that at the beginning of the transition Slovenians were to a large extent left or left-center oriented.[29] In several public opinion surveys conducted between June 1991 and February 1992,[30] about 69 per cent of those interviewed said that they would position themselves on the left-center part of the left–right continuum and only 31 per cent of them would find themselves more on the right of that continuum. Both extreme self-identifications (extreme left or extreme right) were marginal (covering only a few per cent each). By 1996, the left–right configuration had shifted from a predominately left-centrist orientation to a predominantly centrist orientation. In June 1996, 49.8 per cent of respondents positioned themselves exactly in the center, so that it seems that there is almost no asymmetry remaining.

Many of the key determinants of party identification (such as the structure of the party arena, positioning of voters on the left–right continuum, party self-identification) are still in a process of dynamic change. It is probable that identification will not stabilize for at least some time, but recent developments suggest strong occupation of the center (Table 6.1) and possibly a move slightly to the center-right as in the case with the current governing coalition (Table 6.2).

Upper-Class Support

An analysis of Slovenian public opinion poll data from spring 1994 reveals that the upper classes are much more oriented towards the transformed parties from the old regime (Table 6.4).

Fink-Hafner[31] stresses that managers' interests in making and maintaining links with a few of the bigger political parties are not distributed equally. The public opinion survey of 1996[32] revealed that almost the same proportion of managers interviewed were inclined to vote for the two 'old' parties – 23.4 per cent (and 18.6 per cent for the Liberal Democratic Party) – as the proportion

Table 6.4   Party identification according to self-perceptions of respondent's own class status (percentages)

| Parties | Class | | | | | |
| | Low | | Middle | | Upper | |
	1994	1996*	1994	1996*	1994	1996*
Old	12.3	9.5	17.6	15.8	36.3	20.8
New	28.1	25.5	28.5	24.6	28.4	33.8
Don't know	59.6	65.0	53.9	59.6	35.3	45.4
Total	100.0	100.0	100.0	100.0	100.0	100.0

1994: signif. = 0.00000, C = 0.15245

1996: signif. = 0.00000, C = 0.12565

Notes:
* In the 1994 survey, respondents identified their position by choosing one of three possibilities (low, middle or upper class). In the 1996 survey, the scale was different. The three-item scale comprised: low class (the lowest and the working class), middle class, and upper class (upper middle and upper class).

Source: Tos, Slovenian Public Opinion data, spring 1994, 1996 (SPO 96/1 and 96/2).

inclined to vote for all other ('new') parties – 28.5 per cent. It is probable that a new 'ruling' coalition of economic and political forces which will unify the newly-forming economic (private property) and political power is being created, although the successors from the old political and economic elite currently seem to be the main winners of the economic and political transition.

The new parties continue to be more parties of voters from the lower social strata. Still, by 1996 some interesting changes had appeared. While the determined voters from the middle and upper classes felt closer to the reformed old parties (38 to 39 per cent of the middle and upper classes) and the determined voters from the lower class were much more in favor of the new parties (27 per cent in favor of old and 73 per cent in favor of new parties), the undecided cluster had grown. Support for the old parties is probably significantly motivated by the fact that the Liberal Democracy Party has been in power for the longest period of time so far (since 1992) and has thereby gathered support on behalf of interests that would seek close ties with any party in power.

Despite the above-mentioned general situation, there has been a shift toward greater uncertainty among voters and a shift of part of the upper class away from the old parties. The formation of fresh clusters within the political elite has been gaining more political space over the last couple of years and some clusters of the middle and upper classes seem to have shifted their support from the transformed old to the newly-emerging segments of the political elite. Time will tell how strong this tendency is and whether it will grow in the direction of a predominance of new parties in the party arena and in middle- and upper-class support.

Party Capacity for Coalition-building

To date, power has shifted peacefully and democratically after three parliamentary elections (Tables 6.2 and 6.3). First from center-right (1990–92) to the 'grand coalition' including left, center and right (during the important part of the 1992–96 term). After the November 1996 elections, two equal political blocs formed. One was a bloc of center-left and left parties, nationalists and representatives of the national minorities who were ready to support the Liberal Democracy Party leader Janez Drnovsek as the new prime minister. The other is a bloc of center right and rightist parties which supported the Slovenian People's Party leader Marjan Podobnik as the new prime minister. On the basis of individual parties' election successes, after several months of negotiations a center-right coalition was formed in February 1997. It is composed of the Slovenian People's Party, the Liberal Democratic Party and the Democratic Party of Pensioners (DeSUS).

The successor party of the former League of Communists (the United List) then reached its weakest political position thus far with regard to electoral support (Table 6.1) and with regard to its capacity for coalition-building (DeSUS, a former close political ally of the United List now acts as an autonomous political actor, and the United List in the current party power structure it is not a very relevant partner in the building of the government coalition).

Obviously, the figures reveal the growing strength of the newly-established parties and a tendency toward a weakening of two of the three transformed political organizations of the old regime – the successor to the former League of Communists and former Socialist League of Working People. An orientation toward liberalism and the inability of the new parties to cooperate and form efficient coalitions among themselves continues to provide more space to the successfully reformed ('old') parties. Liberal Democracy of Slovenia seems to be able to keep its strong capacity for coalition-building to the left and to the right. However, many of the key determinants of party identification (such as the structure of the party arena, positioning of voters on the left–right continuum and party self-identification) are still undergoing a process of dynamic change. It is likely that identification will not stabilize for some time to come.

6   CONCLUSIONS

The tree of ideologies is always green.[33] The end of the Soviet system did not mean the end of the left, but just the end of the left as it had been defined in a certain historical period.[34] In Slovenia we could also say that the left, in terms of widespread values of social equality, participation of workers and citizens in decision-making as well as the state's relatively strong role in securing welfare, is quite alive although this is not the radical left that favors the abolition of all social inequalities. The left embodied in political parties is also ambiguous. While the reformed communists have been in decline, the former opposition within the old regime (the reformed socialist youth) has been able to establish the most prominent and stable position in the new party arena. Additionally, nearly all the parties in the parliamentary arena nourish some social-democratic ideas which are occasionally very similar to Christian-socialist ones. Paradoxically, the only two parties declaring themselves to be social democratic have not been able to cooperate or even merge due to the deep communist/anti-communist cleavage between them and have so far been able to attract more voters only in times when they have additionally mobilized their voters by introducing elements more common to rightist parties (especially issues concerning the national question and attitudes toward the Catholic Church).

The left that seems to be shaping Slovenian society and politics in the 1990s could be defined in terms of broad support for a soft version of capitalism that maintains an important segment of the welfare state and also implies the participation of ordinary people in a system of economic and political democracy. Given that by the end of 1996 more than two-thirds of the shares in privatized companies in Slovenia were held by a large number of internal owners (mostly workers who received their shares after the internal distribution of so-called 'social ownership'– see note 16), it is difficult to expect that traditional industrial conflicts will escalate in the near future. That would be possible only in the case of shares being concentrated in a smaller number of owners.

In the Slovenian party manifestos and practical politics, 'social-democratic' policy orientation could be and is feasible with both religious and secular values. Therefore, it bridges the gaps created by certain deep ideological and political cleavages in the party arena. Hence, we expect that it will survive in some form or another, but it will probably not be mainly embodied in traditional social-democratic or even communist party electoral support. Perhaps we can describe the dominant Slovenian value and political situation in the 1990s as a mixture of Bobbio's[35] description of 'liberal socialism' (egalitarian and libertarian-oriented center-left), traditionalism and Catholic ethos. In that context, relatively little space can be found for the extreme left parties and even the social-democratic parties based exclusively on left orientations.

NOTES

1. Noberto Bobbio, Levica in desnica [translation of orig. *Destra e sinistra*], (Ljubljana: Znanstveno publicistieno SrediSee, 1994).
2. Charles Derber, et al., *What's Left? Radical Politics in the Postcommunist Era* (Amherst: University of Massachusetts Press, 1995).
3. Klaus von Beyme, *Political Parties in Western Democracies* (Aldershot: Gower, 1985); Jan-Erik Lane and Svante O. Errson, *Politics and Society in Western Europe* (London: Sage, 1987).
4. Oddbjorn Knutsen, 'Value Orientations, Political Conflicts and Left–Right Identification: A Comparative Study', *European Journal of Political Research* **28** (1995): 63–95.
5. Ibid., p. 67.
6. Here we need to stress the difference between the American and European notions of the term 'liberal'. Beyme says that liberal parties originated as bourgeois parties which stressed the value of freedom and the division between the state and civil society (non-intervention of the state) while struggling against the monarchy and feudal systems. As long as the battle was against the privileges of aristocracy, liberalism was egalitarian, and it remained so with regard to equality before the law, in its attitude to legal discrimination and the battle for political rights for minorities even after many liberal parties had become rather conservative, (Beyme, p. 32). Today liberalism is seen mainly as a synonym for support of private property and the market economy as well as strong emphasis on

education policy. The European liberals' program also stresses human and civil rights, pluralism and regionalism. Bobbio, (p. 81) and Beyme, (p. 37) argue that historically, liberal parties in Europe were considered to be either right parties (as in the case of Italy and France) or center parties (as in England or Germany). Only in Scandinavia did the liberals adopt the concept of the welfare state quite early due to a very specific social situation in the region. Otherwise in Europe, neo-liberals made some concessions in challenging the social democrats since the Second World War using the concept of the 'social market economy' (Beyme, pp. 37–9). Contrary to the prevalent notion of liberalism in Europe, the term liberal has been used in the USA to describe the social and economic intervention practiced by the Democratic Party when in power. In that sense, the usual positioning of liberals in Europe would be in the center or center-right, while in the USA liberals tend to be seen as 'left'.

7. Mitja Hafner-Fink, '(Trans)formation of the Idea of Self-management: Slovenian Perspectives', in Frank Brinkhuis and Sacha Talmor, (eds), *Memory, History and Critique: European Identity at the Millennium*, Proceedings of the Fifth Conference of the International Society for the Study of European Ideas, University for Humanist Studies Utrecht, The Netherlands, 19–24 August 1996, CD-ROM (Cambridge: MIT Press Journals, 1998).

8. Alenka Krasovec, *Socialdemokratski stranki v sloveniji (SDSS in ZLSD) v obdobju 1989–1995*, (BA thesis), Ljubljana, Faculty of Social Sciences, 1996, p. 41.

9. Krasovec established that the older generation already constituted about two-thirds of the party's social basis at the time of her research. At the same time, the anti-communist Social Democractic Party had about half of its membership of middle-aged persons and a bigger proportion of young members than the reformed communist party.

10. Samuel P. Huntington, *The Third Wave* (Norman: University of Oklahoma Press, 1993), p. 114.

11. Grigorii Golosov, *Modes of Communist Rule, Democratic Transition, and Party System in Four Eastern European Countries*, Donald W. Treadgold Papers, No 9 (Seattle: Henry M. Jackson School of International Studies, University of Washington, 1996), p. 91.

12. Huntington, p. 276.

13. Maurizio Cotta, 'Building Party Systems after the Dictatorship: The Eastern European Cases in a Comparative Perspective', in Geoffrey Pridham and Vanhanen Tatu (eds), *Democratization in Eastern Europe* (London: Routledge, 1994), p. 115.

14. Golosov.

15. Danica Fink-Hafner, 'The Disintegration of Yugoslavia', *Canadian Slavonic Papers* 37, 3–4 (1995): 339–56.

16. Mencinger describes this privatization in Slovenia with the start of preparations for introducing capitalism with the Federal Amendments to the Constitution and by adopting several other codes and acts before the disintegration of Yugoslavia. During the 1990s, privatization was shifted to the republics which started to prepare drafts of their privatization laws. Slovenia faced a dilemma whether to adopt the concept of a gradual, decentralized and commercial privatization or a concept which insisted on a mass, centralized and distributive privatization. Political controversy over that question caused some shifts in the legislative process, resulting in the delayed adoption of a privatization bill. The Law on the Transformation of Social Ownership of 11 November 1992 provided several methods by which social ownership could be transformed, depending on the decisions of the managing body of the existing enterprises. According to the Law, privatization was attained by restitution of former owners, by debt–equity swaps, by transfer of shares to the Restitution Fund, the Pension Fund, and the Development Fund, by distribution of shares to employees, by management and worker buy-outs, by sales of shares of the company and by raising additional equity capital (Joze Mencinger, 'From Socialism to the Market – the Case of Slovenia', in Adolf Bibic and Gigi Graziano, (eds), *Civil Society, Political Society, Democracy* (Ljubljana: Slovenian Political Science

Association; 1994)). *Slovenia Weekly* reported that by the end of 1996, more than two-thirds of the shares in privatized companies in Slovenia were held by a large number of internal owners (mostly workers who got their shares after the internal distribution of so-called 'social ownership') (*Slovenia Weekly* **44** (7 December 1996): 15.

17. This Social Democratic Party could be considered as a left party when looking at its party manifesto stressing classical social-democratic values with regard to the ideas of worker participation, collective bargaining and social pacts, solidariiy policy in the case of unemployment, general accessibility of the health-care system, humanization of work and improvement of working conditions, better quality of working life, shorter working hours, and a broad conception of democracy. Its image of a right party stems mainly from its stressing the national question and patriotism, support for a rather strict policy with regard to granting Slovenian citizenship, critical attitudes toward immigrants (in the period between 1992 and 1995), an extremely critical evaluation of the communist regime, incorporation of Christian ethics in the party ideology, and cooperation with the Catholic Church. Their close relationship is clearly expressed in a party manifesto of May 1995 (p. 5). The party leader, Janez Jansa, even gives speeches at public religious ceremonies.

18. The Slovenian National Party quite suddenly emerged as the first clearly nationalistic party in the new party arena. It unexpectedly won 10 per cent of the vote in 1992. It could be considered a (extreme) right party because of its nationalist standpoints and some of its policy issues like legalization of gun ownership, creation of professional units in the Slovenian independent military forces, stressing policies relating to the importance of national identity and its protection (for example, support for artistic activities which strengthen national identity, support for the maintenance and renaissance of the cultural and natural heritage of the Slovenian nation and 'Slovenians'), preference for employing Slovenian workers, ensuring social security and education programs for unemployed Slovenians as well as stressing the need to regulate the status of the foreign workforce in Slovenia. The party also supports free initiatives in the field of health care.

The party's conservatism is also seen from several items stressed in the party manifesto especially the attitude toward the family and the role of women. According to the SNP manifesto, the family is the basic unit of society and a strong Slovenian nation. Women should have more time for the development of their family and raising children. A strong nationalist attitude is even stressed by the statement in the party manifesto that obtaining Slovenian citizenship should be difficult. The key party slogan is: 'one's own master on one's own land' referring to two aspects. The first is the status of the Slovenian nation in relation to power (historically, Slovenians lived under foreign rule for a long time), and the second relates to some unresolved questions about the border with Croatia.

Jelincic's opponents criticized him for 'being leftist' and co-operative with former communists. Mainly this is due to Jelincic's positive attitude toward the national liberation movement on Slovenian territory during the Second World War and toward the Partisans. He was also accused of collaborating with the former communists in policy-making processes in the new parliament because of his support for some governmental proposals. Besides that, the party supports critical attitudes toward the Catholic Church in Slovenia and its policy proposals (especially in the field of decentralization) as well as some left ideas of the welfare state such as universal basic health care and social care for the elderly. When the two ideological blocs formed after the 1996 parliamentary elections, the party lent support to the proposal of the center-left government which failed to gain enough support in parliament.

19. Rudi Rizman, 'Radikalna desnica no Slovenskem', *Teorija in praska* **33**, 4 (1995): 259.

20. Krasovec, p. 41.

21. Cotta, pp. 99–127.

22. Brina Malnar, *Zaznava druzbene neenakosti* (Ljubljana: Znanstvena knjiznica FDV, 1996).

23. Ibid.

24. Niko Tos, Slovenian public opinion poll, conducted in April 1994.

25. It is interesting that the Slovenian public opinion longitudinal survey has shown that most respondents would like to identify Slovenia with Germany or Switzerland. Niko Tos, et. al., Public Opinion Polls, Center for Public Opinion Research, Faculty of Social Science, University of Ljubljana, 1986–98.

26. The Liberal Democracy of Slovenia has developed into a party practically supporting the idea of the 'social market economy'. It tends to cover the political space defined as the center. Although in the transition period it has been seen mainly as a center-left party, in the last few years it has been gravitating to the center following the shift in the self-positioning of Slovenian voters toward the center.

27. Statutory rules of the parliamentary parties, December 1994, paragraph 6.

28. Krasovec, p. 43.

29. Tos et al.

30. Ibid.

31. Danica Fink-Hafner, and John R. Robbins (eds), *Making a New Nation: The Formation of Slovenia* (Ashgate: Dartmouth, 1997).

32. Tos et al.

33. Bobbio.

34. Ibid.

35. Ibid.

APPENDIX 6A

ABBREVIATIONS

DeSUS	Democratic Party of Pensioners
DP	Democratic Party (part of former SDA)
GS	The Greens of Slovenia
LDP	Liberal Democratic Party (former League of Socialist Youth, now Liberal Democracy of Slovenia)
LDS	Liberal Democracy of Slovenia (former LDP)
LP	Liberal Party
LSY	League of Socialist Youth (predecessor of LDP and LDS)
PDR	Party of Democratic Renewal (former League of Communists, now United List of Social Democrats)
SCD	Slovenian Christian Democrats
SDA	Slovenia Democratic Alliance (predecessor of Democratic Party)
SDPS	Social Democratic Party of Slovenia (former Social Democratic League)
SFP-PP	Slovenian Farmers' Party- People's Party
SNP	Slovenian National Party
SPP	Slovenian People's Party (former SFP-PP)
ULSD	United List of Social Democrats (former Party of Democratic Renewal, in 1990 it competed as the United List together with the Workers' Party, the Social Democratic Union, and the Democratic Party of Pensioners)

7.   From Red Star to Roses: The Left in Post-communist Romania

Nicolae Harsanyi

In Romania, unlike the other countries of Eastern Europe, post-communism started with a violent phase: the popular uprising of 16–22 December 1989, and its bloody repression. This moment, in some respects, marked a fresh political start: the repression has completely delegitimated the Romanian Communist Party (RCP) in the eyes of the nation. In fact, one of the first decrees of the provisional government stated that the Romanian Communist Party no longer existed. As the RCP had been the only party in Romania for over forty years, its sudden removal left the political field totally barren, and the building of a party system characteristic of a democratic society could proceed from scratch. Parties that had had a rich tradition in Romania's past until their suppression by the communists in the wake of the Second World War, reappeared and made efforts to build national networks and recruit members. New parties registered daily with the law courts. From this perspective, therefore, one can notice a clear discontinuity with the past. All the same, it became quite obvious that in this discontinuity there was a disconcertingly powerful element of continuity: the communist elite used the freedom of party-building to maintain themselves in power positions. A few members of the highest level of the RCP leadership and many more elements of the second and third tier of the *nomenklatura* resurfaced at the top of some of the newly created parties. This chameleonic dispersion of the former communist elite among several parties (mostly self-declared left-leaning organizations) served to legitimate their present status by obscuring their communist past.

   From this point of view, unlike in Hungary, Poland or Czechoslovakia, there was no negotiated transition. None of the parties that appeared on the Romanian post-communist scene claimed to be the successor of the discredited RCP. Former communist leaders set up parties with leftist platforms to save face and to further participate in the process of distribution of power and resources. The party platforms came totally in the cone of shadow cast by the leaders, ideological convictions playing a secondary role. This is consistent with Romania's long tradition of politics dominated by personalities, rather than ideologies.

In Romania the parties claiming a more or less social-democratic profile essentially differ from similar parties in the West. The traditional West European social-democratic parties came to life in order to protect the citizens against the excesses of the market-oriented capitalist system. In Romania, the new post-communist parties that pretend to be social democratic appeared before the capitalist market-oriented system was in place, and they have devoted much energy to preventing the latter from taking root through economic reforms. Therefore, these parties have distinguished themselves as being predominantly anti-reformist. This is a feature that distinguished the Romanian parties of the left, from the Hungarian Socialist Party, for instance, which has been a strong promoter of reform and economic restructuring.

1   EMERGENCE OF A SUCCESSOR PARTY

The origin of the most prominent party on the post-communist political left in Romania can be traced back to the events of 1989 which culminated in the overthrow of the Ceausescus' dictatorship and their subsequent execution. Even nine years after these events, the complete truth about those bloody days at the very end of 1989 has not yet emerged. What in usual parlance is denoted as the 'Romanian revolution' contained elements of both a spreading popular uprising and a *coup d'etat*, the former preceding and serving as background for the latter. Nicolae Ceausescu, faced with the impossibility of quelling both, decided to flee, with his wife, from his headquarters in the Central Committee building of the RCP in Bucharest.

The power vacuum thus created at noon, on 22 December 1989, lasted only one afternoon, being filled in the evening by the National Salvation Front (NSF), a hastily assembled association of reform-minded communist party officials who had previously fallen out of favor with Ceausescu (and therefore full of resentment against the dictator), and a few dissidents. The latter, whose names were known to the country's population from the Romanian language broadcasts of Radio Free Europe and other Western-based radios, were used to give a hallmark of legitimacy to the new leaders. Right from the outset the NSF placed itself at the helm of the country, pretending to be the 'emanation of the revolution'. By this the NSF was able to contain the revolutionary initiative of the crowds: its initial statements called for a reorganization of the country's political structure, seconded by an announcement whereby the RCP and the *Securitate*, the dreaded secret police, were dissolved. The program that the NSF made public late in the evening of 22 December 1989, contained ten points and stipulated the following: the introduction of a pluralist, democratic form of government; free elections; separation of powers within the state; decentralization of economic management; promotion of individual economic initiative; reorganization of agriculture with an emphasis on small farm production; educational reform; promotion of rights and freedoms of ethnic minorities; reorganization of the trade sector and the discontinuation of food exports; a foreign policy which promoted the interests of the people.[1] Moreover, the NSF also pointed out its provisional status, promising it would serve only until the investiture of a freely elected legislative body and of a new government. This platform provided a comprehensive vision of putting the country back on its feet, thus consistent with the idea of 'national salvation' included in the name of the new ruling body. As a result, the public rushed to support such a platform, placing their confidence in the hands of the NSF. However, when it came time for the same public to identify this ideology with the persons who represented the NSF, either at national or local levels, the first seeds of doubt arose.

The majority of the members of the local NSF committees were the same party leaders who, prior to 22 December 1989, had been prominent officials of the local organizations of the RCP. At the top of the NSF the public could see the same organizational formula taking a very obvious shape. The acting head of the NSF Council was Ion Iliescu, a former secretary of the RCP's Central Committee in charge of ideology until 1971, when his climb up the ladder of the party hierarchy was halted by a difference of opinion with Ceausescu on issues of party doctrine. Subsequently, Iliescu held several party appointments in the provinces, ending in the 1980s as the head of the Technical Publishing House in Bucharest. Petre Roman, the acting prime minister, did not have a previous career in the party *nomenklatura*; however, he had strong family links with it. Silviu Brucan, the acting minister of foreign affairs, and a sort of *eminence grise* of the NSF, had been the editor of the communist party newspaper *Scinteia* in the 1950s and held subsequent diplomatic offices. Finally, Alexandru Birladeanu, an expert of command economics, was another former member of the Politburo who accepted an NSF leadership position.

Less than a month after its formation, the NSF Council announced on 23 January 1990, its decision to enter the electoral contest as a political organization and compete in the first free elections since the Second World War. This declaration unleashed angry denouncements of the NSF, and enraged protesters took to the streets of Bucharest on 24 January. The cause of such an upheaval lay in the 180 degree turn of the NSF, which hitherto had maintained that it would exist and serve only as a caretaker, interim government with the main goal of organizing free elections. Formally, this moment appears as the birth of the political party named NSF, subsequently registered as such on 6 February. A Provisional Council of National Unity (PCNU) replaced the NSF Council and included, among its 250 members, representatives of the political parties (National Peasant Party, National Liberal Party) which were the most vocal opponents of the NSF. Nevertheless, two-thirds of the PCNU consisted of NSF members and supporters. Mustering a convenient majority in the PCNU, the country's pre-election proto-parliament, and dominating the government in its entirety, the NSF set out to achieve electoral victory at any imaginable price, grossly disregarding the rules of fair play. Chief among these efforts was to implement its original interpretation of democracy: pluralism meant only an NSF-dominated alliance of parties sharing the same orientation, pitted in a life-and-death fight against the opposition. The latter took shape in the form of all those political forces which attempted to criticize the NSF on the basis of a different approach to reform. The main parties which proposed substantially alternate programs were the 'historical parties', that is, the National Liberal Party, the National Peasant Christian Democratic Party, and the Romanian Social Democratic Party, which, having dominated Romania's political arena until the communists outlawed them in 1948, were resuscitated in the last days of December 1989. These three parties exhibited a strong anti-communist stance and aimed at a radical restructuring of society, while the NSF insisted on a general preservation of the status quo and its power position, embellished only by some cosmetic changes.

Very telling in this respect was the way NSF leaders interpreted such terms as 'democracy' and 'pluralism'. Prime Minister Roman defined pluralism as 'a new form of political coexistence ... where we [sic!] would allow any constructive tendency that will help rebuild the country ... a new form of political pluralism, so to say, based on maintaining and even consolidating the national consensus'.[2] According to Iliescu, 'democracy can exist even in a totalitarian regime, if the despot is a wise man'.[3] Such statements clearly reflect a way of thinking anchored in communist ideology: instead of being a right exercised by society from below, pluralism is a condition granted from above, by the government, which also enjoys 'the prerogative of defining the terms of consensus, according to the government's criteria'.[4] To many Romanians, Iliescu's pronouncement on democracy recalled the concept of 'socialist democracy' whereby party ideologues justified Ceausescu's dictatorial regime.

Although advocating consensus, the NSF, as the governing party, embarked on a path of polarizing Romania's society along a variety of lines, some following the same cleavages existing during the communist era, with a view of turning the divisions into electoral capital. The two most important sets of polarization became visible in the relationships among social classes, on the one hand, and between Romanians and the ethnic minorities, on the other hand. 'We work, we do not think', a popular slogan which originated in the spring of 1990, was used to incite a large segment of workers and peasants against the intellectuals, a strategy which recalled the practice of the communist era, when the working classes were eulogized, and the independent thinkers were persecuted. Repeatedly, the NSF mobilized workers in counter-demonstrations to rallies organized by opposition parties. The NSF propaganda depicted the historical parties as forces that wanted to set back the clock of history to the pre-communist times, reinstate social inequality and exploitation through privatization. Many of Romania's leading intellectuals, gathered in the Group for Social Dialog which published the journal *22*, advocated the reform of Romania's disastrous economy through rapid privatization, making it viable by opening it to free market mechanisms. The same intellectuals called for thoroughgoing democratic reforms, which would entail, first of all, a clear-cut break (both in ideology and leadership) with the communist past. On 11 March 1990, members of the Timisoara Society, a group of young intellectuals from the city where the anti-communist uprising started, issued the 'Timisoara Proclamation' which articulated the political convictions of the city's inhabitants.[5]   In inciting the workers and peasants against the intellectuals, the NSF exploited the fears of job insecurity that the process of privatization and economic restructuring would entail. It constantly presented itself as a guarantor of the status quo. The NSF found a wide audience for such rhetoric in small towns where one large factory employed the entire workforce.[6]

If the bloody events of December 1989 had forged a bond of solidarity between the Romanians and the other ethnic minorities, of which the Hungarians are the most numerous, during the first two months of 1990, ethnic enmity was soon to leave indelible marks on post-communist Romania. The anti-Hungarian themes of the Ceausescu years returned to public discourse, coated in a rhetoric invigorated by freedom-of-speech-as-freedom-to-hate.[7] The grievances the ethnic Hungarians sought to redress (legitimate minority rights to be observed in education, administration and so on) through the agency of their political organization, the Hungarian Democratic Federation of Romania (HDFR), have come, ever since, to be regarded as threats to Romania's national interest and territorial integrity. The initiative of this chauvinist revival rested with *Vatra Romaneasca* (Romanian Hearth), allegedly a Romanian cultural organization, which, however, aimed at mobilizing the Romanian majority in support of a future political platform. In such circumstances, the bloody inter-ethnic clashes in the Transylvanian city of Tirgu Mures on 19–21 March 1990, were an unwanted and tragic illustration of the extent of the radicalization of nationalist discourse and agitation.[8] The NSF government had played neutral at first, then it openly embraced *Vatra Romaneasca's* approach in the interpretation of events: the ethnic Hungarians bore the brunt of the blame because their radical demands had offended the Romanians. This has remained the official interpretation of the Tirgu Mures bloodshed, endorsed even by a parliamentary report. Seven years later, a symposium organized by the Pro-Europe League, a nongovernmental organization committed to promoting human rights and inter-ethnic understanding in Transylvania, addressed the same events and brought to light evidence that NSF leaders at both the national and local levels had been deeply involved in preparing the clashes, in mustering the mob of Romanian peasants to attack the Hungarians peacefully demonstrating in Tirgu Mures, and, finally, in covering up their involvement. The operations were carried out with the help of members of the former *Securitate*.[9] (Inauspiciously, the Tirgu Mures incident became the pretext for the NSF-led establishment to reconstitute the secret police under a new name: the Romanian Service of Information.)

The NSF succeeded in this divisive action because of a very thorough manipulation of the media, chiefly of national television. As the independent press reached only the urban population, and the state-owned distribution network refused to circulate it countrywide, television was practically the only medium through which information could be disseminated to people living in the countryside and in small towns. Viewers in these areas, which comprise the majority of Romania's population, could accept what was being presented on their screens because the post-1989 television (re-named Free Romanian Television) claimed to be a radical departure from the institution of Ceausescu's time. However, most of the programming staff (starting with producers and ending with anchors) were the same people who had put together programs praising the totalitarian regime and its leaders. Contradicting the assumed impartiality of the national TV channel, broadcasts of demonstrations organized by anti-NSF political parties were routinely presented as nefarious actions of forces aimed at destabilizing the new 'frail, democracy' (read NSF), thus plunging the country into civil unrest and threatening the average citizen's domestic tranquility. In keeping with the above-mentioned interpretation of pluralism, the NSF-controlled media exposed any political activity as a danger to stability and democracy. Furthermore, the rhetoric of Romanian TV systematically presented the NSF as the 'good guys' and all the other forces (whether 'historical parties' or civic organizations) advocating a genuine, clear-cut separation from communist practice as the 'bad guys'.[10]

With the same consistency, television helped in the manipulation of ethnic enmity. As early as January 1990, Iliescu, in a TV interview, without providing any concrete examples, asserted the existence of serious disturbances in east Transylvania, where the ethnically Hungarian population committed alleged atrocities against ethnic Romanians. The atmosphere was further vitiated by the biassed TV coverage of the clashes in Tirgu Mures in March 1990, as well as by recurring reports which all implied that the ethnic Hungarian minority constantly threatened the Romanian majority and worked toward the dismemberment of the Romanian national state.

In an atmosphere of general intolerance, the electoral campaign leading to the first free parliamentary and presidential elections on 20 May 1990, only exacerbated these divisions. Instead of deliniating a clear program of reforms in order to win over the electorate, the NSF, which had adopted the socialist symbol of the rose, concentrated all its forces on promoting an image of the chaos into which Romania had plunged following the instauration of democracy and political pluralism. Against this specter of general confusion the NSF appeared as the only force able to restore order and achieve a broad consensus for rebuilding the country. The media affiliated with the NSF (some national dailies, the majority of local dailies and the national TV channel) launched a ruthless crusade against any critic or electoral opponent, while Iliescu and his party were consistently introduced as the only viable political alternative for the country. Iliescu came into view as 'A President For Your Tranquility' on the party's political advertisements. At the same time the NSF mobilized the language and symbols of nationalism to present itself as the sole guarantor of Romania's sovereignty, independence and territorial integrity: a frequently chanted slogan of NSF supporters proclaimed that 'We shall never sell our country!'.[11]

The results of the 20 May elections showed that the NSF was the overwhelming choice of the great majority of voters (voter turnout: 86.2 per cent). In the presidential elections, running against two other candidates (Ion Ratiu of the National Peasant Christian Democratic Party, and Radu Campeanu representing the National Liberal Party), Iliescu received 85.07 per cent of the vote. In the parliamentary elections, the NSF obtained 66.31 per cent of votes (see Tables 7.1 and 7.2). In spite of numerous irregularities signaled by both national and international observers, the elections were pronounced as generally free and fair.[12]

Scholars agree that the NSF owed this electoral victory to its monopoly on government resources, ranging from television to food distribution networks. With such tools the NSF cast itself into the crude image of the saviour of the Romanian people: it rid the country of the Ceausescu dictatorship, it provided food and heat to a people who had been deprived of both before December 1989 and it appeared ready to do away with Romania's backwardness and to lead it back into the European family of nations. At the same time, the NSF was supposed to defend the country and its people from the vile schemes of its electoral opponents which all, ultimately, aimed at selling out Romania, either to the former exploiters who would be the sole beneficiaries of privatization, or to the foreigners whose interests would prevail over national

Table 7.1 Results of parliamentary elections in Romania, 1990 (Eligible voters: 17,200,722)

a. Assembly of Deputies, Voter turnout: 14,825,017 (86.2 per cent)

Political Party	Votes	Percentage of votes	Seats	Percentage of seats[1]
National Salvation Front	9,089,659	66.31	263	68.0
Hungarian Democratic Federation of Romania	991,601	7.23	29	7.5
National Liberal Party	879,290	6.41	29	7.5
Ecological Movement of Romania	358,864	2.62	12	3.1
National Peasant Christian Democratic Party	351,357	2.56	12	3.1
Romanian National Unity Party	290,875	2.12	9	2.3
Agrarian Democratic Party	250,403	1.80	9	2.3
Romanian Ecologist Party	232,212	1.69	8	2.1
Romanian Socialist Party	143,393	1.05	5	1.3
Romanian Social Party	73,014	0.53	2	0.5
Democratic Group of the Center	65,914	0.48	2	0.5
Others[2]	358,983	2.61	16	4.1
Parties failing to win seats	n.a.	4.59	–	–
Total			396	

b. Senate, Voter turnout 14,875,764 (86.5 per cent)

Political Party	Votes	Percentage of votes	Seats	Percentage of seats[1]
National Salvation Front	9,353,006	67.02	92	77.3
Hungarian Democratic Federation of Romania	1,004,353	7.20	12	10.1
National Liberal Party	985,094	7.06	10	7.6
National Peasant Christian Democratic Party	384,687	2.50	1	0.8
Ecological Movement of Romania	341,478	2.45	1	0.8
Romanian National Unity Party	300,473	2.15	2	1.7
Romanian Ecologist Party	192,574	1.38	1	0.8
Parties failing to win seats	n.a.	11.24	–	–
Total			119	

Notes:
1. Rounded figures; column does not total 100 per cent.
2. Sixteen other parties, each of which garnered less than 0.4 per cent of the vote and one seat in the Assembly of Deputies.

Source: Domnita Stefanescu, *Cinci ani din istoria Romaniei*, Bucharest: Editura Masina de scris, 1995, pp. 458–60, 468.

138

ones. In the words of Michael Shafir, 'The NSF thus became the first political formation encouraging xenophobia, which ... was targeted at the West and those said to represent its individualist values'.[13] The NSF also availed itself of the popularity of its leader, Iliescu, with whom most of the voters identified the party, rather than with a clear program for future action. Many voters considered Iliescu, in sharp contrast to Ceausescu, as a benign father figure, a guarantor of Romania's welfare.

Table 7.2 Results of presidential elections in Romania, 1990

Eligible voters: 17,200,722. Voter turnout: 14,826,611 (86.2 per cent)

Candidate	Votes	Percentage of votes
Ion Iliescu	12,323,489	85.07
Radu Campeanu	1,529,188	10.64
Ion Ratiu	617,007	4.29

Source: Domnita Stefanescu, *Cinci ani din istoria Romaniei*, Bucharest: Editura Masina de scris, 1995, pp. 458–60, 468.

Given the still murky, mysterious circumstances which brought it to power in December 1989, for the NSF, the May 1990 elections not only represented the peak of popularity among the voters, but they also represented its genuine, and ultimate, source of legitimation, or in the words of Robert Weiner – an act of 'founding'.[14] In contradistinction, Romanian analyst Vladimir Pasti sees in this victory the end of the NSF, rather than a moment of climax. For Pasti, the NSF was built as 'a simple organization of support for the election campaign .... As a political party it was useless once the elections were over'.[15] This interpretation is consistent with Pasti's view that in Romania political parties appeared in order 'to ensure for a small group of political leaders the legitimacy of holding positions in the state'.[16] Thus Pasti draws a not-so-fine line between the personalities at the top of the party, who enjoy all the visibility in public affairs, and the amorphous mass of rank-and-file membership whose sole *raison d'être* is to promote and maintain the former in leadership positions within the state. What normally would have bonded the leaders and the membership within the party – the existence of a clear ideology – was totally lacking in the case of the NSF.[17] This, in turn, means that party discipline is equated with unconditional support of the leaders, based on their authority, rather than on an ideological common ground. Needless to say, such a pattern comes very near to that of the Communist Party of Ceausescu's time, the only form of party the great majority of

Romanians were familiar with. This is also an explanation for the NSF's popularity with an electorate very much afraid of drastic change in the near future (as offered by the historical parties).

Having won the elections, the NSF comfortably settled into its power positions (presidency, parliament, government), and set out to muzzle any form of radical criticism directed against the new establishment. For this purpose the freshly installed administration relied less on the traditional repressive forces of the police and army, than on violence generated by pitting one segment of society against another. The latter was consistent with the NSF's practice of social polarization and its leaders' authoritarian frame of mind. The most obvious example is the 13–15 June rampage by some 10,000 coal miners from the Jiu Valley in Bucharest. The miners followed Iliescu's call to put an end to the encampment (in University Square) of anti-communist, anti-NSF demonstrators, and critics of the regime, whom he had earlier labeled as 'hoodlums' (in Romanian, *golani*). Armed with crowbars, truncheons and rubber hoses – and led by undercover secret police – the miners kept the city in a virtual stage of siege, ransacked opposition party headquarters, offices of civic and student organizations, attacked Romani-inhabited districts and beat up individuals whose appearance may have suggested the vaguest affinity with the opposition.[18] Such a blatant and gross infringement of basic human rights and democratic principles brought about international condemnation of the NSF government, dealing a harsh blow to the generally positive reputation Romania had enjoyed since the overthrow of communist dictatorship six months before. Inside the country, the opposition parties and civic groups perceived the 13–15 June miners' raid as a stern lesson in the authoritarianism that the newly elected regime stood ready to resort to in order to silence disobedient critical voices.

Beside this use of violence generated by one segment of society against other social groups, equally unexpected was the program of economic restructuring that the new government, headed by Petre Roman, set out to implement in August 1990. It was a program that took by surprise both those who had voted for the NSF and the opposition, for it incorporated the majority of radical pro-capitalist strategies that the opposition had advocated during the electoral campaign, and which the NSF had denounced as a program to sell out the country. It was this program that initiated a warming up of Romania's relations with the West, which had been chilled since June 1990. Nevertheless, as Tom Gallagher has pointed out, the announced privatization measures 'made an impression in west European capitals and financial centers among experts unfamiliar with the fact that government programs and rhetoric often bore even less relation to intentions than in other east European countries'.[19]

The implementation of the privatization program effected several results that were of major importance for the further evolution of the NSF. First of all, the NSF as the government party which set out to carry out economic reforms, was joined by a great number of new members, most of them drawn from all the echelons of state administration and from the former communist party *apparat*, as well as from the managers of economic units waiting to be privatized. As the first concrete steps of the economic reforms (deregulation of prices, cutting back of subsidies) began to take their toll on the ordinary citizen's budget and welfare, a second effect became noticeable: the overwhelming support of the population, whereby the NSF had won the elections with such a landslide, dwindled.

Linked to these two divergent developments, a third effect could be perceived by the end of 1990: the rift at the level of national leadership between the groups centered round Iliescu and Roman, respectively. The latter was interested in promoting a faster pace of economic reform, while the former, afraid of social explosions that might be caused by the newly introduced market-oriented mechanisms, sought to slow down the reforming process. The power struggle between the two leaders and their entourages came to a head at the first (and last) NSF national conference in April 1991 when most of the delegates gave their support to Roman. But this victory proved to be ephemeral for the prime minister. In September 1991, the coal miners from the Jiu Valley invaded Bucharest again, this time protesting against government economic policies. After two days of violent occupation of the parliament building, on 28 September Roman handed in his resignation in order to solve the political crisis. With order restored in the capital city, President Iliescu appointed Theodor Stolojan to form a caretaker government. Henceforth the power struggle between Iliescu and Roman became public, Roman presenting himself as a champion of democracy and associating Iliescu with the communist mentality and methods from Ceausescu's time.[20]

2 FRAGMENTATION OF THE LEFT

The subsequent performances of the NSF in the official confrontations with Romania's electorate showed the consequences of its widening split. The 9 December 1991 national referendum on the new Constitution elaborated by the NSF-dominated parliament showed a weakening of the party's position (on a 69.7 per cent voter turnout, 78.5 per cent of voters approved and 14.1 per cent disapproved the Constitution), though still enjoying a comfortable endorsement. However, until the local elections of 9 February 1992, the NSF witnessed increased difficulties. First, there came a reduced appeal to the voters due to the unpopular austerity measures introduced by the government. Second, a breach opened between Roman and Iliescu, with the president resorting to unconstitutional interventions in the party's struggle in order to mobilize his own supporters (the Constitution prohibits the head of state's membership in any political party). Another serious issue the NSF had to factor into its electoral preparation was the strengthened opposition. Whereas in the general elections of 1990 the poor performance of the opposition had also been conducive to the NSF's resounding victory, by 1992 the opposition significantly enhanced its standing, especially among the inhabitants of large urban centers.

Under such circumstances the 9 February 1992 local elections highlighted the weakened support for the NSF among the electorate: it managed to secure only 33 per cent of seats in local administrative bodies. This percentage was garnered mainly in the rural areas, still home to the greater part of Romania's population, where 'the influence that local power-holders such as the local police chief, the doctor, and sometimes the village priest had over voters often counted in its favor'.[21] This electoral result acted as a wake-up call for the NSF to put up a better show at the national elections in September 1992; it also showed that, unlike in 1990, the country's electorate had become more experienced and demonstrated its readiness to give its votes to political forces other than the incumbent one.

The immediate consequence of the local elections was the breakup of the NSF into two rival parties, as a final expression of the conflict between the factions loyal to Iliescu and Roman. Based on his support coming from territorial NSF branches, the latter succeeded in preserving the same name ('National Salvation Front') and emblem (the rose) for his new party. Nevertheless, the majority of the parliamentary party remained within the old organizational structure, adopted only a slightly different name ('Democratic National Salvation Front' – DNSF) and symbol (three roses). Neither party formulated a clear cut program, rather they embraced catchwords under whose banner they attacked each other. 'Social security' was the DNSF's choice, while the NSF opted for 'democracy'. However, the discourse did not incorporate any further elaboration on how these two concepts would be employed in carrying out the reform of Romania. Although the confrontational rhetoric became quite heated, the energy seemed to go to waste because, rather than being antagonistic, the two terms are interconnected.[22]

In the month-long campaign that preceded the national elections of 27 September 1992, besides the Roman-led NSF, the DNSF had to compete with fairly powerful nationalist parties (the Party of Romanian National Unity and the Greater Romania Party) and a strengthened but not very coordinated opposition (Democratic Convention). Even so, the DNSF still managed to win the elections, garnering 27.72 per cent of the votes for the Chamber of Deputies (where it secured 34.3 per cent of seats), and 28.29 per cent of votes for the Senate (34.3 per cent of seats). Iliescu, running in the DNSF's colors,

Table 7.3 Results of parliamentary elections in Romania, 1992

Eligible voters: 16,380,663. Voter turnout: 12,496,430 (76.3 per cent)

a. Chamber of Deputies

Political party	Votes	Percentage of votes	Seats	Percentage of seats[2]
Democratic National Salvation Front	3,015,708	27.72	117	34.3
Democratic Convention	2,177,144	20.01	82	24.0
National Salvation Front	1,108,500	10.19	43	12.6
Romanian National Unity Party	839,586	7.72	30	8.8
Hungarian Democratic Federation of Romania	811,290	7.46	27	7.9
Greater Romania Party	424,061	3.90	16	4.7
Socialist Party of Labor	330,378	3.00	13	3.8
Others[3]	155,773	1.40	13	3.8
Parties failing to win seats[4]	n.a.	18.60	–	–
Total			341	

143

b. Senate

Political party	Votes	Percentage of votes	Seats	Percentage seats[1]
Democratic National Salvation	3,102,201	28.29	49	34.3
Democratic Convention	2,210,722	20.16	34	23.8
National Salvation Front	1,139,033	10.39	18	12.6
Romanian National Unity Party	890,410	8.12	14	9.8
Hungarian Democratic Federation of Romania	831,469	7.59	12	8.4
Greater Romania Party	422,545	3.85	6	4.2
Democratic Agrarian Party	362,427	3.31	5	3.5
Socialist Party of Labor	349,470	3.19	5	3.5
Parties failing to win seats[4]	n.a.	11.24	–	–
Total			119	

Notes:
1. Rounded figures; column does not total 100 per cent.
2. Thirteen other parties, each of which garnered less than 0.5 per cent of the vote and secured one seat in the Chamber of Deputies.
3. Fifty-nine parties.
4. Fifty-seven parties.

Source: Domnita Stefanescu, *Cinci ani din istoria Romaniei*, Bucharest: Editura Masina de scris, 1995, pp. 458–60, 468.

was re-elected President of Romania, with a comfortable majority of over 60 per cent (see Tables 7.3 and 7.4). These results, although not as stunning as those of the 1990 election, still showed that most Romanians preferred to march along the same old road they had been used to, rather than choose a yet unknown path, that of radical reforms. The old road was paved with promises of social safety and anti-corruption slogans. In the DNSF's interpretation, the issue of social safety meant the preservation of social peace through maintaining the heavily subsidized, state-owned economic sectors, especially the giant industrial units created during the communist decades. In spite of their ever-increasing debt, these inefficient behemoths were kept operating mainly because they provided employment to a sizable segment of Romania's workforce. The declaration of war against corruption was intended to direct attention away from the substantive issue of economic reform to the endemic corruption noticeable at almost all levels of society. Laying the blame of the worsening economic conditions largely on corruption, rather than on faulty policy, betrays, in fact, the same utopian way of reasoning Romanians had been used to since the decades of Ceausescu's communist rule: the policies were impeccable, but those called to carry them out did not behave as 'expected'. On the other hand, the war on corruption itself was a totally empty slogan, because the DNSF had relied on the material support of several 'cardboard billionaires' (who, in two years' time, made their fortunes through dubious transactions facilitated by the NSF-led government). At the same time, the press (in 1992 still the most independent form of the media) had revealed a series of cases in which highly placed members of the ruling party had abused their power with impunity in order to obtain personal gains. It was also the time when the Caritas pyramid scheme flourished and many people had invested their savings in the hope of an eightfold return after six months.

In the countryside, the national elections followed the same pattern as the February 1992 local elections: local officials managed to elicit the majority of votes in favor of the DNSF by 'making it clear that political loyalty was the sole criterion for state resources being granted to them'.[23] One should not forget that local administrations still had their budgets allocated by the central government in Bucharest.

A final major factor explaining the DNSF's electoral victory was, just as in 1990, the total domination of the television by the government, which had hitherto blocked every previous attempt to set up independent TV stations. The DNSF could use television programs to promote its platform and image, as well as to denigrate the other political competitors, not only during the election campaign, but also throughout the entire period since winning the elections in 1990.

Lacking an absolute majority in the newly elected parliament, the DNSF formed a coalition government with two extreme nationalist parties (the Party

Table 7.4   Results of presidential elections in Romania, 1992

First round, 27 September 1992
Eligible voters: 16,380,663; voter turnout: 12,496,430 (76.3 per cent)

Candidate	Votes	Percentage of votes
Ion Iliescu	5,633,456	47.34
Emil Constantinescu	3,717,006	31.24
Gheorghe Funar	1,294,388	10.88
Caius Traian Dragomir	564,655	4.75
Ioan Minzatu	362,485	3.05
Mircea Druc	326,866	2.75

Second round, 11 October 1992
Eligible voters: 16,597,508. Voter turnout: 12,153,810 (73.2 per cent)

Candidate	Votes	Percentage of votes
Ion Iliescu	7,393,429	61.43
Emil Constantinescu	4,641,207	38.57

Source: Domnita Stefanescu, *Cinci ani din istoria Romaniei*, Bucharest: Editura Masina de scris, 1995, pp. 458–60, 468.

of Romanian National Unity and the Greater Romania Party) and an avowed neo-communist party (the Party of Socialist Labor). The new government, headed by Nicolae Vacaroiu, a highly-placed bureaucrat of the Ceausescu regime, maintained through its policies the status quo in the economy: it avoided extensive reforms, favoring instead the formation of a financial oligarchy made up of former members of the *nomenklatura* and the secret police. Corruption continued unchecked. Whatever privatization measures were undertaken, it was only under pressure from international lending institutions. Even in 1995 the private sector had a narrow share, about 12 per cent, of the nation's industrial output. And only at the end of that year was a voucher privatization program begun. At the same time, the official rhetoric became heavily tainted with· the chauvinistic discourse of the DNSF's nationalist allies. Relations between the Romanian majority and the ethnic Hungarian minority became tense again due to the government's reluctance to observe the standards of the Council of Europe concerning minority rights in local administration and education.

At its July 1993 convention the Democratic National Salvation Front changed its name to the Party of Social Democracy in Romania (PSDR), after it merged with three other small parties (the Republican Party, the Cooperatist Party and the Socialist Democratic Party) which hitherto had played a totally insignificant part on the political scene, being mere puppets of the DNSF. Oliviu Gherman, a former professor of 'scientific socialism' at the University of Craiova, became the president of the party; Adrian Nastase became executive president. However, the real guiding force of the party remained Ion Iliescu, the President of Romania, who, according to the Constitution, could not belong to any party.

Until the end of 1996, the PSDR and Iliescu dominated Romanian politics and society. This position materialized in an authoritarian (though not monolithic) regime (called by V. Tismaneanu 'self-styled majoritarianism'[24]), which showed little tolerance for diversity and criticism. This regime was buttressed by eight secret police branches, and by the co-optation of the Romanian Orthodox Church.[25]   Throughout the 1992–96 period of government the PSDR tried to appropriate segments of bureaucracy at both the local and national levels, either by recruitment or by replacement of personnel with party members. Nationalism and populism permeated, and often supplanted, political discourse. All these characteristics prompted scholars to see a similarity between Romania and Argentina under Juan Domingo Peron.[26]

3 THE DECLINE OF THE LEFT

The national elections of November 1996 put an end to the first phase of post-communist transition: the PSDR and Iliescu were voted out of power. In the race for the two chambers of the parliament the PSDR obtained less than one-quarter of all the votes (Chamber of Deputies, 21.52 per cent and Senate 23.08 per cent), while in the race for the presidency, Iliescu won the first round with 32.25 per cent of the votes, but lost in the second round, garnering only 45.59 per cent (see Tables 7.5 and 7.6).

The electoral defeat of the PSDR can be explained by the electorate's ultimate dissatisfaction with the way in which the country was governed and gradually rising aspirations for radical change in society, politics and the economy. By 1996 civil society had become more developed. A sizable segment of the population considered more carefully the existing political choices. The newly developed independent cable TV channels and the press provided alternative sources of information and analyses, thus substantially diminishing the public's reliance on government-sponsored media. Applied successfully in the elections of 1990 and 1992, the formula of playing on the electorate's fears no longer worked out. The territorial distribution of votes also showed that the PSDR's support was limited mainly to less industrially

Table 7.5 Results of parliamentary elections in Romania, 3 November 1996

Eligible voters: 17,218,663. Voter turnout: 13, 088,388 (76.01 per cent)

a. Chamber of Deputies
Valid ballots: 12,238,746 (93.51 per cent). Invalid ballots: 834,687 (6.38 per cent)

Political party or coalition	Votes	Percentage of votes	Seats	Percentage of seats
Democratic Convention of Romania	3,692,321	30.17	122	35.57
Party of Social Democracy of Romania	2,633,860	21.52	91	26.53
Social Democratic Union	1,582,231	12.93	53	15.45
Hungarian Democratic Federation of Romania	812,628	6.64	25	7.29
Greater Romania Party	546,430	4.46	19	5.54
Romanian National Unity Party	533,348	4.36	18	5.25
Ethnic minorities other than Hungarian[1]			15	4.37
Parties failing to win seats[2]	2,437,928	19.92	–	–
Total			343	

b. Senate
Valid ballots: 12,287,671 (93.88 per cent). Invalid ballots: 785,977 (6.01 per cent)

Political party or coalition	Votes	Percentage of votes	Seats	Percentage of seats
Democratic Convention of Romania	3,772,084	30.70	53	37.06
Party of Social Democracy of Romania	2,836,011	23.08	41	28.67
Social Democratic Union	1,617,384	13.16	23	16.08
Hungarian Democratic Federation of Romania	837,760	6.82	11	7.69
Greater Romania Party	558,026	4.54	8	5.59
Romanian National Unity Party	518,962	4.22	7	4.90
Parties failing to win seats[2]	2,147,444	17.48	–	–
Total			143	

Notes:

1. The Constitution provides for each of the registered 15 ethnic minorities to send one representative to the Chamber of Deputies. The Hungarian minority is not included in this group because it is represented by its own party, the Hungarian Democratic Federation of Romania, which competes in elections.

2. Other parties, each of which garnered less than the required threshold of 4.00 per cent of the vote.

Source: http://diasan.vsat.ro/aleg96

149

Table 7.6   Results of presidential elections in Romania, 1996

First Round, 3 November 1996
Eligible voters: 17,218,654. Voter turnout: 13,088,388 (76.01 per cent).
Valid ballots: 12,652,900 (96.67 per cent). Invalid ballots: 426,545 (3.26 per cent)

Candidate	Votes	Percentage of votes
Ion Iliescu	4,081,093	32.25
Emil Constantinescu	3,569,941	28.21
Petre Roman	2,598,545	20.54
Gyorgy Frunda	761,411	6.02
Corneliu Vadim Tudor	597,508	4.72
Gheorghe Funar	407,828	3.22
Tudor Mohora	160,387	1.27
Nicolae Manolescu	90,122	0.71
Adrian Paunescu	87,163	0.69
Ioan Pop de Popa	59,752	0.47
George Muntean	54,218	0.43
Radu Campeanu	43,780	0.35
Nutu Anghelina	43,319	0.34
Constantin Mudava	39,477	0.31
Constantin Niculescu	30,045	0.24
Nicolae Militaru	28,311	0.22

Second round, 17 November 1996
Eligible voters: 17,230,654. Voter turnout: 13,078,883 (75.90 per cent).
Valid ballots: 12, 972,485 (99.19 per cent). Invalid ballots: 102,579 (0.78 per cent)

Candidate	Votes	Percentage of votes
Ion Iliescu	5,914,579	45.59
Emil Constantinescu	7,057,906	54.41

Source: http://diasan.vsat.ro/aleg96

developed counties in the south and east of Romania (53.77 per cent in Calarasi county, 46.69 per cent in Botosani county, 45.34 per cent in Vaslui county and, 45.03 per cent in Neamt county, 44.71 per cent in Vrancea county, 44.7 per cent in Olt county[27]), a situation that first became visible in the elections of 1992; while Transylvania emerged as the area with the fewest backers of the PSDR's policies.

The electoral defeat precipitated a series of defections from the party, mainly at the convention held in June 1997, when several prominent politicians (Teodor Melescanu, Iosif Boda, Mircea Cosea, Viorel Salagean and Marian Enache) left the PSDR. They criticized the party for its lack of a genuine will to expel its corrupt members, as well as for its reluctance to renew itself by adopting a program that would blend social-democratic and social-liberal principles.[28] The defectors set up a new party, the Alliance for Romania, with a centrist platform.

The national convention of the PSDR streamlined the leadership of the party by only five vice- presidents. Iliescu, who rejoined the PSDR immediately after his term as President of Romania ended, was elected the party's leader, and his right hand, Adrian Nastase, became first vice-president. The convention also adopted a new political program which defines the PSDR as a modern social-democratic party. Its doctrine represents a 'synthesis of political democracy and social and economic democracy'. Although the party declares itself to conform to the principles of European social democracy, the program specifies 'that the party's interests are superseded by the long-term interests of the Romanian nation'.[29]

Since its electoral defeat, the PSDR is the main opposition party in the Romanian parliament. Its strategy consists mainly in obstructing the reform process initiated by the new government and in playing up to that segment of the population which might suffer most from the cuts in state subsidies for basic goods and services (for example, retired people; the associations of 'revolutionaries from 1989' whose privileged status was terminated by the new government; potential unemployed workers resulting from economic restructuring). Another strategic line is to endorse different unions in their struggle against the deterioration in living standards. Starting in late 1998, the PDSR escalated its attacks on the ruling coalition and its government, calling for early elections in the spring of 1999. An opinion poll taken in November 1998 shows that the PSDR enjoys 26 per cent of voter support, only 3 per cent behind the Democratic Convention of Romania which is the main component of the governing coalition. However, Iliescu would be supported for president by only 22 per cent of those interviewed.[30]

The PSDR holds the most prominent position on the left side of the political spectrum. Starting off in a more radical position when it was known as the NSF and DNSF, beginning in 1996, it gradually redefined itself as a left-of-center political unit. Throughout the years of post-communist transition other parties can be identified as operating in various sectors of the left. One must state from the beginning that acute rivalry, rather than collaboration based on an ideological affinity, characterizes all the parties of the left.

To the far left of the spectrum one can find the Socialist Party of Labor

(SPL), led by Ilie Verdet and Adrian Paunescu. This party gathers together communist era nostalgics and advocates a Leninist policy, opposing privatization and a market economy, favoring an authoritarian approach which would terminate democratic 'disorder'. Anyone familiar with Romanian communism would recognize from the first glance that the two leaders of the party were important pillars of the Ceausescu regime. Verdet had been a member of the Executive Committee of the Politburo of the Romanian Communist Party, and Paunescu had achieved the dubious fame of being the loudest of Ceausescu's court poets and the leader of a traveling show that extolled the RCP's policies. The SPL gathered its support among the former activists of the Communist Party, many of whom had been rejected by the already existing parties. (The SPL was set up late in 1990.) Also the SPL forged political capital from the discontent generated by the transition period, focussing its activity on the large working-class centers that depended on huge foundries and machine-building plants. By advocating state support for such enterprises and good management by former local party bosses presented as patriots, the SPL managed to build up power bases in the recently urbanized areas in Oltenia and southern Moldavia.[31] At the same time the party rhetoric, especially as delivered by Paunescu, the party's vice-president, draped itself in nationalism. In the elections of 1992, the SPL managed to secure 13 seats in the Chamber of Deputies and five seats in the Senate (see Table 7.3). Given the party's opposition to large-scale privatization and to reform in general, the DNSF co-opted the SPL into the governing coalition. It was the climax of the SPL's evolution: some of its politicians were promoted to important government positions (as state secretaries). Although it did not receive any ministerial positions because of the DNSF's fear that a high-profile alliance with an avowed successor of the communist party might tarnish its image, the SPL supported all the government's initiatives in the legislature. A peculiar situation arose: while permanently endorsing with its votes the Vacaroiu government, the SPL continuously criticized the government. In this way the party leaders could reap all the perks from a government that relied on their votes, meanwhile declining any responsibility for the acts of that government. This symbiotic relationship with the dominant PSDR continued until the end of 1995 when the PSDR, concerned with its image abroad, tried to distance itself from its coalition partners whose positions were either extreme nationalist or extreme left. This marked the beginning of the party's decline. Before the elections of 1996, Tudor Mohora, one of the vice-presidents, split from the PSL and formed his own party, the Socialist Party, which, in its program, recognizes the need to reform the economy on market-based principles. In the 1996 elections, neither the SPL nor the Socialists could get enough votes to rise over the threshold of 4 per cent necessary to enter parliament. In the first round of the presidential race, Mohora received 1.27

per cent of the votes, while Paunescu garnered 0.69 per cent (see Table 7.6).

At the other end of the left sector of the political spectrum. one finds the Social Democratic Union (SDU), an alliance positioned close to the center, leaning only a little to the left. The SDU came into existence in 1996, when the Democratic Party and the Romanian Social Democrat Party (RSDP) agreed to participate on a joint platform in that year's elections. Although united in this alliance, the two parties have quite different roots and histories.

The Romanian Social Democrat Party is one of the country's 'historic parties', that is, those which could look back to a long tradition before the Second World War. The RSDP was revived in the first days of January 1990, and sees itself as a continuation of the traditional party with the same name which was absorbed by the communists into the Romanian Workers' Party in February 1948. In the elections of May 1990 it ran by itself and managed to obtain only two seats in the Chamber of Deputies (see Table 7.1). As the party was committed to upholding the principles of democracy and to struggle for social protection for any category of working people, after the miners' rampage in Bucharest in June 1990, it joined the camp of the opposition parties which were calling for the implementation of thoroughgoing democratic reforms and the removal of former communists then in power. Eventually it became a member of the Democratic Convention, an umbrella organization of the opposition parties, and participated in the 1992 elections as a member of that body. The RSDP remained a member of the Convention until 1995, when it was expelled because of its refusal to recognize the leading role of the National Peasant Christian Democratic Party. In order to be able to compete successfully in future elections, the RSDP accepted the Democratic Party's proposal to run on a joint slate. This electoral union proved beneficial, because it now holds ten seats in the Chamber of Deputies and one in the Senate.

The predecessor of the Democratic Party (DP) came into being in 1992 when Roman and his faction split away from the Iliescu camp. As the latter set up the Democratic National Salvation Front, Roman's group kept the name of National Salvation Front, to which later the name of Democratic Party was appended. After the elections of 1992 the name 'National Salvation Front' was dropped, the party's name remaining that of the Democratic Party. The uncontested leader of the party is Petre Roman, who, since having his own party, had become an advocate of democracy and boasted of his ability to implement reform together with his team of experts. From this standpoint he criticized the Iliescu regime, slowly building up his party's constituency mainly in urban areas. In the elections of 1992, Roman's party obtained a little more than 10 per cent of votes, and its presidential candidate, Caius Traian Dragomir, received 4.75 per cent of the votes in the first round (see Tables 7.3 and 7.4). During the 1992–96 legislature the DP remained in opposition, criticizing the government's slow pace of privatization, as well as the lack of democratic reforms. However, whenever the center-right parties raised the issue of restitution of private property seized during the communist decades, the DP voted against it, an attitude that foreshadowed its voting behavior in the 1996–98 period. The DP's credibility of its intentions and sincere dedication to democracy also came into question whenever it reiterated the need to fight corruption: it is quite well known that Roman and other DP leaders had acquired bits of property at cheap, preferential prices through abuse of office.

In order to have a good showing in the 1996 elections, the DP arranged the alliance with the RSDP, forming the Social Democratic Union. This joint platform strengthened both parties' electoral chances; indeed, the SDU won an average of some 13 per cent of the votes (12.93 per cent for the Chamber of Deputies, and 13.16 per cent for the Senate). In the first round of the presidential race Roman received 20.54 per cent of the votes (see Tables 7.5 and 7.6). Roman became Speaker of the Senate, the third highest office in the country (after that of President and Prime Minister). Because of these results, the center-right alliance of the Democratic Convention of Romania co-opted the SDU, as well as the Hungarian Democratic Federation of Romania, into a coalition government. The DP holds four ministerial appointments.

Although the electorate expected that the new center-right administration, inaugurated in December 1996, would start in earnest to implement the long awaited reforms that the Iliescu regime had failed to initiate, soon infighting among the members of the coalition ground all movement on policy initiatives to a halt. The DP parliamentarians and ministers blocked the Convention's bills concerning the restitution of private property, the redistribution of land among peasants and access to *Securitate* files. This obstruction led to the resignation of Prime Minister Victor Ciorbea in April 1998 and to the formation of a new government headed by Radu Vasile. However these issues have not been solved yet, and the DP started again to accuse the government of not implementing much awaited reform – although the DP uses its parliamentary weight to obstruct reform legislation. Such accusations took the time away from solving substantive issues connected with the implementation of economic reform. Only when the International Monetary Fund exerted pressure on the government, did the DP agree to collaborate in carrying out reforms. The repeated obstruction of the work of the government and the recurrent criticism of its coalition partners makes the DP appear as an opposition party, rather than a direct participant in government. Such behavior certainly lowered the DP's popularity: the poll taken in November 1998 shows merely 14 per cent of those interviewed support the party, while only 9 per cent would like to see Roman as President of Romania.[32]

For Romanians and foreign observers alike, the aims of the left-wing parties still lack clarity. As shown above, the only party that can be called a genuine social-democratic party is the small RSDP. All the others were created hastily, mainly for purposes of legitimating various segments of the population associated with the former communist party. They remained viable by resorting to manipulative tactics that played on the apprehensions of an inexperienced electorate, unaccustomed to democratic practices. As the general elections of 1996 had proved, such tactics are no longer a guarantee of success, nor can they be used as sufficient substitutes for well-delineated plans of action. So far, their professed allegiance to social democracy has not resulted in policies that fit the social-democratic agenda.

The low level of political culture characterizing contemporary Romania can account for a lack in both consistency and doctrinary substance on the part of the country's political parties. Until the communist period, the country had a low level of industrialization and the working class was not too numerous. The social democratic party representing the working class did not cut a significant figure on a political scene dominated by centrist and right-wing parties. The Romanian Communist Party, forced underground in 1924, played a minuscule role in the mobilization of workers, who adhered to the fascist movement of the Iron Guard. After the second World War, throughout the four decades of communist rule, the RCP promoted a consistent Stalinist policy which, in spite of some surface changes, had never been reformed on the basis of ideology. Unlike in Hungary or Czechoslovakia, no attempt to refine or to make more palatable the one party regime was recorded. Starting with the 1960s, the rigid doctrine promoted by the RCP became ever more tinged with the colors of nationalism, evolving into the hallmark of Romania's dictatorial communism under Ceausescu. This unhappy combination of Stalinism and nationalism, whereby a dogma is reinforced by another intolerant ideology, has had deeply-ingrained effects on post-communist Romanian society. Tom Gallagher points out that 'authoritarian conditioning lasting forty-five years meant that many Romanians existed who, at least in 1990, were more at ease with a single political grouping along the lines of a one-party arrangement to be found in post-colonial Africa: dissent might be tolerated provided it was contained under the large umbrella of the single party'.[33] Seen from this perspective, the practice of the post-communist political scene in Romania reveals that the passive political culture, setting little value on participation, emerges as an extension of the four decades of communism. In such circumstances, as Vladimir Tismaneanu noted, the political parties appear as coalitions of personal or group affinities, rather than representing diverse ideologies contending in the political arena.[34]

Although the parties on the post-communist left all claimed to stand for the protection of social interest, the communal values they primarily advocated were those of nationalism. This shows another line of continuity with both

Ceausescu's regime and the interwar period. Nationalism has proved again an efficient 'source of legitimacy for a ruling elite which finds it difficult to appeal convincingly to citizens on the basis of its domestic socio-economic record or fidelity to democratic principles'.[35] The abundant populist nationalist rhetoric promoted mainly by the National Salvation Front, its successor, the Romanian Socialist Democracy Party, or the Party of Socialist Labor, relying on various 'fantasies of salvation' meant to magically solve all the problems of society, only delays the establishment of a truly democratic political public space and renders the newly established constitutional mechanism ineffective.

Against the background of changes brought about by the elections of 1996, the left still has to take into account Romania's special needs. In the economy, the most urgent necessity is privatization; politically, the goal of all parties is Romania's integration into NATO and the European Union. Dealing with these needs, the left can mature and clarify its ideology and objectives, while finally shedding the burden of the communist past.

NOTES

1. Bogdan Szajkowski, *Romania: New Political Parties of Eastern Europe and the Soviet Union* (London: Longman, 1991), p. 220.
2. *Adevarul* (31 December 1989).
3. *22* (11 May 1990).
4. Vladimir Socor, 'Political Parties Emerging', *Report on Eastern Europe* **1** (16 February 1990): 33.
5. Article 7 of the 'Timisoara Proclamation' states: 'Timisoara started the revolution against the entire Communist regime and its entire *nomenklatura*, and certainly not in order to give an opportunity to a group of anti-Ceausescu dissidents within the RCP to take over the rein of political power. Their presence at the head of the country makes the death of our heroes senseless'. *Foreign Broadcast Information Service – East Europe* (4 April 1990): 60–63.
6. J.F. Brown, *Hopes and Shadows: Eastern Europe After Communism* (Durham: Duke University Press, 1994), p. 96.
7. In this respect, see Paul Hockenos, *Free to Hate: The Rise of the Right in Post-communist Eastern Europe* (London: Routledge, 1993).
8. On 19 March 1990, mobs of Romanian peasants, incited and bussed into town by political agitators, attacked the offices of the HDFR. The incidents escalated into vicious street fights, fanned rather than quelled by the police and the army. The noted Hungarian writer Suto Andras was so severely beaten that he lost an eye.
9. *Info PRO EUROPA*, no. 2, 1997.
10. Social psychological studies have shown that repeated categorization of people engenders 'we-feeling' and in-group preference, as well as a corresponding distancing from and bias against out-groups. See Henri Tajfel, 'Experiments in Intergroup Discrimination', *Science* **223**, 11 (1970): 96–102.

11. For a very sensitive analysis of how the NSF used the media in order to achieve its electoral goal, see Georgeta Pourchot, 'Mass Media and Democracy in Romania: Lessons from the Past, Prospects for the Future', in Lavinia Stan (ed) *Romania in Transition* (Brookfield: Dartmouth Publishing Company, 1997), pp. 67–90.

12. For instances of electoral fraud, see 'News From Romania: Election Report', *Helsinki Watch* (May 1990).

13. Michael Shafir, 'The Revival of the Political Right in Post-communist Romania', in Joseph Held (ed), *Democracy and Right-wing Politics in Eastern Europe in the 1990s* (Boulder: Westview, 1993), p. 157.

14. Robert Weiner, 'Democratization in Romania', in Stan (ed), pp. 3–23.

15. Vladimir Pasti, *The Challenges of Transition: Romania in Transition* (Boulder: Westview, 1997), p. 215.

16. Ibid., p. 212.

17. Ibid., p. 215.

18. It was not the first time that Iliescu had relied on the violence of the miners in his attempt to silence criticism of his authoritarian policies: on 29 January and 19 February, in the wake of anti-government protest rallies, several thousand miners arrived in the capital and attacked the headquarters of the historical parties as well the offices of newspapers with an anti-NSF orientation.

19. Tom Gallagher, *Romania after Ceausescu: The Politics of Intolerance* (Edinburgh: Edinburgh University Press, 1995), p. 106.

20. Michael Shafir, *RFE-RL Research Report* 1, No. 3 (24 January 1992).

21. Gallagher, p. 123.

22. For a more detailed analysis of this power struggle see Pasti, pp. 225–6.

23. Gallagher, p. 125.

24. Vladimir Tismaneanu, 'Romanian Exceptionalism? Democracy, Ethnocracy, and Uncertain Pluralism in Post-Ceausescu Romania', in Karen Dawisha and Bruce Parrott (eds), *Politics, Power, and the Struggle for Democracy in South–East Europe* (Cambridge: Cambridge University Press, 1997), p. 422.

25. For the relationship between the Romanian Orthodox Church and political power, see Alina Mungiu-Pippidi, 'The Ruler and the Patriarch: The Romanian Eastern Orthodox Church in Transition', *East European Constitutional Review* (Spring 1998): 85–91.

26. Brown, p. 104; and Tismaneanu, pp. 433, 439.

27. http://diasan.vsat.ro/deputati96/owa/aleg.parlg?idl=1&grp=2 &crp=0

28. *Ziua* (19 June 1997).

29. Programul politic al Partidului Democratiei Sociale din Romania, p. 1, http://www.pdsr.ro/html/index.html

30. *Adevarul* (27 November 1998).

31. Pasti, p. 231.

32. *Adevarul* (27 November 1998).

33. Tom Gallagher, 'The Emergence of New Party Systems and Transitions to Democracy: Romania and Portugal Compared', in Geoffrey Pridham and Paul G. Lewis (eds), *Stabilising Fragile Democracies: Comparing New Pary Systems in Southern and Eastern Europe* (London and New York: Routledge, 1996), p. 212.

34. Vladimir Tismaneanu, *Fantasies of Salvation: Democracy, Nationalism and Myth in Postcommunist Europe* (Princeton: Princeton University Press, 1998), p. 55. In this respect Gallagher states unequivocally that the National Salvation Front, which had emerged from the party apparatus, lacked a clearcut ideology, its primary concern being 'to protect a set of caste interests in an altered set of circumstances'. op. cit., p. 214.

35. Ibid., pp. 221–2.

8. Understanding the Left and Its Future

Charles Bukowski and Barnabas Racz

Clearly, understanding the past, present and future of the political left in post-communist systems represents an enormous challenge. Such a conclusion should be self-evident, but the research presented in this volume provides concrete evidence of the complex nature of the phenomenon of a renewed left in former party-states. In each country examined here the left has traveled a singular path following the collapse of communism, and it continues to play a unique role in the political processes of these countries. Nevertheless, among the differences exist certain parallels, emerging primarily out of the transition from authoritarian rule all of these countries experienced as well as their subsequent attempts to consolidate democracy.

We return first, however, to the issue of defining the left. A broad definition of the left was chosen to permit an examination of more than just the former communist ruling parties. By and large the country studies demonstrate that it has been the direct successors to the communist parties that have enjoyed the most success politically among parties of the left. But, with the exception of Russia, all of the communist successor parties examined in the case studies have remade themselves thoroughly during the transition to democracy. The concept of the political left as it pertains to post-communist political systems is malleable, and it is subject to mutations according to time and place. The country studies indicate that a radical left (that is, communist leaning) renaissance is unlikely, but moderate left principles and economic policies penetrate both centrist and right currents in most countries, as all major political parties realize that they are unable to exclude concerns with social justice from their political platforms. The political climate of Slovenia is most reflective of this phenomenon. As Fink-Hafner notes, a strong current of social democracy pervades Slovenia's political culture, and all of Slovenia's major political parties have incorporated this sentiment into their campaign messages. As a result, a strong concern for social justice does not necessarily translate into automatic support for the successor United List of Social Democrats or for the Social Democratic Party, even though both have had some electoral success. The strong sentiment for social justice in Slovenia is also reflected in the country's privatization program which has permitted a majority of enterprises (more than two-thirds, according to Fink-Hafner) to privatize through employee ownership. Thus while the distinction between traditional left and right is still valid in post-communist systems, it has become considerably more blurred and cannot be defined solely in terms of political parties.

As was argued in Chapter 1, the key categories of challenges raised by attempts at democratic consolidation provide a good starting point for developing some conclusions about the experiences of the left described in the country studies.

1. *Historical legacy* Among the case studies, the left in Lithuania and Slovenia seem to have the most positive historical legacy. In Lithuania the reformed communists of the Lithuanian Democratic Labor Party could point to their break with the Communist Party of the Soviet Union in 1989 as a source of public good will. Similarly in Slovenia it was that republic's League of Communists that broke with Yugoslavia's League of Communists and oversaw Slovenia's transition to democratic rule in 1990. The Hungarian left, particularly the Hungarian Socialist Party, also enjoyed benefits from a reformist past. Racz demonstrates that a moderate amount of nostalgia exists for the communist past, while warning that the electorate possesses unrealistic expectations about the significance of that past. As a result, what appears to be a positive factor has become a negative one. By contrast in Russia the political culture provides less incentive for the communists to seek reform. Cichock argues that much of the Russian electorate is not inclined to reject the historical legacy of communism or of communists. Rather the Communist Party of the Russian Federation continues to advocate traditional communist values in its party platform and to experience considerable electoral success. The one notable modification that is apparent is the rejection by the people (and apparently by the party as well) of the concept of granting a monopoly on power to a ruling communist party.

Ishiyama's research[1] is useful here in understanding the impact of historical legacy. The most successful of the reformed successor parties highlighted by the case studies (Lithuania, Hungary and Poland) emerged out of what Ishiyama identifies as 'national consensus' political environments in which 'internal elite contestation and political pluralism within the old regime helped provide the ex-communist parties with organizational resources and a pool of political talent' that facilitated their electoral successes.[2] In Harsanyi's account of Romania and Cichock's of Russia, the remains of a 'patrimonial communist system' are evident in which the success of the ex-communists can largely be explained by 'the organizational weakness and greater incoherence' possessed by the opposition.[3] This heritage might also explain the lack of success of moderate parties of the left in these countries, since their ability to organize was impaired to the same extent as non-leftist opposition groups.

In all of the case studies past *étatist* traditions are widely and palpably present in transition and consolidation processes. However, the differing historical–social–cultural fabric of the respective societies color their present political cultures. This is evident, for example, in the strong Catholic tradition of Poland or the Habsburg past of Hungary, both of which stand in sharp contrast to an orthodox country like Russia. Nonetheless, the left traditions originating in the late nineteenth-century upsurge of Marxism and its offshoots still exercise a strong influence on these countries' political cultures and social values.

Mode of transition, while useful in understanding the process of consolidation, does not appear to offer much insight into the fortunes of the left. Rather mode of transition might be best understood as a conditioning or environmental factor that all political parties, regardless of ideological orientation, must confront. We can partially understand the success or failure of the left as a function of its ability to cope with the changing political, social, and economic climate.

2. *Economic challenges* Economic reform represents a particularly difficult issue for a post-communist left that must be concerned with issues of social justice. The economic reform requirements that have been all but imposed upon post-communist states by Western institutions and the global market create significant policy dilemmas and leave limited choices for the left. Among the reformed communist parties examined here, we observe a strong tendency to embrace most free market principles. When these parties gained political control, as the studies of Lithuania, Hungary and Poland demonstrate, they pursued economic policies that were not significantly different from their more conservative predecessors. Racz describes the public opinion backlash suffered by the Hungarian Socialist Party after it attempted a comprehensive set of economic reforms in 1995. Wrobel notes a similar experience in Poland leading to the Democratic Alliance of the Left's electoral defeat in 1997. To a large extent, these parties had little practical choice in this matter, but it is not clear whether a party of the left can effectively argue for its future when it supports an economic policy that shows such a limited concern for social justice. In Chapter 1 it was suggested that a possible long-term strategy for the left might be to position itself as a political counterbalance to the political problems of privatization and spreading technological revolution. While the country studies provide no evidence of such a strategy at this time, it does represent an indicator for future observers to monitor. The role played by social-democratic and socialist parties in Western Europe and particularly in the European Union may have a decisive impact on the post-communist countries since it is in Western Europe that such challenges will emerge first.

Much of the post-communist left is likely to take a cue from its counterparts in the West, especially in light of the recent electoral successes by parties of the left in most major West European countries (for example, Britain, France, Italy and Germany).

Looking further into the future, we return to the question raised in Chapter 1 regarding the transformation of the working class in a post-industrial society. Clark and Tucker as well as Racz find little evidence that the left has shown much concern for such long-term trends. Nevertheless, as we try to be forward looking, the political needs of the new working class driven by economic globalization present a challenge that cannot be ignored. The future fortunes of the left will, to a significant extent, depend upon how it is able to cope with the shattering changes of a post-industrial society in a socially acceptable and constructive fashion.

3. *Management of social and political conflict* A key factor discussed in Chapter 1 involved understanding the left's ability to manage and, once in power, control social and political conflict. The case studies suggest that the left has enjoyed a significant amount of success in this area. This success is apparent in the various electoral victories achieved by parties of the left since 1989 and chronicled in the case studies. However, we are equally concerned with the left's political viability in the future. Drawing on the factors discussed in Chapter 1 that might affect the left's ability to compete politically in the future (ability to attract support, idiosyncratic/individual factors, and adaptability), we are led to a somewhat more pessimistic conclusion. A widely noted deficiency in the country studies is the inability of the left to attract support among the young and the working class. Regarding the former, Racz writes that young people in Hungary show a preference for the political right, although this is somewhat tempered by a 'Euro-Atlantic' foreign policy orientation more commonly associated with the Hungarian Socialist Party. Similarly, Cichock notes that the Communist Party of the Russian Federation has so far been unsuccessful in attracting young people to its ranks. With the exception of Romania, the left has not generated much support among the working classes. In some countries this deficiency is exacerbated by the marginal political influence of labor unions. Clark and Tucker find this to be true in Lithuania, where labor unions, a likely political ally of the Democratic Labor Party, have limited membership and equally limited political influence. They find an even more disturbing trend in the small proportion of party members that characterized themselves as recent joiners. Fink-Hafner describes Slovenia's strong tendency toward privatizing firms through employee ownership and a corresponding easing of the gulf between workers and owners. It is likely that such a vested workforce will have a reduced need for parties of the left. It is not surprising that Fink-Hafner sees no room for a radical left in Slovene political culture and observes that leftist parties in

Slovenia have been most successful when they move away from traditional leftist issues, as evidenced by the ongoing success of the Liberal Democratic Party after it emerged from the League of Socialist Youth.

Evidence from idiosyncratic/individual variables yields a mixed evaluation. In three cases, the country studies suggest that individuals have been of great value to the success of leftist parties. Clark and Tucker describe the positive image the Lithuanian public held of Brazauskas, and Racz notes Horn's popularity following his Socialist Party's landslide victory in 1994. However, both of these parties eventually suffered electoral defeat and replaced their once-popular leaders, and neither party has demonstrated an ability to find effective replacements. On the one hand, the lack of popular leaders does not necessarily disadvantage the left since other parties face a similar problem. On the other hand, if such popular leaders are viewed as emerging out of the beneficial historical legacy enjoyed by the left in Lithuania and Hungary, then one could argue that the left has used up this particular benefit and will no longer enjoy a political advantage in this area. Romania represents a different set of circumstances. Harsanyi argues that, at least prior to 1996, Romanian politics could be largely understood in terms of political support for individuals rather than parties or party platforms. Even today the best-known political figures (Iliescu and Roman) remain a part of the left. The future ability of the Romanian electorate to look beyond individuals will partially determine the fortunes of the left in that country.

One indicator of party adaptability suggested in Chapter 1 is level of party democracy. Virtually all of the case studies show that the major parties of the left have achieved a relatively high level of party democracy. This is true even of the Communist Party of the Russian Federation. The ongoing success of these parties may be the result of this democratization which has allowed the left to respond successfully to the needs of the electorate and yet maintain sufficient organizational coherence to run an effective election campaign.

A major intervening variable here concerns the ability of the electorate in a post-communist society to comprehend the complexities of a democratic political process. In short, how politically mature has a particular electorate become since communism collapsed in that country?

Racz writes at length of the mercurial Hungarian electorate that is short-term oriented and has developed a very materialistic view of politics. He finds that few political associations are class based, suggesting that many Hungarians do not yet link their political interests to a particular political party. In fact, Racz argues that Hungary has remained largely a 'one-thirder' political culture, with fluctuating portions of the electorate supporting the right, the liberals and the left. Wrobel writes of the 'confusion' of the Polish voters and Cichock reaches a similar conclusion about the Russian electorate. For example, Cichock suggests that part of the difficulty faced by the politically unsuccessful social-democratic movement is that Russian voters do not yet grasp the distinction between communism and social democracy. Similarly, Harsanyi finds the Romanian electorate slow to mature, although the results of the 1996 elections suggest the long-anticipated awakening of Romanian civil society. In contrast, Clark and Tucker argue that classes do seem to matter in Lithuanian politics. Their research suggests that voters in Lithuania have begun to associate their class interests with a particular political party. The defeat suffered by the Lithuanian Democratic Labor Party in 1996 appears to be the result of social groups that regularly support the left deciding to stay home.

A puzzling consistency throughout the country studies has been the lack of success experienced by social-democratic parties. Our broad definition of the term 'left' was chosen so that the country studies would address more than just the successors to the communist parties. And yet we find little to say about the social democrats because they have been so unsuccessful throughout the post-communist world.

Racz, Clark and Tucker, and Cichock all mention lack of organization as a characteristic of social-democratic parties in their respective chapters. As noted above, Cichock suggests that the average Russian voter is unable to perceive a difference between communists and social democrats and so prefers the better-organized and-publicized communists. Social democrats also seemed to be plagued by poor or fractious leadership. Only in Slovenia have the social democrats experienced much electoral success. But, as Fink-Hafner explains, party development and political culture in Slovenia is idiosyncratic compared to the experiences of other post-communist countries. There exists in Slovenia an unusual public consensus about political values that strongly favor the development of a social welfare society built on the Scandinavian model. Fink-Hafner finds this consensus is reflected in the political platforms of most of Slovenia's major parties and obviously translates into success for the Social Democratic Party.

Obviously any party whose existence was prohibited for over 40 years is likely to have organizational and leadership problems upon reconstitution, but other non-communist parties have enjoyed success in Eastern and Central Europe since 1989, while the social democrats have floundered. Cichock's observations regarding the inability of voters to perceive a difference between the communists and social democrats in Russia may have relevance for several other countries. The reformed communists, going by the label 'socialist', will always be better organized and funded than the social democrats and therefore take the larger share of the undifferentiated vote for the left. However, if this explanation does hold, then, as the post-communist electorate grows more sophisticated politically, the advantage currently held by the socialists *née* communists will disappear. We might expect to see a slow growth in the popularity of social democrats in the future. Indeed, the chapter on Slovenia shows a large and recent improvement in electoral standing by the Social Democratic Party while in Hungary and Poland the Socialist Party and the Democratic Alliance of the Left, respectively, are moving increasingly in the direction of a Western model of social democracy.

4. *External factors*   The external environment emerges as an issue throughout the country studies. Racz suggests that the future success of the left in Hungary will be partially dependent upon the fortunes of the left elsewhere in Europe. In terms of a demonstration effect, it is possible that the electoral failure of Poland's Democratic Left Alliance in 1997 had some impact on the standing of the Socialist Party in the run-up to its unsuccessful showing in Hungary's May 1998 elections. Beyond Eastern Europe, Racz hypothesizes that the Hungarian Socialist Party may be aided by its more internationalist attitude. It has consistently favored the orientation of Hungary toward the West, in contrast to the more nationalist, inward-looking perspective of the center-right parties. The degree to which the European Union, NATO and other regional actors are receptive to that attitude can be beneficial to the standing of the Socialist Party and vice versa. Finally, we have already noted that the success or failure of social-democratic parties in Western Europe might be a harbinger for similar trends in post-communist societies.

Perhaps the clearest conclusion provided by the country studies is that the left is here to stay, whether as a major opposition force, a part of a governing majority, or a majority in its own right. It is also clear that, for now, there is no uniform model applicable to the study of post-communist democratic consolidations or the role of the left in those consolidations. 'Transitology' models and other theoretical abstractions ought not to be used automatically. Such approaches can, however, be of value in helping to ask useful questions and identifying key challenges. Yet in the end it appears that the unique combination of history, geography, commerce and social/cultural values compound our difficulties in constructing more far-reaching generalities. Only time will tell if the science of politics can take us further.

NOTES

1. John T. Ishiyama, 'The Sickle or the Rose? Previous Regime Types and the Evolution of the Ex-communist Parties in Post-communist Politics', *Comparative Political Studies* **30**, 3 (June 1997).
2. Ibid., p. 326. The case of Slovenia is also categorized by Ishiyama as a former 'national consensus' regime. Fink-Hafner's chapter illustrates the organizational talents of the former communists and the initial success of the reformed communist party as the largest single vote getter in the 1990 elections, coinciding with Ishiyama's findings. The party's subsequent fortunes have been less impressive.
3. Ibid.

Index

adaptability, communist successor
  parties 8, 9, 162
Agrarian Alliance (AA) 63
Agrarian Party 16, 28, 31
All Poland Trade Union Alliance
  (OPZZ) 98
Alliance of Free Democrats (AFD) 61,
  66, 75, 77, 81, 83
Alliance of Young Democrats (AYD) 61,
  70, 71, 81, 82, 83
Antall, Jozsef 64, 69, 70, 85
authoritarian conditioning 155
authoritarian regimes 4–5
authority, Polish perception of 104–5
AYD–CP 82, 83, 88

bargaining 6
Bekesi, Laszlo 76–7

capitalism
  KPRF 26
  Slovenia 125
Caritas pyramid scheme 145
Ceausescu, Nicolae 5, 131
Center Union (CU) 40, 43
Chernomyrdin, Viktor 30
Christian Democratic People's Party
  (CDPP) 61, 64, 66, 70, 80
Church
  Polish communism 96–7
  social democrats, Slovenia 116–17
Citizens' Party 64
class politics
  Lithuania 38–9, 40, 41, 42, 44, 45, 48
  Slovenia 122–3
coalitions
  Hungary 64, 66, 75–8, 81, 87
  Russia 14, 15, 31
  Slovenia 123–4

communism
  historical legacy of 4–5
  Poland 96
Communist Party of the Russian
  Federation (KPRF) 15, 16, 21, 22,
  23–8, 29, 30, 31, 32, 33, 161
Communist Party of Slovenia 108–9
Communist Party of the Soviet Union
  (CPSU) 18, 19, 20, 21, 36
Communists, Working Russia 29, 30
continuity, party system
  Romania 130
  Slovenia 113
Cooperatist Party 147
corruption, DNSF war on, Romania 145
criminal aspects, PZPR 95–6

democracy, Romania 133
Democratic Alliance of the Left (SLD)
  95, 98–9, 102–3
democratic consolidation
  challenges for political parties 4–11,
    159–64
  return of the left 2
Democratic Convention 153, 154
Democratic National Salvation Front
  (DNSF) 142–3, 145–7
Democratic Party (DP) 153–4
Democratic Union (UD) 98
Demos 110
DeSUS 110, 124
dictatorships, personal 5
discontinuity, party systems 113, 130
dishonesty, Poland 105
doctrine of social equality 105

economic policy, KPRF 26
economic reform
  class politics, Lithuania 39

165